MW01195704

Indigenous Collective
Rights in Latin America

Indigenous Collective Rights in Latin America

The Role of Coalitions, Constitutions, and Party Systems

Katherine Becerra Valdivia

LEXINGTON BOOKS
Lanham • Boulder • New York • London

Published by Lexington Books
An imprint of The Rowman & Littlefield Publishing Group, Inc.
4501 Forbes Boulevard, Suite 200, Lanham, Maryland 20706
www.rowman.com

86-90 Paul Street, London EC2A 4NE

British Library Cataloguing in Publication Information Available

Library of Congress Cataloging-in-Publication Data Available

ISBN 978-1-66690-910-4 (cloth : alk. paper)
ISBN 978-1-66690-911-1 (electronic)

♾™ The paper used in this publication meets the minimum requirements of American National Standard for Information Sciences—Permanence of Paper for Printed Library Materials, ANSI/NISO Z39.48-1992.

To Emilia. You completed our family.

Contents

Contents

List of Figures and Tables

FIGURES

TABLES

Acknowledgments

The book you have in your hands is an improved version of my PhD dissertation. Therefore, I would like to thank my doctoral committee: Dr. Moises Arce, Dr. Jake Haselswerdt, Dr. Andrea Benjamin, Dr. Vanya Krieckhaus, and Dr. Corinne Valdivia. Thank you for your support during the process of research.

This project allowed me to travel to different countries to look for materials and gather data. I was able to do it thanks to the Department of Political Science (now Truman School of Government and Public Affairs), the University of Missouri and their travel and research fund, and the Graduate School of Mizzou through the John Bies International Travel Award. I appreciate the time of several people who offered knowledge and information regarding this research in Colombia, Peru, and Chile. Thanks to Armando Duran, Beatriz Londoño, Gloria Amparo Rodríguez, Oscar Montero de la Rosa, Virginie Laurent, members of the group of study on indigenous peoples at Universidad Externado de Colombia: Daniel Bonilla, Gonzalo Aguilar, Hugo Rojas, Ricardo Aaron Verona, Gustavo Zambrano, Jessica Bensa, and Cesar Landa. During these trips, I had access to precious resources from the Library at Universidad Externado de Colombia; the library at the Instituto de Estudios Constitucionales Carlos Restrepo Piedrahita; from the CINEP (Centro de Investigación y Educación Popular), Colombia; from the National Archive of Colombia; the library at Law School, Universidad de Chile; and the library at the Universidad Nacional Mayor de San Marcos, Lima.

I would like to thank my family. My husband was a significant part in completing this book; thank you for your love, nourishment, and help. Emilia, you are my inspiration and strength. Dad, mom, Pamela, and Lorena, thank you for all your support. Finally, thank you, Erika Sandoval, for your help and knowledge.

Introduction

INDIGENOUS COLLECTIVE RIGHTS IS ABOUT GOING FURTHER THAN SOCIAL MOVEMENTS

Collective rights are a legal entitlement based on solidarity and self-determination as a group for indigenous peoples. Latin America is one of the regions that have high levels of recognition when referring to these rights, but legal protections differ considerably among the countries of the region. According to several authors, indigenous social movements are the core to recognize different legal instruments related to collective rights. However, the relationship between indigenous social movements and collective rights across the diverse countries of the region is not as strong as some literature suggests, and it is necessary to review other organizational and institutional conditions. So, being contextualized two questions that arise are: Why do some countries in Latin America have a strong recognition of collective rights for indigenous peoples while others do not? and What are the conditions that contribute to enhance the presence of such collective rights?

This book addresses these other conditions, drawing on evidence related to coalitions, constitutions, and party systems in Latin America. The main argument states that indigenous social movements are important to increase the protection of indigenous rights in the region, but they are not enough. The level of recognition of these rights is also influenced by organizational and institutional conditions. This book means what types of rights and stages of autonomy and differentiation indigenous peoples have in diverse legal instruments. It is very well known that indigenous peoples in the region are subject to discrimination and even social segregation that tend to build upon the notion of homogeneity of race or ethnicity. This idea is essential in establishing the nation-state and several legal institutions. Therefore, the concept of collective indigenous rights has included changes in the political and juridical field.

The Struggle of Indigenous Peoples in Latin America

The status of indigenous peoples and the lack of political and juridical representation in the region are a consequence of decisions made by the colonizers in the fifteen centuries and after. Indigenous peoples were unknown to the European conquerors, "[t]here was a good deal of uncertainty about their status, whether they had the use of reason, whether they were real humans, whether they were brutal savages or represented some version of human existence" (Wade, 2010, p. 25). Slavery was usual at that time, and they received support from authorities to enslaved indigenous peoples, based on a "natural slavery" which means indigenous peoples were unable to have autonomy (Wade, 2010). The Spaniard Crown allowed them to be sold as enslaved people, but they decided they were free vassals (Dougnac Rodriguez, 1994).

Moreover, the conquerors had doubts regarding the rationality of indigenous peoples and their lack of Christian values,

[t]his was the substance of the famous 1550–51 debates between Bartolomé de las Casas and Juan Ginés de Sepúlveda, but already by 1542 slavery of indigenous people had been outlawed in Spanish colonies. Portugal followed suit in Brazil in 1570. (Wade, 2010, p. 26)

Even including these changes, indigenous peoples were subaltern. Officially, they were "protected" by some laws, but at the same time they were exploited. The evidence shows that they were protected by stating they were "legally incapacitated" as children and women at the time. For these reasons they were granted several "privileges," for example, in Mexico in 1553, they were declared free but vassal, or if they had any legal issues, such as civil, criminal, or even religious, the procedure will be summary (Dougnac Rodriguez, 1994). These protections show that indigenous people were discriminated against by the Spaniards, Portuguese, and British colonizers.

Indigenous peoples were moved forcefully from the rural areas to urban areas, and the ones that stayed in rural areas became dependents of rural haciendas (Wade, 2010). These were called "encomienda" (Dougnac Rodriguez, 1994), and they were forced to serve Spaniards and creoles. This institution helped to assimilate indigenous peoples into the European norms. For example, indigenous peoples must learn how to write and read, and the Spaniards provided them with a church. The children of the indigenous chief over thirteen years old must be educated in a Christian Convent for four years, among others (Dougnac Rodriguez, 1994).

In the eighteenth and nineteenth centuries, during the process of independence, the "[l]atin American elites wanted to emulate the modernity and progress of [European] nations and accepted in broad terms the tenets of liberalism which saw in science, technology, reason, education, and freedom of the individual the underlying forces of progress" (Wade, 2010, p. 31). Any other kind of knowledge was dismissed, and indigenous peoples were relegated to the end of the social order. The indigenous peoples were military, juridical, political, economic, and cultural subordinated (Aylwin, 2002). By the nineteenth century, indigenous peoples suffered the usurpation of the remaining lands through fraudulent contracts, ridiculous prices, or just moving the fences by non-indigenous peoples (Aylwin, 2002). This process also included a program of assimilation for indigenous peoples in the region.

The twentieth century was a time of political assimilation that was marked by a double approach. The government started to recognize the position of indigenous peoples as oppressed members of society. Still, at the same time, they are an obstacle to the national unity and development of the countries (Aylwin, 2002). These were called "indigenistas" policies. They were made thinking of indigenous, but the elites made them. These policies produce large-scale indigenous movements in some countries in Latin America, claiming a better understanding of the indigenous epistemologies and, in the opinion of some literature, helping to include indigenous collective rights in the legal order.

More Indigenous Social Movement, More Indigenous Collective Rights

The literature that studies this relationship states a straightforward relationship between indigenous social movements and collective rights (Aguilar et al., 2010; Barié, 2003; Hanna et al., 2016; Hodgson, 2002; O'Faircheallaigh, 2012, 2013; Van Cott, 2004; Acevedo De la Harpe, 2021). In general, to have more indigenous social movements and mobilizations will create more collective rights or even reaffirm them in the public realm (Van Cott, 2004). For example, Aguilar et al. (2010) claim that recognizing indigenous peoples in collective rights is an outcome of indigenous mobilizations. They state that

> [f]rom a comparative perspective, it is important to emphasize that the recognition of indigenous peoples in constitutional norms has come to fruition thanks to an arduous defense by indigenous peoples and an active pressure from non-governmental organizations. This process of claims is centered upon the

argumentation and the language of human rights, particularly, in the key issue of collective rights of indigenous peoples. (Aguilar et al., 2010, p. 96)

The current literature heavily relies on the theory of contentious politics, in particular, as an instrument for achieving more indigenous collective rights. According to Hanna et al. (2016),

> "[i]ndigenous mobilizations have a positive impact on the realization of Indigenous rights in that they communicate Indigenous grievances, help to disseminate information about and to build respect for Indigenous cultures, assist in creating pressure for the recognition of their rights, and in enacting new legislation for the further operationalization of their rights" (p. 504), adding that "protests are likely to persist as legitimate, and perhaps the only mechanism, in which communities can gain respect for their established rights, to protect their natural environment, and consequentially to promote their well-being." (p. 504).

These indigenous rights movements "hinge on the right to self-determination and include the right to determine their development and control and protect their cultural knowledge and performances, material remains, languages, indigenous knowledge, and biogenetic material" (Hodgson, 2002, p. 1041). O'Faircheallaigh supports this view stating that "[i]ndigenous control of development can only be achieved by Indigenous mobilisation (sic) in the domestic political sphere, targeting both the state and resource corporations" (O'Faircheallaigh, 2012, p. 541).

The majority of this body of scholarship studying the relationship between indigenous social movements and collective rights explores the topic highlighting the importance of the movements to achieve the outcome, but it does not include other factors or conditions. Furthermore, Van Cott (2004) and Acevedo De la Harpe (2021) use institutional instability as a mechanism for indigenous movements to achieve the recognition of rights. In particular, Van Cott states that indigenous social movements "did so by taking advantage of the conjuncture of institutional crisis and constitutional reform to link their demands to those of the political elite" (Van Cott, 2004, p. 141). However, this explanation does not account for countries that have mid-level institutionalization or no constitutional change, and low-level or mid-level recognition of collective rights as Colombia before 1990, Bolivia before 2007, or Peru before 1993. Thus, institutional instability and constitutional change are conditions that should be considered.

Problems and Challenges

The main problem with the current literature discussed in the previous section is that they do not recognize four substantial and methodological issues. First, there are different types of indigenous rights: individual and collective. It has been easier for governments to work with indigenous peoples' individual rights, which creates a false illusion of recognition. For example, Mexico has a federal legislation that recognizes collective rights, and all the state legislation recognizes individual rights of indigenous peoples; it is possible to think that indigenous peoples have several protections; however, individual rights are not the best way to protect the group (López Bárcenas, 2010). Therefore, this work accounts only for collective rights.

Second, the levels of collective rights as an outcome of indigenous social movements have variations. On the majority of these works, they do not account for this difference (Aguilar et al., 2010; Barié, 2003; Hanna et al., 2016; Hodgson, 2002; O'Faircheallaigh, 2012, 2013; Van Cott, 2004). The same level of recognition is not achieved in all the countries, even if all of them manifest social movements. Indigenous social movements have different levels of success that impact the type of rights recognized in legal instruments. For example, the Chilean case, even showing a high rate of indigenous social movements, has only a couple of rights for indigenous peoples, such as consultation rights; and on the other hand, Colombia showing a low rate of social movements, including self-determination rights for indigenous peoples. This is why this book tries to explain diverse levels of collective rights.

Third, indigenous rights are not only present in constitutions. Several ones are enshrined and incorporated in other legal documents as acts, laws, and even resolutions. Aguilar et al. (2010), Barié (2003), and Acevedo De la Harpe (2021) base their research only on indigenous rights at the constitutional level. However, there are other legal instruments that complement and develop indigenous rights. Adding them into the analysis, it is possible to have a broader look at the state of indigenous rights in the region. For example, Peru has an intercultural bilingual education Act No. 27818, stating the right of bilingual education for indigenous peoples, explaining the term "cultural diversity" as central to all legislation.

Furthermore, the majority of authors did not assess the possibility of showing other conditions as essential factors when recognizing collective rights. They take for granted that indigenous social movements produce more collective rights. However, it is possible to observe the cases of countries with a low level of indigenous social movements and a high level of collective rights, such as Colombia, Bolivia, and Mexico; and others with a high level of mobilization but no rights, such as Chile before the social uprising in 2019 and Ecuador at the beginning of the 1990s. This reality shows that indigenous social movements do not always lead to collective rights and that sometimes when they do, these social movements need to have particular connections. For this reason, it is important to address not only the indigenous movements but also the coalitions they can make with other indigenous and/or other non-indigenous allies, and other factors.

Fourth, regarding the methodological aspects, this body of scholarship also bases its findings only on case studies (Hanna et al., 2016; Hodgson, 2002; O'Faircheallaigh, 2012, 2013; Van Cott, 2004), which has the benefit of presenting in-depth explanations of the circumstances of cases. Nevertheless, it is more complex to generalize the argument for the rest of Latin America. The case-oriented methodology is an essential contribution to the field when it tests theories and hypotheses (Pepinsky, 2019). Also, in the case of Van Cott (2004), she uses countries as a unit of analysis, not accounting for various time frames in the same country. The only work that tries to make a broader analysis is the one from Acevedo De la Arpe (2021). This book will test the theory by using diverse cases for each country; it will work with more units of analysis and look for diverse explanations.

Thus, indigenous social movements are successful in achieving this goal and others that still cannot include these rights into the legal system (Barié, 2003; Benavides-Vanegas, 2009). Van Cott, cited by Barié (2003), states that of all the demands of indigenous communities in Latin America, collective rights are the most difficult to defend and incorporate into the system. Moreover, even if indigenous movements successfully recognize these rights, the movement exists as a tool of legitimate common defense of those rights (Hanna et al., 2016; O'Faircheallaigh, 2012, 2013). Consequently, these expressions become a legitimate instrument to contest when the states or private institutions have threatened their rights when indigenous social movements are not successful in including collective rights, or they persist after the recognition of these rights, other answers must provide a better understanding of the situation.

THE ARGUMENT OF THIS BOOK: STRONG, MODERATE, AND WEAK COLLECTIVE RIGHTS

This research challenges the conventional wisdom about the contribution of indigenous social movements, adding more specifications to the analysis. So, the argument of this book is to give a broader explanation of the problem, specifically searching for collective rights, using diverse levels of analysis, and checking in all the legal systems for those rights and factors to increase the level of recognition. This research states that indigenous social movements are important to increase the protection of indigenous rights in Latin America, but they are not enough. Maybe repeated, but strong enough, organizational and institutional conditions also influence the level of recognition of these rights at the national level. Figure 0.1 shows the argument.

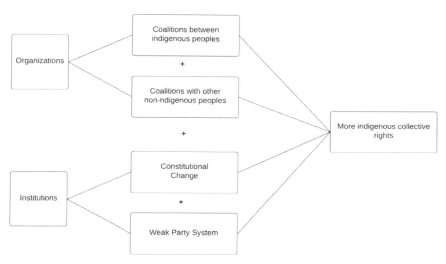

Figure 0.1 Diagram Showing the Argument of the Book. Credit: Katherine Becerra Valdivia.

Regarding the organizational conditions, having in mind that not all indigenous social movements successfully recognize collective rights (Barié, 2003; Benavides-Vanegas, 2009), some coalitions are the critical element of the analysis. Indigenous social movements successfully recognize collective rights when they are capable of creating coalitions between diverse indigenous peoples in a country, building a national association or creating coalitions with other non-indigenous allies, such as other minority groups and left political parties. Using the theory and concepts of bi-racial coalitions, a stable alliance between diverse racial groups, in the United States (Sonenshein, 2006; Williams, 2003), this part of the research notes a coalition-building theory for indigenous peoples in Latin America. The first hypothesis explains that the presence of strong collective rights is associated with the development of coalitions between indigenous peoples when there are also coalitions with non-indigenous allies.

The institutional conditions are related to political and juridical variables. The first condition is related to the functioning of the party system. Party systems that are more institutionalized tend to be closer to recognizing indigenous collective rights because the authorities make more orthodox decisions. The second institutional condition is a juridical-political element that creates conditions for recognizing and increasing the level of these rights, mainly, the constitutional change, as an opportunity to transform the paradigm. This part of the research intends to search for critical institutional variables to answer the problem of recognition of indigenous collective rights. The second hypothesis states that the presence of strong collective rights is associated with a weak party system when there is a high level of constitutional instability.

Institutional and organizational conditions are part of the history to recognize indigenous collective rights in Latin America, and how these conditions related to each other create a diverse level of rights. Thus, this book explains the path to include diversity in the political-juridical system, embracing the role of coalitions in indigenous social movements and the institutional instability of the region. These two sets of conditions clarify the best opportunities for indigenous peoples to dispute for more self-determination in the language of collective rights within a nation-state. A better understanding, focusing on new organizations and formal institutions, will allow us to acknowledge the complex coexistence between indigenous and mestizo-white perspectives. The theory is based on the constantly changing reality in Latin American to account for the processes of recognition of a more diverse cosmovision in the governing systems. However, it does not assess the reality in terms of positive or negative. This research presents a window of opportunity to explore outcomes that can help and build more diversity for minority communities.

It is in this context when all the conditions are present such as coalitions between indigenous peoples, coalitions with non-indigenous allies, weak party systems, and constitutional instability that there is a higher probability, almost near certainty, of having strong collective rights at work in the country. This recognition means that indigenous peoples are entitled to have their organizational system without the opinion of the state and national governments. In this case, the government decreases the level of its power in favor of indigenous peoples. The collective rights considered strong are the right to self-determination and the right to use customary indigenous law. These rights make it easier to wield, exercise, and implement other rights such as cultural diversity and language. Therefore, the third hypothesis states that the presence of strong collective rights is associated with the building of coalitions, between indigenous peoples and with non-indigenous allies, and with also the presence of a weak party system and a high level of constitutional instability.

It is more likely to have moderate collective rights when one set of conditions, one organization and one institutional, are present. Moderate collective rights mean an increase in the level of differentiation. However, indigenous peoples cannot use their organizational system. The government gives up some of its power, but it is controlled by a high level of regulations on strategic topics, such as the right to land and territories, natural resources, bilingual education, and the right to participate in the political field.

It is more likely to have weak collective rights when a country has none of these conditions. This means just a couple of rights related to recognizing a superficial level of differentiation. Even with a high level of indigenous social movements, the culture will be recognized without any autonomy for indigenous peoples. The government is not willing to give up any of its power. In this case of having weak collective rights, it is only possible to find cultural diversity and language rights. These rights are essential because they allow cultural differentiation, but they only show the minimum rights threshold for indigenous peoples.

CASES AND ANALYSIS

To test these propositions, I use qualitative comparative analysis (QCA) and case studies. Specifically, when using QCA, I examine how the conditions behave in a table of truth with seven countries of the region (Bolivia, Chile, Colombia, Ecuador, Guatemala, Mexico, and Peru). It was divided into sixteen cases; each country has several cases according to its historical evolution from 1988 to 2020. Therefore, this research will analyze diverse scenarios in each country. Also, these scenarios help to create a more accurate analysis of each situation. There are objective rules to be used in these countries. Each of them with their unique context and development that helps us to understand the state of the topic of research. For sure, Bolivia and Ecuador are frontrunners in achieving more indigenous collective rights, greatly influencing the decision-making process. However, countries such as Chile, Colombia, Guatemala, Mexico, and Peru also have an exciting trajectory on the topic. Some of them have increased their level such as Colombia and Peru; others show a significant change such as Chile, Guatemala, and Mexico.

Additionally, I present three cases—Colombia, Peru, and Chile—for a better understanding of the process and causal mechanisms. All these countries show underlooked cases of indigenous collective rights and give examples of diverse outcomes and processes. Colombia is a case of innovation in including collective rights having a low level of indigenous social movements, but with coalitions, a weak party system, and a constitution that was changed at the beginning of the 1990s. Peru is a diverse case, it shows all the conditions, it has strong collective rights, but the process of achieving them is different from Colombia. Chile shows a weak level of indigenous collective rights with an institutionalized party system, with a liberal constitution from 1980, and a high level of indigenous social movements that do not form coalitions between indigenous peoples and other non-indigenous groups. The case of Chile shows to be paradigmatic for the theory of weak collective rights. All the results support these propositions.

PLAN OF THE BOOK

Chapter 1 addresses the concepts of this book: collective rights and indigenous social movements; regarding collective rights, terminology, definitions,
and explanations of its classification; and emphasizing the concept of indigenous peoples and the role of international instruments. In the case of indigenous social movements, it explains their contexts and the impact of the term
in Latin America. Chapter 2 explains in-depth argument of this book, stating
the role of each condition. First, it develops the role of indigenous social
movements, the concept, and theoretical approaches for building coalitions
between indigenous nationalities and other non-indigenous allies. At the end
of this first section, an explanation is provided of how these two conditions
work together to include a different level of collective rights. Second, chapter 2 illustrates two institutional conditions that enhance this protection: the
political party system and its institutionalization and the constitutional change
as a tool of recognition of collective rights. At the end of the second part, the
role of the interaction of these two conditions will be analyzed to incorporate
more indigenous rights. Also, chapter 2 intends to set out how circumstances,
coalitions, and institutions work together to achieve the outcomes creating
a complete theory. Chapter 3 presents the main conditions and the empirical results of the analysis, including the discussion and findings. So, all the
results support the argument. Chapters 4, 5, and 6 present the cases of Colombia, Peru, and Chile, respectively. Finally, the research conclusion explains
the general findings and future research related to the subject of analysis.

Chapter 1

Collective Rights and Indigenous Social Movements in Latin America

This chapter presents collective rights as the object of analysis for this work and the condition that the literature points out as the most important for generating indigenous social movements. This chapter explains the essential concepts and clarifies the terms of this research. The analysis will start with the notion, elements, and classifications of collective rights, explaining their importance of them as an active subject: indigenous peoples. Finally, it will develop the concept, the role of indigenous social movements, and their importance in Latin America.

COLLECTIVE RIGHTS: CONCEPTUALIZATION AND IMPORTANCE IN LATIN AMERICA

"Right" is a vastly studied principle for diverse disciplines and areas of knowledge. Prominent scholars study the distinction between individual and collective rights. However, collective rights "generally have remained ill-defined, especially in relation to the more theoretically meaningful conceptualization of individual rights, both human and civil" (McHugh, 2010, p. 2). According to Van Dyke (1974), several French and British political philosophers assumed that people were homogenous with no racial, linguistic, or cultural differences within the state. That is the case with classic authors such as Locke, Rousseau, and John Stuart Mill (Van Dyke, 1974).

Historically, the term collective right was used to particularize rights for institutions. Specifically, they referred to benefits belonging to members of specific groups (Bellamy, 2000), "[i]n international law 'collective rights' are accepted as belonging only to states, corporations, associations, including such entities as universities and churches" (Malloy, 2005). The notion of collective rights as human rights began to be studied post World War II, and it

> is often used to refer to the human right of self-determination included in the common Article 1 of the two 1966 UN Covenants, the [International Covenant on Civil and Political Rights] ICCPR and the International Covenant on Economic, Social and Cultural Rights (ICESCR), and has also been used in connection with the Genocide Convention. (Malloy, 2005)

The mention of collective rights in the Genocide Convention is related to the right to the physical existence of diverse peoples (Dinstein, 1976). Thus, this legal construction from the international law is used in international human rights law to refer to "cultural rights of ethnic minorities, indigenous groups, religious minorities, immigrant minorities, and racial groups as well as with the social rights of economically disadvantaged groups" (Malloy, 2005). Until today, the notion of collective rights is disputed between these two systems of international law and creates problematic approaches.

However, I will refer in this book to the term used in international human rights law. Therefore, collective rights are a legal entitlement based on solidarity and self-determination as a group (Saito, 1996; Squella, 2000) for communities that share a particular point of view. Thus, they are part of the "groups rights" and "third generation of rights" in opposition to the individual rights of the first generation, liberties, and political rights, and the second generation or social rights (Saito, 1996; Squella, 2000). Among different authors such as Jack Donnelly, there is the idea that solidarity cannot be the source of human rights; therefore, these rights are not human rights, and they should be categorized differently (Donnelly, 1989). However, the dignity concept is seen as a source of human rights and solidarity; these two concepts can be engaged with the role of human beings in different aspects: one is personal, as the value that everyone has for being a person, and the other one is relational, stating how we should behave among people.

According to Kane (2002), the group rights, such as collective ones, try to search for the defense and preservation of culture, a distinct way of life, and attempt to prevent or correct some exclusions or discriminations against a particular group, such as indigenous peoples. This distinctiveness may sound odd in a globalized world, where assimilation and universal characteristics are the trends (Lauderdale, 2009; Ndahinda, 2007). However, the tendency is to protect people from hostile development policies that do not consider cultural identities (Ndahinda, 2007). This new tendency is essential for Latin America, one of the continents with a high level of protection of collective rights for indigenous peoples at the aggregate level.

The Problem of Conceptualization of Collective Rights

Collective rights are a legal category for protecting groups of peoples who have access to communal or collective goods (Green, 1991) which are produced and enjoyed by a specific community (Soriano González, 2019) such as language; cultural, political, and social traditions; land protection, among others. These rights are against the classical notion of individual rights (Badger, 2010; Buchanan, 1993; Green, 1991; Hsieh, 2006; Jovanović, 2005, 2012; Kreimer, 2000; Schilling-Vacaflor & Kuppe, 2012; Soriano González, 2019; Van Cott, 2000a; Xanthaki, 2000). Jovanović (2012) states that "collective rights, particularly those held by groups [. . .] cannot be adequately grounded in this [individual] normative-moral point" (Jovanović, 2012, p. 200). The main feature of this category of rights is that they must be exercised jointly as a group. Thus, these rights are not entitled to one particular person in the community, but to every person in a group, tribe, or nation as an assembly (Jovanović, 2005, 2012; Kane, 2002; Seymour, 2017; Xanthaki, 2000). The exercising of collective rights is for the community. There are also other characteristics of collective rights, such as sex and gender, although these rights do not configure a threat to the notion of the nation-state (Seymour, 2017).

One definition of these rights states that

> [c]ollective rights could refer to the right of a group to limit the liberty of its own individual members in the name of group solidarity or cultural purity [. . .]; or it could refer to the right of a group to limit the economic or political power exercised by the larger society over the group, to ensure that the resources and institutions on which the minority depends are not vulnerable to majority decisions. (Kymlicka, 1995, p. 7)

A more straightforward definition states that "Collective rights are typically rights to collective goods" (Raz, 1988, p. 210; also, Jovanović, 2012). Both definitions and their authors believe in the individual's autonomy as the center of any right. This view is also accurate for collective rights. The difference is the role that these rights play. Will Kymlicka centers his analysis on the freedom of the citizens (Kymlicka, 1995). Thus, collective rights may be necessary for individual autonomy; this is called a moderately liberal theory of collective rights (López Calera, 2003). For Joseph Raz, the principles of autonomy and liberty are central. However, other principles and rights make them possible, for example, the provision of many collective goods (López Calera, 2003). Hence these other principles are not secondary elements for the individual. This has been called the moderate collectivism theory of collective rights. (López Calera, 2003).

Furthermore, from a liberal point of view, Seymour (2017) provides four essential characteristics in understanding what collective rights are. He states,

That a collective right is a right such that (1) the subject of the right is a group, (2) The object of the right is an institution (created and enjoyed by many individuals), (3) the institution concerns some collective aspect of the group, and (4) it plays a major role in the maintenance or development of the group as a whole. (Seymour, 2017, p. 164)

All of them are characteristics that point out the participatory elements of the collective rights, which embrace the importance of the group in the concept. The collective rights are an application of the principle of solidarity because the open contexts are an essential element for them; the diversity and cultural characteristics of the peoples are at the center of the analysis (Buchanan, 1993; Guerrero, 2018; Mosquera Caro & Hinestroza Cuesta, 2017). In the same line of analysis, Kymlicka (1995) states that collective rights are a consequence of multiculturalism because individual rights cannot consider cultural diversity.

In particular, indigenous collective rights are defined as recognizing cultural diversity. These rights state that indigenous peoples are political subjects, inhabiting the territories even before the nation-state, using their self-determination (Millaleo, 2019). Thus, political power and authorities guarantee indigenous peoples their lives and development under their terms (Guerrero, 2018) and cosmovision. Therefore, indigenous collective rights are one category of collective rights. Other groups or collectives can also be subject to them, for example, the afro descendants and other minorities in Latin America.

In essence, this research utilizes the notion of indigenous collective rights as an entitlement of the community of collective good, using the principle of solidarity to develop their culture and cosmovision in spaces of oppression.

Diverse Types of Collective Rights

Adding more technical elements to the definition, Buchanan (1993) explains that it is possible to find two different types of these rights: collective rights in the strong sense and dual-standing collective rights. The author explains that collective rights in a strong sense

Can only be wielded (a) by a group through some collective decision process (majority rule or a consensus process) or (b) by some agent (or agents) that wield(s) the right for the group (that is, by representative or leaders of the group). (Buchanan, 1993, p. 93)

This definition is the more classical approach to these rights and agrees with other authors' definitions, such as Jovanović (2005, 2012) and López

Calera (2003). An example of this right is the self-determination of the peoples. The dual-standing collective rights are those that

> [a]ny individual who is member of the groups can wield [them] . . ., either on his or her own behalf or behalf of any other member or members of the group, and the right may also be wielded by a collective mechanism or by an agent or agents of the group. (Buchanan, 1993, p. 94)

Segal (2010) calls this type of rights collective-oriented individual rights. For example, the right to participate in cultural or religious ceremonies. The critical element of each of these classifications is that the people have them because they belong to a group or community that shares a specific culture. Moreover, their protection of them is essential for the community.

Placing these ideas in their historical context and connecting collective rights to multiculturalism, which means multiple nations and ethnicity, co-habit the same society. Kymlicka (1995) explains three types of collective rights: rights to self-government (political autonomy, even secession); polyethnic rights related to the respect of ethnic identities; and rights to the representation of diverse groups. This idea of multiculturalism is central to the analysis because different cultures or heritage are part of it. Every society has diverse groups of people who connect, live, and interact, creating different demands for the political and juridical system.

This book uses the term indigenous collective rights broadly, including all the classifications explained in the previous paragraphs. Having a complete understanding of the types of collective rights allows to analyze their real level of recognition in diverse countries throughout Latin America. Accounting for collective rights in the strong sense, it is important to point out that dual-standing collective rights, right to self-government, polyethnic rights, and rights of representation will help to explain the level of recognition for these rights.

Active Subject: Concept of Indigenous Peoples

It has been challenging to find a universal definition for "indigenous peoples"[1] (Gagliardi, 2019). The conceptualization can be troublesome for the states and governments, who are careful regarding the claims of these ethnic groups as a nation or "peoples." The United Nations (UN) is the institution that has built a body of scholarship related to the notion of indigenous peoples. This institution defines them as

> Inheritors and practitioners of unique cultures and ways of relating to people and the environment. They have retained social, cultural, economic, and political characteristics distinct from those of the dominant societies in which they

live. Despite their cultural differences, indigenous peoples from around the world share common problems related to the protection of their rights as distinct peoples. (United Nations, n.d.)

However, the term "indigenous peoples" is broadly used in Latin America, but other concepts are most accurate for political use. In some Latin American areas, indigenous people prefer to be called "pueblos originarios," translated as "original peoples." Since the 1990s, this concept has been more widely used in the region for three main reasons. First, it is challenging to use the term as a noun. It is incorrect to call them just "originarios," thus, this facilitates calling them by the name of their nationalities in their native language, creating a strong political statement. For example, it is not "pueblo originario Wayuu," it is just Wayuu. The same with Nahuas and Mapuche, among others. Second, it eliminates the concept of "indigenous" as an expression of racism against them. Third, it creates a clear language that embraces plurality and inclusion (Semo, 2017). In other parts of the world, the denomination has also changed. For example, in the United States, indigenous peoples are called "American tribes"; in Australia, they are called "Aboriginal Peoples" (Bowen, 2000).

The United Nations Working Group on Indigenous Populations (WGIP) established four criteria that are important to interpret the concept of indigenous peoples:

(1) priority in time, with respect to the occupation and use of a specific territory, (2) the voluntary perpetuation of cultural distinctiveness, (3) self-identification, as well as recognition by other groups and by state authorities, as a distinct collectivity, and (4) an experience of subjugation, marginalization (sic), dispossession, exclusion or discrimination, whether or not these conditions persist. (Kenrick & Lewis, 2004, p. 4).

In the same sense, the International Labor Organization (ILO) in its Convention No. 169, article 1.1[2] declares who are the indigenous peoples for applying the instrument, having a binding effect on the countries that signed it (Gagliardi, 2019). These definitions and criteria focus on their marginalized cultural identity outside of the leading stream society and the idea of indigenous peoples as political actors.

Indigenous peoples can be considered a minority group. However, there are two differences between them. Minority groups are a creation of our system, which are assigned to the political and legal characteristics (Ketley, 2001). They are a small group in a society that lives in diverse territories; they are culturally homogenous and do not have a right to self-determination (Andrade, 2018). Indigenous peoples existed before creating the nation-state (Ketley, 2001). They can be the majority of the population in a country

(Andrade, 2018). Also, they have a special connection with their lands (Cruz-Saco, 2018; Gagliardi, 2019). Each indigenous people have their own culture, language, and cosmovision (Cruz-Saco, 2018). Moreover, they wield the right to self-determination (Andrade, 2018). Therefore, more than being a minority group, indigenous peoples have built relationships based on their distinctiveness (Warren & Jackson, 2002) as a central element related to and belonging to their ancestral lands (Gagliardi, 2019).

Therefore, it is more accurate to use the term "pueblos originarios" in the Latin American context. There is not an exact translation of the expression; thus, this research will use the term "indigenous people(s)" as a non-dominant group, formed by persons who have identified themselves as indigenous and who share a cultural identity that is different from the dominant in the specific territory. They want to preserve their culture, and they have a sense of belonging to the lands of their ancestors. They have an economy of survival and a communitarian organization while living in poverty and marginalization (Andrade, 2018).

The Impact of Collective Rights for Indigenous Peoples in Latin America

Collective rights are central for indigenous peoples for two main reasons: first, they are an institutional instrument to protect indigenous peoples who work better than other institutions. Second, they provide a racism-sensitive safeguard. Regarding the former, the creation of the legal category of collective rights is a consequence of the lack of protection of individual human rights. Also, individual rights were an imposition of institutional and legal structures that were inappropriate for indigenous peoples (Ndahinda, 2007). Another institutional tool example is to be seen as an individual political representation of indigenous peoples at the Legislative branch through the proportional system (PR) and indigenous quotas. The critics of these instruments state their lack of efficiency in resolving problems for indigenous peoples (Htun, 2016; Union Interparlamentaria, 2014).

Furthermore, they force indigenous peoples to use individualistic-western institutions to participate in the political field. According to Hall and Fenelon (2009), when a group becomes a minority one without any special legal protection, it is more likely to become fully absolved by the dominant state. Therefore, collective rights are helping to maintain the culture of indigenous peoples and develop the group, participating in the political field with their traditions, enhancing their differences.

Individual human rights are non-effective to protect indigenous peoples as they protect non-indigenous peoples. The experience of domination and internal colonialism was central to this problem (Andrés Santos & Amezúa

Amezúa, 2013; Guerrero, 2018). From the sixteenth to the eighteenth century, indigenous peoples were dominated, and their institutions and cultural practices were abandoned and destroyed by the Europeans (Rousseau, 2016). The emancipation of Latin America at the beginning of the nineteen century created a "forced inclusion" of indigenous peoples in the new constitutional states, building a fiction of equality that never existed (Andrés Santos & Amezúa Amezúa, 2013). Thus, human rights are a consequence of a Eurocentric cosmovision that excludes any difference from other cultures. This approach is one of the hurdles that collective rights can overcome.

One of the main characteristics of collective rights is that they play an essential role in maintaining or developing a group (Seymour, 2017). These rights become a critical institutional factor for establishing, maintaining, and developing the group's identity. Specifically, for the indigenous peoples, they protect cultures and reject assimilation and integration of indigenous culture (Xanthaki, 2000). Consequently, these rights are an example of the co-creation of society through the recognition of the differences between several groups within a state (Xanthaki, 2000).

Collective rights provide a racism-sensitive safeguard. According to Williams (2003), one of the central principles in eliminating the privilege of non-indigenous peoples is to have these safeguards. One of these safeguards is collective rights. The protection of these rights becomes permanent, giving a space of autonomy when they are present in a legal instrument. Collective rights are especially crucial as the enforcement of non-discrimination. Jovanović (2005) states correctly that collective rights are more than the measurement of affirmative action to improve the situation of historical discrimination against indigenous groups. The difference between affirmative actions and collective rights is that the former is a temporary measure, so when the problem is solved, they are no longer needed. Collective rights are permanent to enhance the identities of indigenous peoples (Jovanović, 2005),

> [t]herefore, once certain specific legal arrangements for the minority protection are introduced in a domestic legal system, that state is no longer allowed to abolish, restrict, or diminish the scope of these rights, for they are treated as acquired minority rights. (Jovanović, 2005, p. 639)

In that context, the question then arises: why are collective rights necessary for Latin America and indigenous peoples? Because they have been one institutional framework that works for indigenous peoples in the region, giving space for developing their collective culture with significance in the political field. These rights provide an understanding of their cosmovision and cultural norms, and they are also part of a western approach. As a racism-sensitive safeguard, these rights are a tool for recognition and non-assimilation in democratic societies. It allows indigenous peoples to have legal instruments to protect their differences, becoming permanent tools to embrace their diverse way of living, making a political and juridical environment with conditions related to ethnic diversity, in a continent where indigenous peoples have been excluded, even in countries with a high level of the indigenous population.

The International Recognition of Collective Rights for Indigenous Peoples

As stated previously, the role of international human rights law is central in recognizing the importance of collective rights for the indigenous peoples (Aylwin, 2014; Badger, 2010; Del Toro Huerta, 2008; Estupiñan Silva & Ibáñez Rivas, 2014; Hsieh, 2006; Ketley, 2001; Kreimer, 2000; Van Cott, 2000a; Warren & Jackson, 2002). There are general and specific provisions for indigenous peoples in the international order (Ketley, 2001). The general provisions give recognition of collective rights to any minority group. Examples of these kind are the UNESCO Declaration on Race and Racial Prejudice; the 1969 International Convention on the elimination of all forms of racial discrimination; the Rio Declaration; and the Convention on Biological Diversity. The most critical and specific instruments for the collective rights of indigenous peoples are the ILO Convention No 169, the 2007 UN Declaration on the Rights of Indigenous Peoples (UNDRIP), and the 2016 American Declaration on the Rights of Indigenous Peoples.

The indigenous peoples are recognized as "peoples'" who wield collective rights in all these instruments. The Convention No. 169 establishes "that indigenous peoples have the right to preserve their own identity and makes clear the distinction between those rights that are enjoyed collectively, and those that are inherent in the individual" (p. 44). The ratification of this instrument gave indigenous communities a set of tools to mobilize for the inclusion of collective rights at a national level (Van Cott, 2000). The UNDRIP states that

> [d]espite the continuing debate, one of the main goals of the Declaration is to clearly signal to the international community that internal self-governance should be recognized as a collective indigenous right and left in the control of the indigenous group itself. (p. 494)

Aguilar et al. see these instruments as minimum standards: "[t]hese minimum standards will serve as a basis for the recognition of indigenous peoples and the proclamation of their rights within the constitutional norms" (Aguilar et al., 2010, p. 21). The international instruments of human rights claim to have a universalistic point of view, but in this case there is a specification of the protection; this specification claims that equality requires treating people differently from others. Moreover, indigenous peoples deserve these rights because some rights belong to groups of peoples who were the first settlers in a territory (Bowen, 2000).

There are several cases in which the Inter-American Court of Human Rights (IACHR) has explained the importance of indigenous collective rights. The cases are Mayagna (Sumo) Awas Tingni Vs. Nicaragua (2000); Comunidad Indígena Yakye Axa Vs. Paraguay (2005); Partido político Yatama Vs. Nicaragua (2005); Comunidad Moiwana Vs. Surinam (2005); Comunidad Indígena Sawhoyamaxa Vs. Paraguay (2006); Comunidad Indígena Xákmok Kásek Vs. Paraguay (2010); Pueblo Indígena Kichwa de Sarayaku Vs. Ecuador (2012); Caso Masacres de Río Negro Vs. Guatemala (2012); Kuna de Madungandí y Emberá de Bayano y Sus miembros Vs. Panamá (2014); Pueblos Kaliña y Lokono Vs. Surinam (2015); Comunidad Garífuna Triunfo de la Luz y sus Miembros Vs. Honduras (2015); Comunidad Garífuna de Punta Piedra y sus Miembros Vs. Honduras (2015); Comunidad Campesina de Santa Bárbara vs. Perú (2015); Miembros de la Aldea Chichupac y comunidades vecinas del Municipio de Rabinal Vs. Guatemala (2016); Pueblo Indígena Xucuru y sus miembros Vs. Brasil (2018); and Comunidades indígenas miembros de la Asociación Lhaka Honhat (Nuestra Tierra) Vs. Argentina (2020).[3] In the majority of them, the main problem was the access to the land and the exploitation of natural resources (Sauca & Wences, 2015). One of the most famous cases is the "Pueblo Indígena Kichwa de Sarayaku Vs. Ecuador." In this case, the IACHR has changed its jurisprudence to recognize that the indigenous peoples are the collective subject of the International Law system. Before this, the opinion of the court was to give rights to members or individuals of the indigenous peoples using an individualistic point of view (Carmona Caldera, 2013; Sauca & Wences, 2015). Thus, in previous cases, indigenous peoples wielded rights as individuals belonging to a community. The case "Indígenas Kuna de Madungandí y Emberá de Bayano y Sus miembros Vs. Panamá" reaffirms the idea of "Pueblo Indígena Kichwa de Sarayaku Vs. Ecuador," expressing indigenous peoples as a wielder of collective rights (Sauca & Wences, 2015).

However, they have not been entirely successful at recognizing collective rights in the national legislation with the same level of protection, even with all the benefits these international instruments and jurisprudence bring to indigenous peoples. For example, these standards are not binding for private corporations that exploit natural resources, and the states do not necessarily align their national legislation to the international standards. Therefore, indigenous social movements are present to bring awareness regarding the realities of indigenous peoples (O'Faircheallaigh, 2013), but other multiple factors help to recognize them in the domestic order. So, this is the reason that the book wants to address.

ANTI-NEOLIBERAL MASS MOBILIZATIONS IN LATIN AMERICA: EFFECTIVENESS OF INDIGENOUS SOCIAL MOVEMENT FOR PROTECTING COLLECTIVE RIGHTS

This section will address the role of social movements and indigenous social movements in Latin America. The role of social movement in the region is essential to understand the rise of new political actors. In the case of indigenous peoples, social movements and their tools of mobilization create a common identity for these (new) political actors.

Social Movements: Becoming a Political Actor in Latin America

The last decades are impressive because for the young democracies of the region, there has been one new actor who influences how the authorities make decisions in the public realm: the peoples (Almeida & Cordero Ulate, 2017; Bellinger & Arce, 2011; Boulding & Holzner, 2015; Madrid, 2012; Moseley, 2015; Rossi & von Bulow, 2016; Stahler-Sholk et al., 2014; Yashar, 2005). Latin America has experienced much change through the models of development, political power, and the building of an off-centered political field theory where the focus is on actors rather than the state (Krupa & Nugent, 2015). For different reasons, there has been an increasing number of mobilizations in the region. Now, social movements are a reality, and the political literature has assumed this fact.

In the political field, apart from Cuba and Venezuela, Latin America has consolidated electoral democracies in all countries, as Moseley (2015) states. However, this is still not enough to strengthen the democratic institutions in the region due to multiple factors that continue to create social instability, for example, poverty, exclusion, and lack of work. Therefore, in many countries of the region, the rules of the game change very quickly and provoke instability. These factors create a fragile political system built only for the participation of a few citizens. Furthermore, those left behind try to find ways of participating in the political field (Moseley, 2015). Thus, "protest emerges due to the inability of formal political institutions to adequately channel and respond to the voices of active democratic citizens" (Moseley, 2015, p. 11). This is important to understand the Latin American context when exploring people's possibilities in democratic participation.

The repoliticization literature states characteristics of this process of participation: collective actors take action in this capitalist era when democracy is present; class-based actors mobilize against market policies; there are new actors in the public field that want to participate; and economic liberalization must provoke protest of different sectors of the population which authorities change their decision (Bellinger & Arce, 2011). This idea is evident in countries like Ecuador and Bolivia, where the "pink tide," a mix between electoral left and discredit of neoliberal policies, brings governments that support and potentiate social movements (Stahler-Sholk, Vanden & Becker, 2014). Bellinger and Arce postulate that "the presence of democracy enhances the opportunity for collective political activities" (Bellinger & Arce, 2011, p. 691). This postulate is valid for the Latin American reality, specifically for indigenous social movements, and the literature confirms it (Moseley, 2015).

Indigenous Social Movements: Creating Identity

In the context of democracy and economic liberalization, the indigenous mobilizations are one of the actors who have found their way to participate (Aylwin, 2014; Boulding & Holzner, 2015; Madrid, 2012; Moseley, 2015; Rousseau, 2016; Stahler-Sholk et al., 2014; Van Cott, 2003, 2004; Yashar, 2005). This participation becomes a surprise considering that indigenous peoples represent 8% of the total population in the Latin American region, according to the Economic Commission for Latin America and the Caribbean (CEPAL, 2014; ECLAC, 2008). These movements are part of the "new social movements" that focus on conflict regarding lifestyle, identities, and solidarity (Almeida & Cordero Ulate, 2017; Wade, 2010). Indigenous social movements started to become stronger at the end of the 1980s (Wade, 2010). According to Benavides-Vanegas (2009), indigenous social movements result from diverse factors such as local mobilizations, networks with international organizations, and a new understanding of the indigenous legal position.

The critical characteristics of indigenous social movements are two: the actors are indigenous peoples, and they focus on the recognition of their cultural identities. Hsieh states that "[t]he indigenous movement is a wave of politically active peoples who have, with market success, asserted their rights over the last three decades all over the world" (Hsieh, 2006). This idea points out the fact that they are not a minority who wants to participate in the political realm. Instead, it is confirmed the idea of indigenous peoples as politically active, focusing on the fact they had existed even before there were western organizations and authorities present in the region, as several scholars state (Barié, 2003; Jovanović, 2012; Ketley, 2001), thus they are not outside of the system, and indigenous peoples have rights that are unquestionable and irrevocable.

Regarding identities, these indigenous groups want to move away from the political agenda, which dictates that they need "development" as a social group. Furthermore, they want to decolonize the liberal thinking and recognize their many ways of life (T. Hall & Fenelon, 2009; Stahler-Sholk et al., 2014). The indigenous peoples want to live the concept of buen vivir (well-being). This concept must be understood as a framework of a non-capitalist way of life, where there is a society in a direct and harmonic relationship with the natural environment (Stahler-Sholk et al., 2014; Warren & Jackson, 2002; Yashar, 2005). This sacred relationship is part of their dignity and pride as a community of people. This approach has been called a "Pan-American discourse" that celebrates the indigenous distinctiveness (Warren & Jackson, 2002) based on their cultural identities.

Thus, their cultural identities are in a close relationship with the inclusion of these ideas into the political-juridical system. Indigenous peoples are outsiders from political, social, and economic realms. Mainly because their communities are generally poor and lack the resources necessary to participate, indigenous communities have lower levels of education when compared to non-indigenous peoples (Boulding & Holzner, 2015; Cruz-Saco, 2018; Stahler-Sholk et al., 2014).

This goal is related to recognizing indigenous as collective entities (Jovanović, 2012). Their cosmovision is a manifestation of a common culture. There is mutual recognition of their members, and, at the same time, there is self-identification through the general characteristics of the groups. This situation is associated with the culture as a mark of their personal preferences (Jovanović, 2012). Consequently, national and international instruments codified these characteristics, using rights and human rights (Badger, 2010; Hsieh, 2006; Ketley, 2001; Kreimer, 2000; Van Cott, 2000; Warren & Jackson, 2002), as it was stated in previous sections. The indigenous social movements coincided with an international movement to codify social, economic, and cultural rights (Van Cott, 2000) based on the international instrument of Public Law.

The indigenous social movements represent an alternative for indigenous peoples to the traditional model of political representation based on political parties and civil society that represent the white and mestizo interests (Van Cott, 2004). This alternative model was especially true for the Andean region of Latin America—Peru, Bolivia, Ecuador, Colombia, and Venezuela (Van Cott, 2004). The indigenous social movement introduces a more inclusive national identity, debating the concept of citizenship and showing the failure of the assimilation project of the nation-state (Van Cott, 2004; Yashar, 2005). Thus, the social and indigenous movements are a consequence of the instability of political institutions that push citizens to a more radical model of participation in Latin America (Moseley, 2015). Moreover, it creates a new way of participation and citizenship (Van Cott, 2004; Yashar, 2005).

Having all this present, some actual demands from the social movements express the recognition of their collective identities. Indigenous peoples claim self-determination and autonomy, cultural distinctiveness, political reforms rebuilding the notion of state, right to the land and natural resources, and reforms of how military and police behave toward indigenous peoples (Benavides-Vanegas, 2009; Van Cott cited by Warren & Jackson, 2002). Thus, most of these demands can be expressed in legal language as collective rights. Therefore, the literature sees a clear connection between them. However, this research will add new factors and evidence to contribute to a profound and detailed analysis.

NOTES

1. The Spanish and French colonizers who arrived in the Americas coined the term "indigenous," and it is used mainly in the Americas and Australia (Bowen, 2000). This term derived from the Latin term *"indigena,"* which means born in a country or native (Hodgson, 2002).

2. Article 1.1. This Convention applies to:
   (a) tribal peoples in independent countries whose social, cultural, and economic conditions distinguish them from other sections of the national community and whose status is regulated wholly or partially by their customs or traditions or by special laws or regulations;
   (b) peoples in independent countries who are regarded as indigenous on account of their descent from the populations which inhabited the country, or a geographical region to which the country belongs, at the time of conquest or colonization or the establishment of present state boundaries and who, irrespective of their legal status, retain some or all of their own social, economic, cultural, and political institutions.

3. There are other cases related to indigenous peoples in which the complainant is individual not the community, as example: "Masacre de Mapiripán" Vs. Colombia (2005); Tiu Tojín Vs. Guatemala (2008); Rosendo Cantú y otra Vs. México (2010); CFernández Ortega y otros. Vs. México (2010); Chitay Nech y otros Vs. Guatemala; Norín Catrimán y otros (Dirigentes, miembros y activista del Pueblo Indígena Mapuche) Vs. Chile (2012); and Familia Pacheco Tineo vs. Bolivia (2013).

Chapter 2

Constructing the Theory

The New Role of Indigenous Social Movements and Explaining Other Institutional Conditions for Increasing the Collective Rights of Indigenous Peoples

This chapter explains the backbone of the book. Indigenous social movements are more likely to include collective rights when they become a strong national actor, creating coalitions between indigenous peoples to influence the political system, mainly if anti-systems movements or left parties create coalitions with other non-indigenous allies. According to the previous observation of the cases in Latin America, there are also two ways indigenous peoples can increase protection: A weak party system that allows the authorities to make more radical decisions in the economic field and the constitutional instability that allows to change the constitutional model, including the indigenous cosmovision. The difference in the level of inclusion of collective rights depends on the interaction of the conditions, creating weak, moderate, or strong collective rights.

In several sections of this book, this argument unfolds. First, this research explains the role of indigenous social movements, the concept, and theoretical approaches for building coalitions between indigenous nationalities and other non-indigenous allies to include these rights. The first section concludes by explaining how these two conditions work together to include a different level of collective rights. Second, this chapter explains two institutional conditions that enhance this protection: the political party system and institutionalization and the constitutional change as a tool of inclusion. At the end of this second section, I analyze the role of the interaction of these two conditions to incorporate more indigenous rights. Finally, I explain how these two sets of conditions, organizations, and institutions work together to achieve the outcomes creating a theory that includes diverse paths for a diverse level of collective rights. This is called equifinality theory.

INDIGENOUS SOCIAL MOVEMENTS: ARE INDIGENOUS MOBILIZATIONS SUCCESSFUL, IF SO THEN WHEN?

In general, indigenous peoples are more likely to attain collective rights when they can build coalitions between themselves, such as organizations and confederations, and form permanent alliances with other non-indigenous peoples. Indigenous social movements that do not form coalitions, specifically, are not strong enough to change the political system. The problem of indigenous social movements in the region is the lack of organizational strength (McAdam, 1982). Also, the low number of indigenous populations can be a problem that weakens the movements. They are not "able to maintain and successfully utilize their . . . acquired political leverage to advance collective interest" (McAdam, 1982). However, creating coalitions with other indigenous peoples and non-indigenous people, such as minorities, social movements, or left parties, generates the opportunity to include their demands as part of a packet of modifications with potential compromises and eventual loss of some of their demands. This part of the research uses the literature related to bi-racial coalitions in the United States, taking a few of their elements to contextualize how they work in Latin America to note a coalition-building theory.

Coalitions and Their Different Theoretical Approaches

The most seminal definition of coalition states that it "is the joint source of resources by two or more social units" (Gramson, 1991, p. 374). Social movement coalitions exist when "two or more social movements work together on a common task" (Van Dyke & McCammon, 2010, p. xiv). One organization cannot achieve any political goal by itself (Goy, 2008; Meyer, 2005; Obach, 2004). Thus, coalition formation is more common for groups that are not influential, such as indigenous peoples. These coalitions aim to transform society through actions (Smith & Bandy, 2005) and pursue social justice to end several forms of oppression (Bystydzienski & Schacht, 2001). It is easier to find natural allies in some cases, such as other movements with the same interest. Nevertheless, to advance in common political goals, cooperation within social movements is usual (Obach, 2004).

The literature on coalitions and social movements has developed several theoretical approaches: resource mobilization, which explains the structure, strategies, institutions, and opportunities of these coalitions; and identity politics, which addresses the internal dynamics of social movements and their shared identity, helping to build coalitions (Bystydzienski & Schacht, 2001). There is a third approach from the stance of "the critical social theory" that emphasizes coalitions as a tool for fighting against oppression and unfair ideas and practices. In this type of approach, the differences in peoples are central to creating coalitions (Bystydzienski & Schacht, 2001). These multiple identities produce enough flexibility for the participants in social movements to connect from diverse "positionality" with other groups to form coalitions (Barvosa-Carter, 2001). A sense of belonging to more than one community (Barvosa-Carter, 2001) is helpful to create a united front. Barvosa-Carter states "that multiple identities can increase links between individual citizens and a range of politicized groups. It can underpin a synergistic process of identity and community (trans)formation that can become the basis for radical political alliances" (Barvosa-Carter, 1999, pp. 123–124). Having diverse identities can build a more vital organization to pursue social justice. I will expand this concept with one example in a further section.

The concept of a coalition does not mean the same as other related terms. Coalitions are a long-term commitment to achieve social justice. They can start as alliances and networks. However, these relationships between social movements develop and expand to be more stable and produce changes. For example, alliances are a short-term relationship, ad-hoc effort to work together, and network is the informal exchange of information or ideas between social movements (Smith & Bandy, 2005). This research uses the concept of coalition as a long-term relationship and it will be based on the theory of identity politics. I will focus on the idea of coalitions of indigenous peoples as a collective identity and add elements of the multiple identities in the coalitions that indigenous peoples create with non-indigenous peoples.

Contribution of the Coalition-Building Theory for Indigenous Peoples

In this case, the specific contribution of the coalition-building theory is the lack of studies that analyze these coalitions between indigenous peoples and non-indigenous allies in the context of recognizing more collective rights in Latin America. It is possible to find literature on coalitions with general social movements. The main characteristic of these works is their focus on the outcome of these relationships, and they often study the reality of the United States or other regions (Beamish & Luebbers, 2009; Meyer, 2005; Obach, 2004; Smith & Bandy, 2005; Stearns & Almeida, 2004). For example, there are studies of cross-movement alliances in the United States pointing out the tension for positional differences reflected in race, class, gender, among others (Beamish & Luebbers, 2009); the role of social movements coalitions in the institutionalization of concerns in the United States (Meyer, 2005); and, the coalitions between state agencies and social movements in Japan (Stearns & Almeida, 2004). Other studies focus on transnational cooperation that can form coalitions, transforming into long-term relationships (Smith & Bandy, 2005), such as the international coalitions of lesbian, gay, bisexual, and transgender (Ungar, 2001) and coalitions working for social justice with NGOs and international governance (Cullen, 2001).

The work of Grossman (2001) in terms of ethnic coalitions explains the alliances between Native Americans and rural whites in Northern Wisconsin. Since 1970 it is essential to understand the common purpose of these alliances. As stated in chapter 1, the most influential studies that research the indigenous movements and their achievements are by Van Cott (2004, 2007) and the collective book coordinated by Postero and Zamosc (2006) using case studies, the latter researchers look for the relationship between coalitions and indigenous rights in Latin America. The authors' inquiry is to regard the rights of indigenous peoples who should have as citizens in several Latin American countries, each of the eight authors mentioned explaining one country. Some other studies focus on this topic, but the majority of them refer to the success and creation of ethnic-political parties, such as Madrid (2012) and Van Cott (2000, 2004). It is possible to see a mix between indigenous social movements and left parties in those political parties. Specifically, Madrid (2012) states that the successful electoral performance of indigenous parties is due to ethnic and populist appeals. Van Cott (2004) argues that three factors increase the likelihood of having indigenous parties: decentralization, improved access to the ballot for novel parties, and reserved seats for indigenous in several institutions. In both cases, the authors found that these characteristics are present in the case of the MAS party in Bolivia and the Pachakutic party in Ecuador. Therefore, to add more studies to the Latin American case becomes essential.

This research adds coalitions as a requirement to create more indigenous collective rights in the region. It provides evidence of the results of these coalitions between indigenous peoples and non-indigenous allies. Therefore, the following sections will explain how indigenous peoples create coalitions between themselves and other non-indigenous allies to recognize more collective rights.

Coalitions between Indigenous Peoples: Become a Strong Actor

The indigenous social movements are a significant influence for including collective rights in countries where there is a collaboration among different groups of indigenous peoples. In each country, it is possible to find diverse indigenous peoples. For example, in Brazil, there exist 305 different indigenous peoples, tribes, or nationalities; in Colombia, 102; Peru, 85 (CEPAL); and in Chile, 10. It is possible to achieve their goals when they work together. In this case, they build coalitions that are more likely to secure collective rights at the political and social level, when indigenous peoples can develop a group interest related to a common fate and recognize that all indigenous peoples in a country share a collective cultural identity. Further paragraphs will explain this in more detail.

These coalitions pursue a group interest, with the two elements: social and economic components (Dawson, 1994). Regarding the former, the social aspect of these coalitions is based on group interest, which is fighting against discrimination. Here we can see a linked fate (Dawson, 1994). The idea of linked fate is present in the characteristics of this group. This concept was first used by Dawson (1994) to explain the discrimination against African Americans in the United States. It defines "as an acute sense of awareness (or recognition) that what happens to the group will also affect the individual member" (Simien, 2005, p. 529). In this case, this idea is applied to the diverse indigenous peoples who share several elements such as language, cultural practices, and levels of education. These characteristics create a sense of oppression not only because they are indigenous but also because they are poor and do not have the resources to be influential in the political field outside of a coalition. Thus, what happens with one group or tribe, or one individual, would befall all of them.

The World Bank has studied the level of poverty across the indigenous population to illustrate this reality of deprivation for indigenous peoples. This study spans five countries, with the most indigenous peoples in Latin America (Bolivia, Ecuador, Guatemala, Mexico, and Peru). The findings of this report are impressive and remarkable. The study conducted from 1994 to 2004 shows few gains in terms of income poverty reduction, and indigenous peoples recover more slowly from an economic crisis. They also concluded that being indigenous increases an individual's probability of being poor. Their labor earnings are far below that of non-indigenous peoples, and indigenous peoples often have fewer years of formal education than non-indigenous peoples. Education results are substantially worse for indigenous peoples. Indigenous peoples, especially women and children, have less access to essential health services (G. P. Hall Harry Anthony, 2004). All these findings, oriented by economic data, explain the role and place of indigenous peoples in the Latin American racial and social order. This is the reality in countries with a high level of indigenous populations. In that case, it can be assumed that the scenario is more precarious for countries with low populations of indigenous peoples with less influence in the political field, such as

Argentina, Chile, and Costa Rica. For such a problem, indigenous peoples need to fight against discrimination and influence the political and juridical system to make the changes.

Regarding the economic aspect, indigenous peoples are bonding to change the understanding of the liberal paradigm. The liberal paradigm states the value of freedom as the center of all relationships. It advocates for the prosperity of the people promoting civil and economic liberties, all of them based on individual rights. In this paradigm, the government regulates only the public sphere, non-addressing the private life of citizens. The liberal ideas have been crucial for Latin America since the period of independence at the end of the nineteenth century (Rivera, 2016). After two centuries of applying this paradigm, the countries of Latin America are not developed countries (Bulmer-Thomas, 2017). In most indexes, these countries have "medium income," with an improvement in industrialization and urbanization, and an increase in the exportation of resources, such as sugar and coffee, even at the expense of the natural resources of the region (Bulmer-Thomas, 2017). In this liberal paradigm, the state's role is minimum, with a high level of private investment. These policies of non-intervention of the country have brought a stagnant economy, a high unemployment rate, and a high level of poverty (Quijano, 2004). Therefore, there is an increase in social mobilization in the region to focus on changing the liberal politics implemented since the 1990s (Bellinger & Arce, 2011; Silva, 2009). These new actors in the public field want to participate by provoking protests, which will impact authorities to change the system through several instruments (Bellinger & Arce, 2011; Moseley, 2015; Silva, 2009).

The cultural identities that they exhibit are the other element that helps to form coalitions between indigenous peoples. Indigenous peoples are collective entities (Jovanović, 2012). Even if they belong to different indigenous nationalities, they bond together because their point of view of life is a manifestation of a common culture. There is a mutual recognition of their members, and, at the same time, there is self-identification through the general characteristics of the group. This situation is associated with the fact that even the personal preferences of indigenous peoples are marked by this culture (Jovanović, 2012).

The cultural identities behind their social mobilization are a crucial element of the analysis. Although all the indigenous peoples in the region are different, they have common identities that make them work hand to hand. In Latin America, according to Hooker, indigenous peoples "are generally better positioned than most Afro-Latinos to claim ethnic group identities separate from the national culture and have therefore been more successful in winning collective rights" (Hooker, 2005, p. 285). As a group that is a minority in comparison to the rest of the population, they are in a better place than others, but they are still excluded from the political field. Here we can see the apparent tension between the themes of distinctiveness and inclusion (Sniderman & Piazza, 2002). Distinctiveness means the characteristics that make a person or group different. Inclusion

> entails greater access to power and public and private resources and improves the way society views group members. Inclusivity is realized when historically or currently marginalized groups feel valued, when differences are respected, and when weak and fundamental needs and rights—relative to those society's dominant groups—are met and recognized. (Haas Institute, 2016, p. 4)

These two concepts are not pulling to opposite sides. They are working to potentiate minorities, in the case of this research, to enhance the cultural differences of indigenous peoples and increase participation in the political field.

Linked fate and cultural identities must interact to form an indigenous national organization. Sometimes, there are barriers to create these organizations: the lack of political willingness to create a coalition and the lack of incentives to form national organizations. Regarding political willingness, the indigenous leaders can be skeptical regarding the importance of coalitions if, in the past, some alliances or coordination between groups did not work. Sometimes, there is a lack of incentives to create national organizations because there is no political or juridical culture of associativism, so creating a coalition is more complicated and less beneficial for the group. In these cases, the indigenous people decide to try to influence the system, but the results will be less auspicious.

Having a cohesive indigenous group is a tool of pressure for different policies. A national or regional organization that unites all, or at least the majority of indigenous peoples in the country, can act as a political actor with the government, pushing for achieving shared interest in the social and economic realm, including their collective identities in the language of collective rights. Indigenous peoples can directly influence the political field, when confederations, organizations, councils, and coordinators are created. The narrative of the relationships between indigenous peoples and government changes. The government has to face an organized group of peoples who request held demands. This occurs no matter how big or small the indigenous population in the country is at the time. Countries with a high number of indigenous peoples such as Ecuador, Bolivia, Guatemala, and Mexico count on national or regional coalitions between indigenous peoples. Moreover, it is possible to find a robust national confederation in countries like Colombia, with a low level of the indigenous population.

Coalition with Non-Indigenous Peoples:
The Process of Binding with New Allies

For building coalitions between diverse actors, these "must be conceptualized as fluid sites of collective behavior where the blending of multiple personal identities with political activism interacts with structural conditions to influence the development of commitments, strategies, and specific actions" (Bystydzienski & Schacht, 2001). These elements, multiple identities, political activism, structural conditions, and mobilizations are present in the case of relationships between indigenous peoples and non-indigenous allies.

In this case, indigenous social movements are not strong enough to change the political system. The number of indigenous populations is an important part of weakening the movements. However, collaboration with non-indigenous peoples, such as other actors like anti-system social movements or alliances with left political parties, creates the opportunity to include their demand, which can consist of collective rights of indigenous peoples. In particular, the cooperation with the left parties has been documented in the case of Mexico and Bolivia (Disney & Williams, 2014) and Ecuador (Madrid, 2012) and also the importance of collaborators in the Colombian case (Rappaport, 2005).

In this scenario, the help of "other allies" (Denzin et al., 2008), the nonindigenous population, especially the mestizo population, is central to achieving the objective. Being mixed race or "*mestizo*" means a racial-ethnic mixing into the communities, which impacts two characteristics. First, this is a biological process in which people from European descendants and natives from Latin America bring into the world mixed-race children. Second, it is a process of cultural assimilation and subjugation in which indigenous peoples lose their cultural practices and identity as a group (Madrid, 2012; Wade, 2010). Thus, becoming allies of indigenous peoples shows a recognition between groups as equal. The power of social movements as a political actor comes from the union of several sectors of the society who negotiate together, pursuing a change. In these cases, this is the only option to keep the level of insurgency and social control with their demand to achieve a collective attribution (McAdam, 1982).

According to the literature that explains bi-racial coalitions in the United States, several elements allow these different groups to work together. These elements can be appreciated differently in indigenous/non-indigenous coalitions. Sonenshein (2006) describes three requirements for these coalitions: ideology, shared interest (or at least not a conflict of interest), and leadership. The following paragraphs explain these elements, starting with the problem of the denomination.

It is not possible to use the term bi-racial coalitions in the region. The terms race and ethnicity are entangled with the idea of mestizaje. Both terms denote cultural differences or even class differences more than just phenotypic characteristics (Cadena, 2001; Wade, 2010). According to De la Cadena, "[c] ulturalist visions of race have been pervasive among Latin American thinkers, and their efforts have not necessary (sic) been aimed at separating race from culture" (De la Cadena, 2001, p. 23). The process of mixed race does not make it possible to find distinct racial groups in Latin America. Thus, being indigenous means being part of an ethnicity more than a race.

Ideology is one of the factors helping to create coalitions (Sonenshein, 2006). It is the most important within the realm of Latin America. However, it works in two diverse directions. First, there is a need to have a wider concept about the state, which means that the state and government need to have more power to develop more functions, such as providing free health care and education. Other minority groups and left parties share with indigenous peoples the idea that human rights are central to a government. The states must secure those rights for the people to achieve their common good or have the minimum for living and development. This idea is related to anti-neoliberal politics. There is a new role for the state based on the well-being of the citizens. These indigenous social movements have found allies in liberal labor groups and political parties that embrace these ideas. Thus, in this case, indigenous or non-indigenous are mobilized against a system of beliefs. It seems like the Washington Consensus, the implementation of neoliberal policies as the only instrument to achieving economic development, is broken (Grugel & Riggirozzi, n.d.; Stahler-Sholk et al., 2014).

Second, Latin American citizens demand more participation, particularly marginalized groups. The people want to participate actively in the decision-making process. This scenario focuses on actors who influence the political field rather than the state that takes these decisions by itself (Krupa & Nugent, 2015). This model is called "horizontalism" (Stahler-Sholk et al., 2014), which means that Latin America has experienced much change through the models of development, political power, and the building of an off-centered political field theory.

According to Sonenshein (2006), the second element for coalitions is the shared interest or absence of conflict of interest. In these cases, each of the new social mobilizations in Latin America wants to achieve new public policies that benefit them. There is a vital factor of self-interest, but also, those groups know that they are stronger together. In the case of left parties, depending on the country, they become allies because they can find strong support for the election of indigenous peoples, depending on the size of the population. This is a true reality particularly in Ecuador, Bolivia, and Peru, where the size of the indigenous population is unusually large, and the left parties can be united with ethnic parties, making the influence stronger (Madrid, 2012).

Finally, the last element is leadership (Sonenshein, 2006). This is the most complex element to consider in Latin America because there is no straight rule of how leaders work to unite indigenous peoples with non-indigenous communities. There are cases where the leader has identified himself as an indigenous one, such as Bolivia. The leadership proved successful when the indigenous population took the presidential office with Evo Morales. In other cases, such as Ecuador, the guidance has been in the hands of mixed race and indigenous peoples. They were able to influence essential topics, including the case of two presidential resignations, under pressure from the indigenous and non-indigenous coalitions (Salinas de Dosch, 2012). Behind this flexibility is the idea of multiple identities concerning the process of mixed-race peoples (*mestizaje*).

Multiple identities mean every person has an "array of social identities" (Barvosa-Carter, 2001, p. 24) related to gender and sexual identities, cultural, ethnic, racial, and ideological identities, along with identities based on nationality, lifestyle, socioeconomic status, among many others. These identities are integrated and mutually conditioning (Barvosa-Carter, 2001). Everyone performs or shows the character that best fits each moment's social context. This phenomenon is visible in the process of leadership between indigenous peoples and non-indigenous allies in Latin America. The mixed-race condition allows the leader to use the element of indigenous and white identity to become more appealing in running a coalition. The notable example of Alejandro Toledo in Peru is evidence of this phenomenon. He embraced his highland origin and Quechua symbols, and he also used his education at Stanford University, being a former World Bank employee (Garcia-Huidobro, 2016); furthermore, the diverse use of symbols allowed Toledo to lead coalitions filled with people from diverse ethnic backgrounds, using his multiples identities and cultural symbology.

According to Ture and Hamilton (1992), the coalition does not work when its members have a different status in society, the political field, and the economic sphere. The "new social movements" (NSMs) in Latin America focus on excluded groups from the political and economic areas. NSMs mean mobilization of groups related to gender, race, ethnicity, sexuality, spirituality, countercultures, environmentalism, and animal rights, in contrast with the old movements of the working class (Buechler, 2013). The neoliberal politics have been complicated for several minorities groups, especially indigenous peoples. They are the most disadvantaged group (Boulding & Holzner, 2015; Stahler-Sholk et al., 2014) working together and often attaining help from other groups, especially left parties. Therefore, these groups articulate their demands as new social policies related to the welfare state. They gain more support to increase their likelihood of influencing the political field when non-indigenous groups form coalitions with indigenous peoples.

Furthermore, if the coalition is made with left political parties, they gain more support and make a statement about what political program they believe in, a more progressive one. Therefore, the coalition works, even if they have more wealth and power than indigenous peoples. Also, it is possible to find other preconditions stated by Ture and Hamilton (1992) in these coalitions. The coalitions deal with specific and identifiable goals, and in the case of indigenous peoples, it is the inclusion of rights at the national level. Each group has its independent base power that lies in its constituents called to mobilize. In the end, groups form coalitions to gain something in the political field, not losing what they already are and their expectations. Generally, these expectations are related to changing aspects of societies that are not working correctly for them. The modifications in the legal field are part of these changes, pursuing recognition and rights.

The Role of Coalitions in the Process to Include More Collective Rights

Coalitions between indigenous peoples and coalitions with non-indigenous allies are two critical ones by themselves to increase the probability of getting more collective rights in the countries. However, if they both are present in the system, there are more opportunities to include collective rights. This change occurs because to become a coherent movement that provides for all or most nationalities forming coalitions with other non-indigenous allies makes a strong political actor. The consequences are having more power to negotiate, more representation and knowledge of how to use the language of traditional politics.

Indigenous peoples and their new organizations have more power to negotiate in extraordinary events when there are national organizations of indigenous peoples and coalitions with other groups. They become a relevant element in spaces of deliberation and peace processes in violent countries. This power of negotiation happened in the case of Colombia via the National Assembly of 1991 (Rathgeber, 2004) and Guatemala in their post-conflict agreements (Torres-Rivas, 2006). Thanks to indigenous confederations and their coalitions, these processes recognized collective rights successfully.

Related to the capacity to negotiate, these coalitions represent a broader number of people. In particular, there are more citizens who are participating in the political field, exposing their concerns. The coalitions create more extended topics to focus on, bringing more people who want to collaborate and cooperate. Their interest of them becomes more transversal to diverse organizations. This happens with issues related to lands. For example, territories and land are not just a concern for indigenous peoples but also for peasants and general citizen organizations. Mexico and Ecuador are examples of diverse organizations that work toward the same objective, protecting lands (Dietz, 2004; Zamosc, 2004).

Creating coalitions with left parties produces a new way of navigating the political field for social movements. They learn and understand the political language to negotiate effectively with the government and start to use the institutional path to push for changes related to their demands. The evidence of this new understanding is found in countries such as Bolivia, Colombia, and Ecuador. The fluidity between indigenous social movement leaders and left party politicians shows a close connection between them (Postero, 2004; Rathgeber, 2004; Zamosc, 2004), helping them navigate the political field.

In these cases, in which the two conditions work together, it is possible to recognize strong collective rights in juridical-political systems. This recognition means that indigenous peoples are entitled to have their organizational system without the opinion of the state and national governments. In this case, the government decreases the level of its power in favor of indigenous peoples. Also, there is a high level of differentiation among indigenous peoples. This means that society is recognized as diverse. Therefore, the difference between groups is visible, sharing their diverse ways of living in a respectful context. The collective rights considered as strong are the rights to be considered a nation, self-determination, and the right to use customary indigenous law. These rights make it easier to wield, exercise, and implement other rights such as cultural diversity and language.

Suppose that there is an absence of coalitions between indigenous peoples and other non-indigenous allies. In that case, the outcome will be a weak presence of collective rights of indigenous peoples, which means only a couple of rights related to recognize a superficial level of differentiation. Even with a high level of indigenous social movements, it will be a recognition of the culture with no autonomy for indigenous peoples, and the government is not willing to give up any of its power. In this case, the difference between diverse groups in society is not visible, with a high degree of assimilation in a hegemonic group. In this case of weak collective rights, it is only possible to find rights such as cultural diversity and language. These rights are essential because they allow starting in cultural differentiation, but they only show a minimum threshold of rights for indigenous peoples.

There is an increment in the inclusion of collective rights when there is only one of these conditions, coalitions between indigenous peoples or with non-indigenous allies. It is possible to see a moderate level of these rights. Moderate collective rights mean an increase in differentiation, making the difference among more visible groups, but indigenous peoples cannot use their organizational system. The government gives up some of its power, but with a high level of regulations on strategic topics, such as the right to land and territories, natural resources, the right to bilingual education, and the right to participate in the political field. Table 2.1 shows all these expected outcomes.

Table 2.1   Coalition Conditions under Study and Outcomes Regarding Collective Rights

Coalitions		With Non-Indigenous Peoples	
		Present	Absent
Between indigenous peoples	Present	Strong collective rights	Moderate collective rights
	Absent	Moderate collective rights	Weak collective rights

Hypothesis 1: Strong collective rights are associated with the development of coalitions between indigenous peoples when there exist also coalitions with non-indigenous allies.

THE INSTITUTIONAL CONDITIONS TO TELL THE STORY: PARTY SYSTEM AND CONSTITUTIONAL CHANGE

Particularly in the Andean Region during the past years, there have been changes in politics related to a new way of thinking about the concept of power. In many countries in the region, the rules of the game change very quickly due to a series of causes: personalistic governments, economic instability, corruption, among others, and provoke general instability. This degree of institutional uncertainty often has direct consequences on the quality of public policy (Moseley, 2015). According to the theory of this book, having a weak party system and constitutional instability will create better conditions for including collective rights for indigenous peoples. These conditions show the instability of the political system; however, they are an opportunity to improve the political and juridical system, opening them for diverse cosmovision.

Institutional Conditions: The Types of Institutions for Having More Indigenous Collective Rights

According to North, "[i]nstitutions are the rules of the game in societies or, more formally, are the humanly devised constraint that shape human interaction" (North, 1990, p. 3). These rules are not only crucial for society as an abstract element but also to institutions, which are necessary for the political and juridical fields. Institutions can be formal when there are rules and informal when there are norms, conventions, or codes of conduct (North, 1990). The difference between them is not a problem of a kind, but how they show different degrees of constraints, from traditions to written constitutions

(North, 1990). This part of the research focuses on formal rules that give organized solutions and structure to collective actions (Whitley, 1999). Uncertainty will be decreased by providing structure to the relationship between people. Political and juridical institutions are constraints because they establish procedures and limitations that all the actors involved must respect to a certain extent (North, 1990). These institutions impede the actors from destabilizing the political status quo (Pepinsky, 2013).

The institutionalization of the party system and constitutional change in Latin America are two present conditions in this research, and they both are formal institutions that explain how the political-juridical game develops between political actors and state and the relationship between citizens and the people with public institutions. These conditions present a better or worse opportunity for indigenous peoples to include their collective rights, depending on how they receive a diverse worldview in their systems.

Several studies examine the relationship between institutional stability and compliance with human rights (Biddulph, 2015; Peerenboom, 2005; Potter, 2006). According to Peerenboom, "stability is a pre-requisite for the enjoyment of all right" (Peerenboom, 2005, p. 80). This is true regarding individual civil and political rights—rights that are compatible with a liberal system. However, it is essential to have some level of instability to include a new understanding of them in the political and legal system, when it is the time to enshrine and, later, comply with indigenous collective rights, based on solidarity with a group perspective. The following paragraphs will explain this interaction.

Institutionalization of Political Parties: A Radical Approach for Having More Indigenous Collective Rights

According to Powell and Whitten (1993), party systems[1] are designed to provide representation and clarity of responsibility in a democratic context. According to Sartori (1976), a party system is an interaction between political parties[2] that compete for power. According to Van Cott (2007), political parties are the essential connection between state and society in our representative democracies.

An important question arises: what does it mean to have an institutionalized party system? According to Mainwaring, institutionalization means "the process by which a practice or organization becomes well established and widely known, if not universally accepted" (Mainwaring, 1998, p. 68). This process provides value and stability to any organization (Huntington, 1968). In the case of the party system, all the actors have clear and stable expectations regarding the behavior of other actors and the rules of party competition (Mainwaring, 1998). An institutionalized party system presents several characteristics: it has a high level of stability patterns of party competition; political parties present deep roots in the society; and the actors agree on the legitimacy of political parties and the importance of their organization (Mainwaring, 1998; Mainwaring & Torcal, 2006). A recent reconceptualization of party system institutionalization focuses on only two elements and defines it

> As one in which a stable set of parties regularly interacts in stable ways. Actors develop expectations and behavior based on the premise that party competition's fundamental contours and rules will prevail in the foreseeable future. An institutionalized party system shapes the future expectations and behavior of political elites, masses, and other actors. (Mainwaring, 2018a, p. 4)

If a party system presents these two characteristics, the stability of competition between political parties and trustworthy organizations, the system is considered institutionalized. However, if not, the party system is weak or inchoate.

Weak party systems "are less stable and less predictable. These conditions generate less certainty, which affects the logic of major actors in the system" (Mainwaring, 2018a, p. 2). A system in which it is possible to find new significant competitors for the political power and old political parties with no support reflects weak institutionalization (Mainwaring, 2018a). The level of institutionalization of a party system shows stability to make consistent and firm decisions. Murillo (2001) states that an institutionalized party system is more likely to preserve the pro-market status quo, creating only moderate economic transformation. Similarly, Flores-Macias (2012) states that having a weak party system increases the likelihood that authorities decide on more radical reforms and policies. Thus, a more institutionalized party system will result in moderate economic decisions while maintaining pro-market policies.

The Latin American party system is characterized as an organism with differentiating ideological profiles and a different competition structure (Altman et al., 2009). According to Carreras (2012), the evolution of the party system in the region developed in conjunction with the process of democratization, including former armed groups as political parties. Thus, there was more plurality than in other areas. However, at the same time, in the last decades, there has been a process of moderation within political parties which means that a series of constraints were created to push polarized political parties to act underground, not in mainstream politics (Carreras, 2012). In general, party systems in Latin America are unstable and weak (Van Cott, 2007). The literature states that countries such as Ecuador, Bolivia, Colombia, Peru, and Venezuela have experienced the process of deinstitutionalization (Sanchez, 2008). Countries such as Brazil and Chile have shown an increase in the institutionalization process.

The role of institutions to incorporate the collective rights of indigenous peoples is central to this theory. The first institution that impacts this recognition is political parties. Therefore, the authorities are more likely to make more radical decisions when the party system is weak. The addition of indigenous cosmovision is radical because it is organized in different principles. There is more recognition of collective rights for indigenous peoples when there is a radical decision.

So far, studying this condition is important because there is no analysis regarding the relationship between the party system and the collective rights of indigenous peoples. A body of scholarship studies the impact of the party system on other variables in Latin America. These include the effect of the institutionalization of party systems on the level of protests (Arce, 2010), the relationship between political parties and the size of indigenous populations (Van Cott, 2000b), and the impact on the decisions that authorities choose and implement in Latin America (Flores-Macias, 2012; Murillo, 2001; Roberts, 2013). Although for this research, the latter is the most important, the role of the party system, in general, is interesting to assess. The relationship between a weak institutionalization of the political party system and the size of the indigenous peoples has been used to explain how the elites in countries with high percentages of indigenous peoples use the political parties to dominate and control the indigenous populations (Van Cott, 2000). In the case of protest, Arce states, "countries with low levels of party system institutionalization and high levels of legislative fragmentation experience greater levels of protest activity" (Arce, 2010, p. 670). In this proposal, the explanation is focused on the role of a weak political party system for including collective rights that expand the liberal paradigm with more radical decisions and even influence the economic field.

Another important question arises: why is this relationship important to include the collective rights of indigenous peoples? The indigenous cosmovision is a more radical approach, with the protection of nature as a critical element of their relationship with society (Stahler-Sholk et al., 2014; Yashar, 2005). Indigenous peoples see themselves and nature as part of a whole, an ecological family with the exact origins and ancestry; they have respect for it and a deep sense of belonging (Salmón, 2000; UN Environment, 2017). This idea is the base of collective rights, not only for people, but it is also entitled to these rights.

The protection and respect given to the environment are in constant tension by the many ill-witted and environmentally risky decisions authorities and corporations make. The neoliberal policies related to environmental management are highly criticized because free trade, deregulation, privatization, and commodification are more likely to destroy the environment than protect it (Barlow, 2001; Koop & Tole, 2001; Robbins, 2012; Wheeler, 2001). The natural resources also increase conflict with indigenous peoples, notably the hydrocarbons (Oil and Gas) dispute (Vasquez, 2014). The expansion of the paradigm to include the collective rights of indigenous peoples requires that authorities make decisions against the status quo or neoliberal approach, and by making more radical decisions, such as not allowing resources extraction in sacred land for indigenous peoples or expropriating indigenous lands to return them to their ancestral owners.

If collective rights are included in the juridical-political system, it means more protection of the environment to respect the new paradigm in which indigenous peoples can enjoy their rights along with nature. This change has an actual effect on economic decisions by considering that most of the resources in Latin America are from sectors such as forests, agriculture, and fisheries (Liverman & Vilas, 2006).

The argument relies on the idea of the conflict between the indigenous cosmovision and the neoliberal approach. If the political system is stable, there are fewer chances of including indigenous collective rights because the authorities will not put at risk their political capital and prefer to keep the status quo based on neoliberal measures. Authorities are more open to include diverse perspectives in the political and juridical order when there is a weak party system, because they have less to lose. The rules of the game change quickly, so if they are in power, they can make a more radical decision like less exploitation of natural resources to embrace indigenous collective rights.

Constitutional Change: More New Constitutions, More Indigenous Collective Rights

Another important institution of study is the constitution and its duration. The argument of this section states that constitutional change, more specifically constitutional replacement, helps to include new elements into the liberal system. These elements are part of the indigenous cosmovision and enshrine collective rights as a consequence of this.

The significant element in the analysis is the concept of constitutional stability and constitutional instability which allows us to understand the endurance of constitutions. Constitutional stability is the lifespan of a constitution, and it is the length of time that passes between the enactment of a constitution and its formal replacement by another (Negretto, 2008). Constitutional stability can be compromised, producing instability when it is necessary to make a change in the juridical-political system. Constitutional change or constitutional transformation (Lorenz, 2016; Negretto, 2016; Nolte & Schilling-Vacaflor, 2012; Van Cott, 2000a) is understood as any alteration a constitution suffers from being an adaptable instrument for the new necessities of the society and the state. These alterations can be partial or total. If the modification is partial, that is called a constitutional amendment. Negretto (2016) states that this adaptation preserves the revision of the constitution in a changing environment. If the alteration is total—a constitutional replace-ment—it is a political decision to replace the legal order with a brand-new constitution. These constitutional changes are instruments to adapt the legal order to new social realities, especially the constitutional replacement. These changes move from the permanence of the constitution to the dynamics of society, and they can also produce instability.

One of the incentives to change the constitution is the failure of this legal instrument to achieve the public good (Negretto, 2016). The public good is a state of well-being for most of the population. Consequently, if the state does not effectively embrace several groups of the population in the constitution, it is logical that these groups will protest to be part of that public good. In the case of indigenous peoples, it is a particular type of public good produced and enjoyed by a group (Jovanović, 2012).

The central aspect of this part of the theory is how constitutional replace-ment produces instability, creating an active inclusion of diverse elements in the liberal paradigm while collective rights are protected. Three main reasons are derived from constitutional replacement:

- A new constitution can generate better spaces to negotiate a modification among national actors.
- The tendency in Latin America is to change constitutions more often than in the United States and Europe.
- Changing the constitution produces several changes in other rules inside a country.

The institutional change of replacing a constitution is fundamental to effec-tively include the new way of thinking that creates the recognition of collec-tive rights. A constitutional replacement is the only approach to incorporate new onto-epistemologies (Barad, 2007) in the legal system. This concept expresses that our culture and ways of relating to others are influenced by who we are. According to Barad, "[t]he entangled practices of knowing and being are material practices" (Barad, 2007, p. 379). Thus, to know and to be are part of the same tradition and how we get closer to the world. In the case of indigenous peoples, their material practices of knowing and being are not appreciated by the western culture. Therefore, a constitutional replacement can be an opportunity to expand the western paradigm, negotiating new ele-ments. The way of being and the systems of beliefs of indigenous peoples (Kovach, 2009) are included through a change in the most important legal instrument. The incorporation of indigenous cosmovision creates flexibility in the paradigm.

It is easier to change some paradigm elements with a constitutional replace-ment than with amendments. If the constitution states easy rules to change some parts of itself, the tendency would be to have more constitutional endurance (Nolte & Schilling-Vacaflor, 2012). The constitution would last longer with several amendments. For example, this is the case in Chile, with the highest rate of amendment in the region (Negretto, 2016). None of them are related to indigenous peoples because of the liberal principles of the Chilean constitution conflict and the collective perspective of indigenous peoples.

Also, the element of negotiation is indispensable when changing the constitution. Generally, the discussion of a new constitution allows the development of National Constituent Assemblies with representatives from all sectors. This process occurs in the cases of Colombia, Bolivia, Ecuador, and Venezuela (Rathgeber, 2004; Van Cott, 2007). In those cases, indigenous peoples had representatives to address their cosmovision and search for coalitions to recognize the collective rights of indigenous peoples.

There is a high tendency to create new constitutions more often, to change the game's rules than in other regions of the world. Also, the focus on constitutional replacement is because the evidence shows that in Latin America this occurs more often. Studies made by Negretto (2016) state that from 1789 to 2001, Latin America has had 193 constitutions, compared with 51 in Western Europe. In contrast, the amendments level is comparatively inferior: compare from 141 amendments in Latin America to 240 in Western Europe (Negretto, 2016) in the same time frame. This information shows the constitutional instability of the region.

Enshrining a new constitution creates the need for the rest of the rules and provisions in several legal instruments to be coherent with the new constitution orders. Thus, the rest of the legal system needs to be modified to fulfill the constitutional mandate, developing its provisions fully. This change is a consequence of the constitutional supremacy principle, which states the constitution as the first and foremost crucial legal instrument, above all others. This principle claims the superiority of the constitution and the importance of making coherent the legal system with it. The idea was born in the United States with the case of Marbury vs. Madison in 1803. Justice Marshall stated, "If, then, the Courts are to regard the Constitution, and the Constitution is superior to any ordinary act of the legislature, the Constitution, and not such ordinary act, must govern the case to which they both apply." The case was also the beginning of judicial review or "the power of courts to examine law and determine whether it is constitutional" (Walsh & Hemmens, 2008, p. 80).

Applying this principle to indigenous peoples some issues will provoke a series of modifications and create a new body of legal rules to fulfill the new constitutional standards. These modifications will develop and enforce new constitutional provisions. In the case of this research, including some level of indigenous collective rights will produce other legislation and rules related to those rights, increasing the level of protection.

Constitutional instability is a sign of profound institutional conflict. However, it can be an opportunity to introduce new elements to the constitutional system, finally allowing diverse groups in society to negotiate. The inclusion of new elements can help to create other rules in the name of the constitutional supremacy principle, making these changes stronger. Constitutional instability is a reality in Latin America, and indigenous peoples can use it to include new ideas to protect their rights in the constitution.

Institutional Conditions and the Inclusion of Collective Rights

The two factors—weak party system and constitutional instability—are essential for achieving more inclusion of collective rights. However, they both must be present to have strong incorporation of collective rights in the long run. Although having a weak party system and constitutional instability produce a complicated political scenario, having them simultaneously increases the potentiality of creating collective rights. The scenario promotes the adoption of radical decisions for the authorities having no problem adopting indigenous cosmovision in contrast to more orthodox economic decisions. The opportunities to develop a constitutional replacement increase the likelihood of having indigenous representatives in the process of discussion for a new constitution. If they create alliances in the process, succeeding in including indigenous topics at the constitutional level, it is more likely that the whole legal system will change. This change would create better conditions for indigenous peoples, including securing collective rights.

Constitutional stability and an institutionalized party system would mean integrating weak collective rights into the legal and political system. The national authorities will not be willing to make radical decisions challenging the status quo. Furthermore, the stability of the constitution, maybe only with a partial amendment, will not meet the requirements for the indigenous concerns to be formally heard. It will not create a coherent and sympathetic legal order for indigenous peoples. The presence of institutional stability, in this case, means keeping a system where indigenous peoples are excluded from the political system.

In other cases, constitutional instability with the institutionalized party system, or constitutional stability but a weak party system, the outcome would be a moderate presence of collective rights. At least the presence of one of the conditions makes a difference in the collective rights of indigenous peoples. The presence of one of the conditions increases the probability of having more, but they cannot achieve a high level of autonomy. This moderate progress occurs because the opening for achieving more rights is not that durable; there are fewer spaces for negotiation and influence from indigenous

Table 2.2   Institutional Conditions and Outcomes Regarding Collective Rights

		Party System	
		Weak	*Institutionalized*
Constitution	Instability	Strong collective rights	Moderate collective rights
	Stability	Moderate collective rights	Weak collective rights

peoples. Table 2.2 explains the relationship between the conditions and the expected outcomes.

Hypothesis 2: The presence of strong collective rights is associated with a weak party system when there exists a high level of constitutional instability.

THE EQUIFINALITY THEORY:
ORGANIZATIONS AND INSTITUTIONS
CREATING MORE COLLECTIVE RIGHTS

Equifinality "[a]llows for different, mutually non-exclusive sufficient conditions, or paths, for the outcome" (Schneider & Wageman, 2012, p. 326). The theory presented in this research explains diverse ways of achieving the outcome of more indigenous collective rights across Latin America. At the same time, this theory allows us to see those paths in several levels of collective rights. The interaction between the conditions is complex and presents different levels of recognition.

Coalitions among indigenous peoples, coalitions with non-indigenous allies, weak party systems, and constitutional instability are present; there is a higher probability, almost near certainty, of having strong collective rights at work in the country. This increase in collective rights occurs because organizations and institutions open a possibility to include rights that allow indigenous peoples to develop a higher level of self-determination. A national organization of indigenous peoples shows a coherent and robust political actor. Furthermore, it is easier to find allies in the social and political field to present a more comprehensive proposal to the national authorities.

Protest is a response to weak institutions (Arce, 2010). However, in this case, the indigenous social movement can create a more stable relationship, organizing coalitions between diverse indigenous nationalities or other non-allies with a weak party system. The exciting part of this last relationship is that even with a high level of volatility within the party system, the ideologies behind parties and movements can endure while pushing for more collective rights.

The coalitions can also push for a constitutional replacement, looking for the opportunity to make changes to the national constitution. In the discussion process, in Constituent Assemblies, these coalitions can influence alliances among diverse actors to include the indigenous collective rights in the new constitution. Also, indigenous social movements and their coalitions are essential to keep influencing the legal system to include more collective rights, following the principles stated at the constitutional level, institutionalizing the legal system for indigenous peoples with more rights for them. The weak party system enables indigenous coalitions to push for more collective rights with national leaders who are more willing to make radical decisions to change some aspects of the liberal paradigm, recognizing indigenous collective rights. This change can be seen mainly in the form of a new constitution and other legal instruments.

It is more likely to have moderate collective rights when one of each set of conditions, one coalition and one institutional, are present. In this case, it will present one type of coalition, with indigenous peoples or non-indigenous allies, and one institutional condition, weak party system, or constitutional instability. Regarding coalitions, one of them is present, but it is not strong enough to develop more relationships. The most essential coalition is the national organization among indigenous. It is easier to establish, and this one leads to coalitions with other non-indigenous allies.

Regarding institutional conditions, countries with moderate collective rights will have more stable political systems, but they are not entirely institutionalized. Therefore, it would leave space for making more radical decisions. However, the national authorities will try to keep some liberal institutions that are not all compatible with the indigenous perspective. The national indigenous organizations will push for more rights. They will have some opportunities to include their cosmovision even if national authorities keep a high level of power when they develop necessary collective rights, such as land and natural resources, maintaining the exploitation of resources.

It is likely to have only weak collective rights when a country has none of these conditions in place. The expectation in these countries is that indigenous peoples are not political actors who can form coalitions among themselves or other non-indigenous allies. In these countries, there can exist high levels of indigenous social movements. However, fragmentation is too high to look for those connections that create a union among groups. In countries with weak collective rights, the stability of the institutions does not offer a possibility for modifying the status quo. The party system is highly institutionalized. Thus, the decisions made are moderate and follow capitalism's rules in contraposition with indigenous cosmovision. The constitutional stability does not allow any opportunity for including collective rights, even if the constitutional amendment occurs often. In these cases, the constitution excludes any other

Table 2.3 Presence/Absence of the Conditions to Obtain Collective Rights

Conditions	Collective Rights		
	Strong	*Moderate*	*Weak*
Organization: coalitions between indigenous peoples and with others	Both	Only one	Neither
Institutions: weak party system and constitutional instability	Both	Only one	Neither

type of onto-epistemology, enduring the view of indigenous peoples as outsiders of the political realm. Table 2.3 shows the argument, with the relationship between conditions for the three levels of collective rights of indigenous peoples.

Hypothesis 3: The presence of strong collective rights is associated with the building of coalitions between indigenous peoples and with non-indigenous allies, as well as with the presence of a weak party system and high levels of constitutional instability.

NOTES

1. Party system refers to the set of patterned connections in the struggle among institutionalized parties (Mainwaring & Scully, 1995).

2. A political party provides a core of ideological beliefs to the people. It is a channel of expression for the demands that the people want to expose in the public field (Sartori, 1976), establishing how the public policies should be designed, following those ideological beliefs.

Chapter 3

A Trade Off

More Organizations and Less Institutional Stability for Strong Indigenous Collective Rights

This chapter seeks to clarify the reason why the level of recognition of indigenous collective rights is different in each country and what factors besides indigenous social movements help to increase the recognition of collective rights in the political and juridical order. By level of recognition, this chapter reveals what kinds of rights, stages of autonomy, and differentiation indigenous peoples have. The operating assumptions of the analysis from previous chapters may be summarized as a series of propositions and hypotheses as follows:

H1: Strong collective rights are associated with the development of coalitions between indigenous peoples when there exist also coalitions with non-indigenous allies.
H2: The presence of strong collective rights is associated with a weak party system when there exists a high level of constitutional instability.
H3: The presence of strong collective rights is associated with the building of coalitions between indigenous peoples and non-indigenous allies, as well as the presence of a weak party system and high levels of constitutional instability.

This chapter will also provide the analysis and results from the Qualitative Comparative Analysis (QCA) for testing these hypotheses to assess the conditions or factors that originate more collective rights. The analytical tool QCA shows the table of truth and the Boolean minimization for each level of collective rights.

COUNTRIES UNDER STUDY AND METHODOLOGY, USING QCA AND CASE STUDY

The analytical tool QCA is a technique used to study data related to the causal contribution of different conditions to an outcome of interest, in this case, indigenous collective rights. The QCA's "home base is comparative sociology/comparative politics, where there exists a strong tradition of case-oriented work alongside an extensive and growing body of quantitative cross-national research" (Ragin, n.d.). A synthetic strategy that combines the two traditions requires addressing a large number of cases, using comparative logic of experimental design, and providing parsimonious explanations (Ragin, 1987). The QCA is a framework that is suitable for those requirements. It works with small, medium, and large N comparisons to generalize the factors that influence an outcome (Ragin, 1987; Ragin & Rihoux, 2009; Schneider & Wageman, 2012). Case-oriented comparative studies use the logic of the combination of conditions, allowing for multipart and conjunctural causation (Ragin, 1987). Parsimonious explanations are a goal of social science in the majority of cases. Thus, QCA allows for simplifying the data, reducing its complexity guided by the theory (Ragin, 1987). According to Peters, "this method allows the use of some of the genuine advantages of cases, while still being able to systematically examine the cause-and-effect relationship existing in the outputs of many cases" (Peters, 2013, p. 176).

This study covers some countries in Latin America, and the approach of Barié is used (2003). It does not include the Caribbean countries because their ethnic configuration is different. In addition, the indigenous population in the region is minimal, and the challenge is related to the African descendant population, an exciting topic but outside the scope of this analysis (Barié, 2003). The study also leaves out small countries in Latin America whose population is 10 million or less, such as Guyana, Surinam, Belize, and Uruguay. The study with QCA includes seven countries in the region: Bolivia, Chile, Colombia, Ecuador, Guatemala, Mexico, and Peru. For sure, Bolivia and Ecuador are frontrunners in achieving and developing more indigenous collective rights, with a high level of influence in the decision-making process. Nevertheless, countries such as Chile, Colombia, Guatemala, Mexico, and Peru also have an interesting trajectory on the topic. Some of them are increasing the level of achievement such as Colombia and Peru and others with important political or social changes such as Chile, Guatemala, and Mexico. In the end, these countries will show us diverse cases, trajectories, and elements to be analyzed.

Diverse Cases for QCA

Each country may experience several cases according to its historical evolution. Therefore, this research will analyze diverse scenarios in each country. Besides, these scenarios contribute to create a more accurate analysis for each particular situation. The ILO's Convention No. 169 will be essential to reach this goal. There will be three possible time frames for each country. The first period (see table 3.2) began in 1988 up to the ratification of this convention, which is different in each country. The year of ratification is different because each country must follow its national process to ratify this international instrument. The convention was supposed to change the understanding between indigenous peoples and national authorities. However, this is untrue in all cases, as this research will show it. The second period started with the ratification of the convention until 2007. This year UNDRIP was approved, creating a new understanding of the role of the state and indigenous peoples, called plurinational constitutionalism. There is a decolonized perspective of politics, including indigenous norms and an equal system to the nation-state rules (Yrigoyen Fajardo, 2011). The 2007 UNDRIP is a declaration; so, it is not binding for the signatory's countries, but it introduces principles that the countries that signed must follow. It was adopted by the General Assembly on 13 September 2007, with 144 states in favor, 4 votes against, and 11 abstentions, Colombia included. Therefore, the date of this instrument is the same for all countries. Table 3.1 shows the year of ratification of the ILO's Convention No. 169.

Most countries achieve the first and second periods because they all ratified the ILO's convention on different dates. The third one was achieved by only two countries: Bolivia and Ecuador; these countries signed the UNDRIP and changed the understanding of how the government should function from a decolonized perspective (G. A. Rodríguez, 2015; Yrigoyen Fajardo, 2011). Even if the other countries signed the international instrument, they have not made a change from this perspective. Table 3.2 shows the cases for each country.

Table 3.1   Ratification ILO's Convention No. 169

Country	Year
Guatemala	1996
Mexico	1990
Bolivia	1991
Chile	2008
Colombia	1991
Ecuador	1998
Peru	1994

Source: International Labor Organization.

Table 3.2   Cases under Study for QCA

Country	Before Convention Nro. 169	After Convention Nro. 169	After UNDRIP (Plurinational Constitutionalism)
Bolivia	Bolivia 1 (1988–1990)	Bolivia 2 (1991–2006)	Bolivia 3 (2007–2018)
Chile	Chile 1 (1988–2007)	Chile 2 (2008–2018)	
Colombia	Colombia 1 (1988–1990)	Colombia 2 (1991–2018)	
Ecuador	Ecuador 1 (1988–1997)	Ecuador 2 (1998–2006)	Ecuador 3 (2007–2018)
Guatemala	Guatemala 1 (1988–1995)	Guatemala 2 (1996–2018)	
Mexico	Mexico 1 (1988–1989)	Mexico 2 (1990–2018)	
Peru	Peru 1 (1988–1993)	Peru 2 (1994–2018)	

Source: Own elaboration.

This table shows sixteen cases, each of them with different dates. This by no means expresses that a country that achieves the second or third time frame has more collective rights than the previous one. It is only a categorization to study the cases in a less complicated method and relate them to the two most important international legal instruments for indigenous peoples: ILO's Convention No. 169 and UNDRIP.

The Reality of Different Countries: Case Study: Colombia, Peru, and Chile

The QCA will expose the more likely conditions to produce the outcome in a parsimonious method. This simple way of showing the information "can be a problem if there is an interest in knowing "the process" or the "how" of the causal combinations that explain the outcome" (De Meur et al., 2009, p. 159). The solution to this "apparent" problem is to have more data about the cases and the conditions. So, this research will present case studies to solve that apparent problem.

The case study is a method that allows researchers to know more deeply the variables and conditions behind any phenomenon or the development of a process (Swanborn, 2010). In this method, "the researcher writes general questions that reflect the research objective and that these questions are asked of each case to guide and standardize data collection, thereby making systematic comparison and cumulation of the findings of the cases possible" (George & Bennett, 2005, p. 67). One of the recommended tools is the process-tracing method, to recognize the causal chain and causal mechanism between the variables and the outcome (George & Bennett, 2005). Process-tracing is "the examination of 'diagnostic' pieces of evidence within a case that contribute to supporting or overturning alternative explanatory hypotheses" (Bennett, 2010, p. 208). With this method, it is possible to carefully describe trajectories and sequences of different variables (Bennett, 2010; Collier, 2011).

Geddes (1990) states that selecting the cases based on the dependent variable can arrive at a biased conclusion because the researcher tends to choose instances in which the outcome is what he/she expected. To avoid this, the selection of cases in this research will cover most of the relationships between the conditions and the typological representatives of the outcomes. Moreover, a few of them will cover deviant cases.

Having involved indigenous peoples, Van Cott (2010) states that biased case selection is related to two problems. The first one is a focus on the cases. Scholars usually choose "particularly unusual or successful cases and ignore cases where indigenous peoples have had little or no success" (Van Cott, 2010, p. 400). That is the reason why most of the literature explains the Ecuadorian case, where social mobilization has been successful. Another problem of a biased case study is the population of indigenous peoples. The preoccupation "is with countries with numerically or proportionally large indigenous populations" (Van Cott, 2010, p. 400). Researchers study in-depth cases such as Bolivia and Ecuador. Nevertheless, they entirely neglect multiple instances in which small groups of the indigenous populations, but Colombia, achieved massive success in a democracy (Van Cott, 2010).

This chapter analyzes three countries applying the approach of Van Cott (2010), in which there are not many previous studies. The cases are Colombia, Chile, and Peru. They all present a diverse combination of conditions with diverse outcomes in different time frames. Some are typical cases, which means they are representative, with a stable relationship between the variables (Seawright & Gerring, 2008), for example, Colombia. There are diverse cases (Seawright & Gerring, 2008) showing all the conditions to have strong collective rights, but the process to achieve them was different, like Peru. Others are deviant cases, meaning an anomalous relationship between the variables, challenging the theory (Seawright & Gerring, 2008). In these deviant cases, the context gains more value as an explanation of the outcomes, like Chile. The context is "the relevant aspects of a setting in which an array of initial conditions leads to an outcome of a defined scope and meaning via causal mechanisms" (Falleti & Lynch, 2009, p. 1143). This unique element is different in every case.

These three countries have commonalities. All of them are countries with a presidential system with high powers granted to the executive (Ginsburg et al., 2010). Chile and Colombia have a bicameral Congress (Vanden & Prevost, 2015), and Peru has a unicameral Congress (Cedillo Delgado, 2018). Furthermore, all these states are unitary, which means that they have one political and juridical power center. They also present economic stability with a high level of regional development (Diario Financiero, 2019).

Currently, these are democratic countries with an authoritarian past. Chile and the authoritarian Pinochet's regime ruled from 1973 to 1989 (Bresnahan, 2003; Silva, 2015). In the case of Peru, the Revolutionary Government of the Military Forces ruled between 1968 and 1980, and they had a competitive authoritarian regime from 1990 until 2000 with the government of Alberto Fujimori (Hernández Chavés, 2018). Colombia and the Military junta of government ruled from 1957 to 1958. At the moment of the second wave of democratization in 1960–1970, Colombia was one of three countries considered a liberal democracy (Lorente, 2010). The process of erosion in 1980 was due to political, economic, and social factors that deteriorated democracy (Lorente, 2010). These factors are related to the increase of guerrilla activities in the country, mainly the groups known as FARC (Fuerzas Armadas Revolucionarias de Colombia) and EPL (Ejército Popular de Liberación) showing a high level of violence. The main difference between them is the number of indigenous populations. They keep various percentages of indigenous peoples in the country. Peru has a 24% of indigenous peoples population, 11% for Chile, and Colombia with a 3.4% of indigenous population (CEPAL, 2014, p. 43).

Thus, the political context creates a vast difference between the three countries. These differences play an important role in how the conditions under study in this research behave to create more collective rights in the case of Colombia and Peru or to maintain the same level of weak collective rights, for example, the Chilean case. These countries were treated as two cases in the QCA analysis. In this chapter, they will be treated as one case to show how these conditions changed, modifying the level of indigenous collective rights and the causal mechanism.

In the study of every case, I will look at the analysis by conditions and causal mechanisms. Sometimes, this can coincide with a chronological study. However, in the majority of the cases, the conditions are coexistent, or the explanation requires going back and forward for a better understanding of the process.

Currently, Colombia and Peru are cases of innovation when including collective rights with a low level of indigenous social movements, but with coalitions, a weak party system, and a change of constitution at the beginning of the 1990s. From 1987 to 1991, Colombia is a typical case of moderate indigenous collective rights, with a national organization of indigenous peoples and a weak party system. From 1987 to 1993, Peru was a deviant case because it showed the absence of any coalitions, a weak party system, and no constitutional replacement. However, the outcome of that time is a moderate level of collective rights. The transition in those two countries, from weak to strong collective rights, and moderate to strong, needs to be studied in-depth. The two cases of Chile show to be paradigmatic for the theory of weak collective rights. Chile shows a weak level of indigenous collective rights with the institutionalized party system, with a liberal constitution from 1980 and a high level of indigenous social movements that do not form coalitions between indigenous peoples and other non-indigenous groups.

To study these cases, the data was collected in those countries from different sources: interviewing scholars and experts who study indigenous peoples and gathering primary information such as archival documents, official reports, and laws. But also, secondary sources of information were used, such as articles and books. These materials were gathered in Bogota, Santiago, and Lima between September 2019 and January 2020.

THE CONDITIONS INFLUENCING MORE
INDIGENOUS COLLECTIVE RIGHTS

To conduct the QCA research, this study uses a V-Dem v11.11 data set (Coppedge et al., 2021) on party systems. This study codes several variables using primary and secondary data for the rest of the conditions. All these conditions are coded from 1987–1988 to 2020. It is important to highlight that the coding data took place after the democratization process and new social movements in the region.

The Outcome: Level of Collective Rights in Latin America

There are nine critical collective rights for this analysis. Each of them allows indigenous peoples the use of their cosmovision in different areas: the right to cultural diversity, the right to practice their language, the right to have a bilingual education, the right to participate in the political field, the right to be considered as a nation, the right to have access to natural resources, the right to their communal lands and territory, the right to self-determination, and the right to use their customary indigenous law.

According to the United Nations' Universal Declaration on Cultural Diversity, this concept means having the right to access and participate in the enjoyment of culture. This is directly related to their right to practice the language by indigenous peoples. In this case, "[i]ndigenous languages are more than a means of communication: they are central to the sense of identity and the culture of their speakers" (De Varennes, 2012, p. 39). Thus this right protects the oral culture of indigenous peoples as an expression of their identities. Language is also an expression of the right to have access to bilingual education,

This right implies the ability to receive a quality education in the maternal language, that which is culturally suitable and responds to the fundamental needs of indigenous peoples. In practice, one speaks of intercultural bilingual education or simply bilingual education for indigenous peoples. (Aguilar et al., 2010, p. 81)

In chapter 1, I discussed the notion of indigenous peoples as political actors who intervene in the political sphere. This idea believes in the independence of indigenous peoples as a nation. The political participation of indigenous peoples requires not only votes, elections, and being candidates in those processes but also their inclusion in government institutions (Aguilar et al., 2010). One of the most important rights for participating in the political field is the right to free, previous, and informed consultation enshrined in the ILO's Convention Nro. 169, in which indigenous peoples must participate in any decision related to their interests. Moreover, the right to be considered a nation implies this political status of being actors for indigenous peoples and their capability of self-determination.

Indigenous rights to land, territories and natural resources protect a variety of possibilities in which they relate to the natural environment. According to Aguilar et al., "[s]everal examples include property, possession, occupation, control, administration, conservation, development, utilization, and access" (Aguilar et al., 2010, p. 70). According to the right to territories, the definitive characteristic is the idea of collective or communal property; this means that indigenous peoples share the ownership of the land.

The right to self-determination proposes that peoples should be free to have their self-government and institutions with a level of autonomy. The UNDRIP states in article 3 that "[b]y virtue of the right, indigenous peoples will have self-determination over their politics, and be able to freely pursue their economic, social and cultural development." This is the most critical right for indigenous peoples. One consequence of self-determination is using their customary indigenous law, which means they use their oral norms and judicial system to resolve conflicts within the community. This right is recognized in articles 8, 9, and 10 of ILO's Convention No. 169. If the nation-state recognizes the indigenous system as having "parity with traditional state jurisdictions" (Sieder, 2012, p. 110), it is customary indigenous law. If not, the country only recognizes some indigenous practices in legal procedures, playing a secondary role. In these cases, the weak recognition of these practices does not satisfy the customary indigenous law standard. This option is highly used in several countries in Latin America.

Development of These Rights in Latin America

In Latin America, there exists a significant variation of collective rights across the different countries, even if most of them signed and ratified the

ILO's Convention No. 169 and the UNDRIP. Each of the cases is complex and follows different rules for introducing these international instruments. There are countries where the threshold for having weak, moderate, or strong collective rights is easy to determine, such as Bolivia 3, Colombia 2, Ecuador 3, Mexico 2, and Peru 2. In other cases, the scenario is complex and requires more explanation, such as the case of Bolivia 1, Chile 1 and 2, and Peru 1.

In the cases of Colombia 2 and Ecuador 3, they present all the rights stated in table 3.3: the right to cultural diversity, to practice their language, to have a bilingual education, to participate in politics, the right to be considered as a nation, rights to natural resources, rights to their collective lands and territories, right to self-determination, and the right to use their customary indigenous law (Aguilar et al., 2010; IWGIA, 2010; López Bárcenas, 2010). In the cases of Bolivia 3, Ecuador 2, and Peru 2, the majority of these rights are present including self-determination and the use of indigenous customary laws (Aguilar et al., 2010; Chuecas, 2008; Ministerio de Justicia y Derechos Humanos, 2013), the most important rights to recognize autonomy to indigenous peoples. However, these cases do not present the right to consider indigenous peoples as a nation. Moreover, Peru 2 in 2011 enacted an act that preserves the territorial, economic, and ecological integrity of land from voluntarily isolated groups (Ministerio de Justicia y Derechos Humanos, 2013), which means durable protection for the lands of indigenous peoples. Ecuador 2 recognizes the right to participate in the decisions related to national resources, but it did not recognize another type of participation in the 1998 Constitution. In all these cases, all the countries in those time frames are strong, allowing a high level of autonomy for indigenous peoples.

The set membership score for each moderate collective right is more complex to establish. Mainly because the rights that are part of that category are diverse and completely asymmetric in the content of their protection. For example, it includes rights related to education and rights related to natural resources or land. It is not easy to equate their contents for this classification. Colombia 1 has a moderate level of collective rights because all the protection in the time frame was related to bilingual and ethnic education and cultural diversity in Decrees 88 and 1142, 1978, and the Resolution 3454-1984 from the Education Ministry (Ayuda en Acción, 2018b; G. A. Rodríguez, 2007). There were a few decrees in 1988 regarding the land of indigenous peoples and the priority rights of indigenous peoples regarding the exploitation of mines. All these rights are considered moderate collective rights. The case of Guatemala 1 and 2 is also in this category. The 1998 Constitution includes cultural diversity, the right to land and territories, indigenous language, bilingual education consultation, and indigenous justice (ACNUR, n.d.; Aguilar et al., 2010). This protection was developed for other legal instruments, such as decrees and ministerial agreements that increase protection for indigenous justice, respect for indigenous sacred land and communal lands, and participation in public affairs (ACNUR, n.d.). Even if this case presents indigenous justice related to customary indigenous law, it is a case of moderate collective rights because the evidence shows only an application of indigenous institutions for resolving the case, not a full development of their norms as a nation-state legal system.

Bolivia 1 and Bolivia 2 are also moderate collective rights for different reasons. Bolivia 1 only presents a few collective rights in the constitution: indigenous justice, special protection for indigenous territories, and autonomy (Barié, 2003). Even though they can be related to strong collective rights, it applied the same explanation for indigenous justice in the Guatemalan case. The indigenous peoples only have those rights and other weak or strong collective rights. They have more autonomy, but they cannot exercise any other rights. The same explanation applies to Bolivia 2, adding the incorporation of the Decree Supreme 25,894-2000 regarding indigenous language (Barié, 2003). All these cases show a better level of differentiation, but indigenous peoples cannot use their system of organizations, having a great level of regulation from the country.

In the cases of Chile 1, Chile 2, Ecuador 1, and Peru 1, they show a weak level of collective rights. Chile 1, Chile 2, and Ecuador 1 present cultural diversity as the primary right in their cases. They can add a few others from the same category or even a few moderate rights, but the inclusion is not strong enough to be moderate. In Chile 1, it is possible to find in the Indigenous Act 19,253 the right to indigenous culture, land (individual and collective), indigenous language, and the right to intercultural and bilingual education. These rights are a blend of weak and collective ones, but the presence of individual lands makes the difference. Even if collective land is present, the preference is for individual lands producing disincentives for having the former. In Chile 2, the only additional rights explicitly incorporated for indigenous peoples is the right of the previous consultation since 2015. Even if this is a success for participation, the recognition threshold is too weak for changing it to a moderate level of collective rights.

Ecuador 1 only has the right to land in all its forms, individual and collective, in the 1979 Constitution, and the law 50 in 1994 enshrined the right to indigenous traditions (Comisión Interamericana de Derechos Humanos, 1997). Regarding the lands, the same explanations regarding Chile 1 must be applied in Ecuador 1, and indigenous tradition is one expression of the right to cultural diversity. In this case, only weak collective rights are present.

The case of Peru 1 is thorny. This case only presents the use and, in some cases, the property of the land by the decree-law 1974 modified in 1978 (Chuecas, 2008). The property of communal land is only for peasants in Act

24,656 in 1987 (Ministerio de Justicia, 2013). The 1979 Constitution gives the right of autonomy to indigenous peoples and peasants. In this time frame, indigenous peoples are seen as native communities, considerably limiting their rights (Chuecas, 2008). This scenario is confusing and troublesome, enshrining some rights but disincentivizing the role of indigenous peoples and enhancing the role of peasants. These cases show only recognition of indigenous culture but no autonomy.

The case of Mexico 1 and Mexico 2 is complex to calibrate because the 1917 Constitution includes indigenous collective rights, but only after constitutional amendments. Further, state legislation only presents individual rights, not collective rights, for indigenous peoples (López Bárcenas, 2010). In the original 1917 Constitution, the only right present in Mexico 1 is indigenous peoples' collective land (López Bárcena, 2010). Even if this right is a moderate collective right, it allows some level of autonomy for indigenous peoples, but it does not allow indigenous peoples to express their cosmovision in the country adequately. Therefore, it is calibrated as a weak level of collective rights.

In Mexico 2, there are more collective rights, but after the 1992 amendment, the collective property of lands became suppressed (López Bárcenas, 2010). In 2001, another amendment created better conditions for indigenous peoples. It added a series of collective rights, such as self-determination, with conditions that federal entities will impose; recognizing indigenous as peoples; norms of social organization; indigenous justice; indigenous authorities; linguistic and cultural rights; protection to their lands (no collective), with priority use for natural resources; and proportional representation at local levels (Aguilar et al., 2010; López Bárcenas, 2010). The lack of full self-determination, the lack of communal lands, the absence of bilingual education as collective rights—even if it is present in state legislation as an individual right (Blanco Gómez, 2010)—and recognition of some indigenous practices at the legal procedure (not the right to use their customary indigenous law) make Mexico 2 a case of moderate collective rights.

Table 3.3 shows all this information in a more transparent and precise manner. Moreover, table A shows the legal instruments, rights, level, and source for each case in the appendix.

More Organizations: Indigenous Social Movements and Coalitions

There exist two main conditions related to organizations: the coalitions between diverse indigenous peoples in one country and the coalitions with non-indigenous peoples. The next chapter will explain how they work in Latin America in detail.

Table 3.3 Presence of Collective Rights in Each Case (1988–2020)

Collective Rights	Cases[a]															
	Bolivia 1	Bolivia 2	Bolivia 3	Chile 1	Chile 2	Colombia 1	Colombia 2	Ecuador 1	Ecuador 2	Ecuador 3	Guatemala 1	Guatemala 2	Mexico 1	Mexico 2	Peru 1[b]	Peru 2
Right to cultural diversity			X	X	X	X	X	X	X	X	X	X		X		X
Right to practice their language		X	X	X	X		X		X	X	X	X		X	X	X
Right to have a bilingual education		X	X			X	X		X	X	X	X				X
Right to participate in politics			X		X[e]	X	X		X	X		X		X		X
Right to natural resources			X	X[d]		X	X		X	X	X	X		X		X
Right to their collective lands and territory			X	X[d]	X[d]	X	X	X	X	X	X[f]	X	X		X[g]	X
Rights to be considered a nation		X					X			X				X		
Rights to self-determination		X	X			X	X		X	X					X	X
Right to use their customary indigenous law	X[c]	X[c]	X				X		X[c]	X		X[c]		X[c]		X
Level of collective rights[h]	MoCR	MoCR	StCR	WeCR	WeCR	MoCR	StCR	WeCR	StCR	StCR	MoCR	MoCR	WeCR	MoCR	WeCR	StCR

Source: own elaboration.

[a] Cases: number 1 means before ILO's 169 Convention; number 2 means after ILO's 169 Convention; number 3 means the declaration of plurinational state. For more information see table 3.2.

[b] Indigenous peoples are called native communities and peasant communities.

[c] They have a weak recognition of some practices in legal procedures.

[d] Individual and collective land for indigenous peoples.

[e] Previous consultation.

[f] Special protection to territories.

[g] Only the use of land for indigenous peoples not property. The property is for peasants.

[h] Levels: WeCR Weak; MoCR Moderate; StCR strong.

Development of Indigenous Coalitions in Latin America

Ecuador and Colombia claim to have the best-organized confederations of indigenous peoples. In these confederations' associations, there are elements of collective interest and collective culture that unfolded in the negotiation of indigenous issues. All of their organizations share the idea of representing indigenous interests as a united front for discussing important topics with the government.

Ecuador claims to have the most influential indigenous movement in Latin America, with a presence in the Amazon area and the Andes Coast. They are united in one large organization called CONAIE (Confederación de Nacionalidades Indígenas del Ecuador) (Yashar, 2005). Since 1986, with the National Counseling of Indigenous Nationalities of Ecuador, this organization has grouped the fourteen indigenous nationalities fighting for social justice (Becker, 2014). In the 1990s, the confederation brought 80% of the country's indigenous peoples together (Van Cott, 2004). They endeavored to make their communal-based society visible. They included a collective vision of the world in national policies, blocking neo-liberal reforms, and a high level of support from non-indigenous peoples (Van Cott, 2004).

In the case of Colombia, the national organization of indigenous peoples is called ONIC (Organización Nacional de indígenas de Colombia), created in 1982 and representing the majority of indigenous peoples in the country. Before this organization, other indigenous coalitions were created in the Cauca region called CRIC (Consejo Regional Indígena del Cauca) in 1971. Some years after others were created, for example, the OPIC (Organización de los Pueblos Indígenas de la Amazonía Colombiana) that has been established since 1995 (Rathgeber, 2004). These indigenous organizations were crucial for the 1991 Constitutional Assembly that originated a new constitution and brought peaceful solutions to the armed conflict with paramilitary groups and guerrillas in the country (Rathgeber, 2004).

Countries such as Bolivia, Guatemala, Mexico, and Peru have been more cautious with the role of their national indigenous association. Despite the fact they work collectively for the interest and culture of indigenous peoples, their processes have been more unstable, with diverse strategies of mobilization concentrated on majoritarian indigenous peoples. There have been problems of legitimation, fragmented participation of some indigenous peoples, and even revolutionary associations in all these cases. I will explain these cases in the following paragraphs.

Bolivia has had two indigenous organizations: the CSUTCB (Confederación Sindical Única de Trabajadores Campesinos de Bolivia) since 1979 and the CIDOB (Confederación de Indígenas del Oriente de Bolivia) (National

Indigenous Federation) since 1982. These organizations have a central role in presenting indigenous peoples' demands to the government, especially the Sub-secretary of Ethnic Affairs (SAE), in making decisions that benefit indigenous peoples in the country (Postero, 2004). It is not a stable relationship, and it has problems of legitimation with the government (Van Cott, 2004). However, CIBOB has created spaces for dialogue to keep mutual understanding and trust between indigenous peoples and the state for resolving indigenous issues since 1994.

Mexico has several organizations that work with diverse strategies of mobilization. The CNPA (Coordinadora Nacional Plan de Ayala) since 1979, The Mexican Council for 500 years of indigenous resistance since 1992, and the EZLN National Liberation Zapatista Army since 1994. The CNPA is formed by indigenous peoples, peasants, and afro descendants, gathering thirty-two federal entities from diverse fields in the country. The Mexican Council for 500 years of indigenous resistance is an organization located in the region of Guerrero, a key actor in spreading the culture of indigenous peoples in Mexico, achieving several improvements for indigenous peoples, even with an unstable performance over time (SICETNO, 2013). Finally, one of the most known indigenous organizations in Mexico is EZLN in Chiapas, fulfilling significant achievements such as the creation of the autonomies in several local governments in the area called MAREZ (Municipios Autónomos Rebeldes Zapatistas) (SICETNO, 2013), but it has been highly criticized for using violence as a tool of mobilization.

In the case of Guatemala and Peru, both have indigenous organizations; the former consolidates one highly influential and known indigenous peoples: Mayan (Fischer, 2004). In the case of Peru, the organization of indigenous peoples is more fragmented and slower, and it was organized in the last twenty years (M. E. García & Lucero, 2004; Van Cott, 2004). In Guatemala during the late 1980s, pan-Mayan groups started organizing around non-political issues, especially language and culture. During the 1990s, leaders of pan-Mayan groups created the COMG (Consejo de Organizaciones Mayas de Guatemala) as a coordinator for diverse indigenous groups that cover language, culture, and political issues (Fischer, 2004). In 1994, pan-Mayans organizations were invited to participate in the negotiation of the Peace Accords; not surprising, as indigenous peoples were the most impacted population by the internal armed conflict that the country experienced in the process of democratization in the mid-1980s (Torres-Rivas, 2006). For participating in this negotiation, pan-Mayan groups established the COPMA-GUA (Coordinación de Organizaciones del Pueblo Maya de Guatemala) to represent Mayan interests at the table of negotiation (Fischer, 2004).

The process was different in Peru. According to Yashar (2005) and Van Cott (2007), the indigenous movement was almost nonexistent in the country.

This notion is contested by García and Lucero (2004). They state that "indigenous peoples in Peru have experienced and gone beyond the full range of the indigenous organizational model that has been identified by scholars in Latin America" (García & Lucero, 2004, p. 181). The difference focuses on the strategic adaptation that these organizations have developed. Since 1998, the COPPIP—the Peruvian Coordinator of Indigenous Peoples—was created as a space of discussion and organization in the country (García & Lucero, 2004). Further, CONAMI—Coordinadora Nacional de Comunidades Afectadas por la Minería (1999)—represents communities affected by the mining industry in the highlands (Van Cott, 2004).

Finally, countries such as Argentina, Brazil, Venezuela, and Chile do not have coalitions between indigenous peoples; Argentina, Brazil, and Venezuela do not have indigenous social movements (Coppedge et al., 2021); and they are unable to create any coalitions that are stable enough to present indigenous issues to the government. Although Chile is a case with high levels of indigenous social movements (Coppedge et al., 2021), the fragmentation of the ten indigenous peoples legally recognized by the government cannot produce a stable and effective coalition yet. There is no visible construction of collective identities between all ten indigenous nationalities. According to historical research, the coalitions between indigenous peoples were important for defending territory during the colonial period, building a united front of peoples from the coast, plains, pre-mountain, and mountain range (Goicovich Videla, 2004). This need to create a united front based on absolute survival, and security is no longer the driving force. Today, we can see and measure a series of indigenous social movements and indigenous peoples who work alone and are dispersed throughout the political field.

Tables B and C in the appendix show the sources used in each case.

Coalitions with Non-Indigenous in Latin America

There exist indigenous social movements in Latin America with solid ties to peasant movements and left parties such as in Bolivia during specific times: Colombia after 1991 and Ecuador, Mexico, and Peru after 1993. Other countries such as Bolivia in the late 1980s and Colombia before 1991. Chile and Guatemala do not present substantial evidence of coalitions with other non-indigenous allies.

Through the CONAIE, Ecuador has negotiated coalitions with non-indigenous peoples, especially left political parties. The culture of indigenous peoples in Ecuador has coalitions with other sectors (Gutierrez Chong et al., 2015). For example, they were able to overturn three presidents: Abdalá Bucarám, Jamil Mahuad, and Lucio Gutierrez (Gutierrez Chong et al., 2015). The last presidential overturn occurred in 2002 and resulted from a coalition between the CONAIE, the indigenous movement Pachakutik, and the Patriotic Society Party. This coalition was looking to consolidate a plurinational state (Gutierrez Chong et al., 2015), having shared interest, a prevailing ideology, and leadership. It is essential to point out the formidable links between the CONAIE and Pachakutik. The confederation was one of the actors behind creating the political party (Madrid, 2012). Before 2000, there was evidence of coalitions between the CONAIE and the agrarian sector. It was involved in creating Coordinadora de Movimientos Sociales, including unions throughout the public sectors, neighbors' associations, human rights activities, NGOs, associations of truckers, and small and medium entrepreneurs (Zamosc, 2004). All of them were created to influence the national debate regarding land and constitutional amendments, along with several types of mobilizations, including national uprising, protest, national debates, among others (Zamosc, 2004).

In Bolivia, the main coalitions between indigenous peoples and nonindigenous allies are with left parties. The CIDOB has relationships with the MNR party (Movimiento Nacionalista Revolucionario), and MAS (Movimiento al Socialismo) political party (Postero, 2004). The main aim of these coalitions was to bring a multicultural approach to the country (Postero, 2004). In the case of MAS, the coalitions have been successful because they appeal to indigenous peoples and mestizos that may or may not come from an indigenous background and the local white population (Madrid, 2012). The most significant success of this coalition was the election of President Evo Morales in 2005, who led the coalition since its first steps in the public field (Madrid, 2012). There was a period between the beginning of 1990 and mid-2000 in which these coalitions fell apart, mainly because a conservative alliance took the presidency (Postero, 2004), closing the possibility of negotiation. This lack of coalitions changes the narrative: formally, the legislation regarding indigenous peoples was there, substantially, having a multicultural society flip to a more conservative stance (Postero, 2004).

After 1991, in Colombia, there were several coalitions between the national and regional organizations, such as ONIC, CRIC, OPIC, and left political parties such as ASI (Alianza Social Indígena) (later changing "indígena" to "independiente") and the MIC (Movimiento Indígena de Colombia) (Rathberger, 2004). This coalition focused on indigenous problems, sharing ideologies, and global conflicts with the community in a highly convulsed country by the violence of paramilitary forces.

In Mexico, the coalitions are mainly formed by peasants and other movements. In the early 1990s, it was created the coalitions between CNPA and the CIOAC (Central Independiente de Obreros Agrícolas y Campesinos) (Dietz, 2004). Later, the EZLN formed coalitions with other movements to build the

Democratic Convention and the "Transition Governor in Rebellion," mainly human rights organizations (Dietz, 2004), in which the demands were pluralistic and involved all the citizens. The coalitions in Peru started after 1994 and mainly with a left political party called "Perú Possible," which was fruitful in bringing indigenous representation into influential political positions, such as the minister of states and President Alejandro Toledo (García & Lucero, 2004). Tables B and C in the appendix show the sources used in each case.

Less Institutional Stability: Political Party System and Constitutional Change

Some other conditions to have more indigenous collective rights are related to institutional instability. Therefore, I will analyze the party system and the constitution replacement in Latin America in the next section.

Expressions of the Party System in Latin America

Latin America is "a dynamic, complex and rapidly changing reality" (Vanden & Prevost, 2015, p. 1). This changing reality also affects the political field and party systems. According to Mainwaring (2018) and his measurement of party system institutionalization, countries such as Mexico and Chile were two of the most institutionalized systems during the 1990–2015 period. Guatemala, Peru, and Bolivia ranked on the opposite side: countries with lower levels of institutionalization in the same time frame (Mainwaring, 2018a). These differences result from the dynamic power and political structure in the region.

In Chile, the authoritarian government of Augusto Pinochet (1973–1989) originated the greatest crisis of political parties in the history of the country, closing the Congress, banning several political parties that supported the former president Salvador Allende, and suspending other right parties (J. S. Valenzuela et al., 2018). In 1990, the country quickly acknowledged the importance of elections and political parties to transition to a more democratic system (Valenzuela et al., 2018). This new reality creates two main political actors who articulate their programs in terms of left and right, generating coalitions between the one that supports the dictatorial regime and the one that supports democracy (Alcántara Saez, 2013a). The political system of Chile shows a low index of electoral volatility, even if they have a high number of political parties and a stable offer of political parties (Alcántara Saez, 2013a). However, even if the indexes are increasing the stability of the party system in the country, there are still some visible symptoms of problems: misalignment between citizens and party identity, presenting doubts regarding the roots of political parties in society, and the lack of new political parties. This is due to a series of institutional bans that do not allow these new forces to arise (Altman & Luna, 2015).

In the case of Mexico, the context is entirely different. In 1988, a series of legislation reforms included a genuine regime of political party system able to place alternate people in power (Alcántara Saez, 2013b). Before that date, the PRI (Partido Revolucionario Institucional) was a hegemonic and dominant political party, configuring an indistinct line between the party and the government (Alcántara Saez, 2013b; K. Greene & Sánchez-Talanquer, 2018). According to Greene and Sánchez-Talanquer (2018), the stability of Mexico is a result of this authoritarian past, stating that

> [i]In our view, biased but competitive elections under dominant-party authoritarian rule blunted the potentially fragmenting effects of social cleavages and federalism, and instead encouraged partisan elites to invest in nationally oriented parties, craft differentiated economic policy platforms, and establish close links to core electoral constituencies. Subsequent negotiations between the then-dominant PRI and its two primary challengers over electoral rules and party finance regulations locked-in advantages for these existing parties at the onset of fully competitive democracy, helping them survive and dissuading potential new competitors. (Greene & Sánchez-Talanquer, 2018, p. 203)

However, this legacy did not last forever, and it is now possible to see lower trust in political parties due to criminal violence, human rights violation, poverty, and political corruption (Greene & Sánchez-Talanquer, 2018).

The Andean countries of the region present fewer levels of institutionalization regarding their party systems than Mexico and Chile, with Peru as the weakest system in the region. The system has decreased over time in Ecuador and Bolivia, and Colombia has a stable but weak political party system. In the Peruvian case, the political party system collapsed at the end of the 1980s and at the beginning of the 1990s, creating space for the election of Alberto Fujimori as president, and with that an authoritarian turn (Levistsky, 2018; Sanchez, 2008). This authoritarian turn debilitates the political party system even more by creating more fluidity and personalism, which is still happening even with democratization: "[f]ar from experiencing a rebirth in the 2000s, then, Peru's party system decomposed. Not only were established parties displaced by personalistic vehicles, but, at the local level, national parties of all types were displaced by ephemeral candidate-centered "movements." The result was a level of partisan fragmentation and fluidity unparalleled in Latin America" (Levistsky, 2018, p. 331). The stable political parties disappear from the public scenario (Alcántara Saez, 2013a), bringing new anti-political parties authorities with a high level of informal networks (Tanaka, 2015).

In Ecuador, the political parties are fragile, non-effective in processing the citizens' inputs, fragmented, personalists, and besides the electoral game, they have been absent from the society (Alcántara Saez, 2013a). There are traces of patronage, clientelism, and a high level of personalism (Alcántara Saez, 2013a). According to Sanchez,

[b]y the late 1990s Ecuador displayed some of the lowest levels of trust in political parties and Congress among all Latin American countries, a trend exacerbated by the economic collapse of 1999. From the mid-1990s onwards street politics became the major arena in determining political outcomes. (Sanchez, 2008, p. 327)

As well as Peru, this lack of institutionalization brings to power presidents who are outsiders from the party system, as Lucio Gutierrez in 2002 and Rafael Correa in 2006 (Sanchez, 2008). In these cases, political movements were essential for success (Alcántara Saez, 2013a).

On the other hand, Bolivia presents a stable party system, not as institutionalized as Mexico and Peru, but with mid-level institutionalization at the beginning of the 1990s, with active main political parties and a few secondary groups (Tanaka, 2015). This changed with the eruption of MAS in the political arena in 2002, after a tremendous economic crisis (Tanaka, 2015). The MAS has been the only party that survived in the political system with a certain level of representation (Sanchez, 2008). The party system has reached a new level of weakness, with great fluidity and uncertainty, volatility, and high abstention rates (Sanchez, 2008).

The main characteristic of the Colombian system is a process of deinstitutionalization, but without creating a collapse (Albarracín et al., 2018). This process started in 1991 and is a stable continuum into the modern day. Before 1990, it existed as a stable system with very strong left and right parties (liberals and conservatives, respectively) (Alcántara Saez, 2013a). The change occurred because a "mismanagement of the security situation by both traditional parties and a severe security threat in the early 2000s fostered profound change in the competition for the presidency and altered national party competition" (Albarracín et al., 2018, p. 228). Nowadays, the system is weak and fragmented, with a high level of personalism with *caudillos* and low electoral participation of citizens (Alcántara Saez, 2013a). These characteristics produce a fragile party system, index level between −0.222 and 2.593 of party system institutionalization.

According to Jones, "Guatemalan political parties are primarily clientelist in orientation, with limited programmatic differences among the major political parties. Furthermore, even this constrained level of programmatic politics is undermined by the extreme volatility of the Guatemalan party system" (Jones, 2011, p. 15). The fragmentation level increases over time, allowing a significant number of new political parties (Jones, 2011) and new actors who frequently change the politics.

All the information of these countries is coherent with the index of the V-Dem data set v11.1 (Coppedge et al., 2021). Table D in the appendix shows this information and the code used.

Constitutional Replacement and the Changing Reality of Latin America

Constitutional replacement is part of the changing reality of Latin America. There have been nine new constitutions in the seven countries between 1988 and 2018. Bolivia has done more constitutional replacements with four in total occurring between 1995 and 2009. The other country with several new constitutions is Ecuador, with the 1998 Constitution and the 2008 Constitution. Colombia, Guatemala, and Peru also prevailed in instituting new constitutional replacements throughout the 1990s: Colombia in 1991, Guatemala in 1998, and Peru in 1993.

Mexico and Chile are the only countries that did not present any constitutional replacement during this period; however, both present a high level of constitutional amendments. In the case of Mexico, the amendment of 1992 and 2002 was essential to introduce indigenous collective rights at the constitutional level (López Bárcena, 2010). The Chilean case shows a high level of constitutional amendments, one of the highest in the region, according to Nolte (2013). However, none of those amendments included indigenous collective rights at the constitutional level. Table E in the appendix shows the cases, the standing constitution for each time frame, the number of new constitutions, and the presence or absence of constitutional replacements.

CONDITIONS AND OUTCOMES: CONSTRUCTING A TRUTH TABLE

The truth table is the main characteristic of any QCA. According to Schneider and Wageman, "[i]t contains the empirical evidence gathered by the researcher by sorting cases into one of the 2k logically possible combinations, aka truth table rows, of k conditions. Each row linked to the outcome can be interpreted as a statement of sufficiency" (Schneider & Wageman, 2012, p. 334). With the truth table, it is possible to work with the Boolean minimization of Boolean algebra, which states the diverse conditions or factors that are present, showing the variation of the dependent variable or outcome of interest, in this case, collective rights showing all the possible combinations (Peters, 2013; Toshkov, Dimiter, 2016).

The truth table contains the empirical evidence, grouping the cases that share the same set of conditions and outcomes. To complete this table, it is imperative to have a row data table containing the evidence for each case. This table is in appendix, table F. The data from table F are grouped depending on the same outcome, collective rights, and conditions. Therefore, the cases with the same conditions and outcome will be in the same row in the truth table.

The truth table (table 3.4) shows the conditions organized by the outcomes: weak, moderate, and strong collective rights. As a reminder, strong collective rights are those that indigenous peoples are entitled to have in their organizational system without the opinion of the state and national governments. In this case, the government decreases the level of its power in favor of indigenous peoples. Strong collective right is coded as 2. Moderate collective rights mean an increase in the level of differentiation, but indigenous peoples cannot use their organizational system. The government gives up some of its power, but with a high level of regulations in strategic topics. Moderate collective rights are coded as 1. Ultimately, weak collective rights mean recognizing the culture with no autonomy for indigenous peoples, and the government is not willing to give up any of their competencies. Weak collective right is coded as 0.

As table 3.4 shows, in the case of strong collective rights (row 1), the conditions are consistent and coherent. Bolivia 3, Colombia 2, Ecuador 3, Peru 2, and Ecuador 2 have coalitions between indigenous peoples, coalitions with non-indigenous allies, weak party systems, and constitutional replacement. The set of conditions for cases with moderate collective rights (rows 2 to 5) is diverse and requires an in-depth analysis, which will be explained in the following sections. In the case of weak collective rights (rows 6 to 8), the conditions of Ecuador 1, Chile 1, and Chile 2 are similar, so we can state:

- Lack of indigenous coalitions creating national organizations and alignments with non-indigenous groups.
- Lack of constitutional replacement.
- Mid or high level of institutionalization of the political party system.

In those countries, the difference is a matter of degree in the level of the party system. Peru 1 also presents a lack of all conditions, except for the weak party system. Only Mexico 1 presents a diverse path for weak collective rights.

In the following sections, the analysis regarding the sets of conditions, organizations, and institutions, and by each level of collective rights, will be done by applying the Boolean minimization, which states the diverse conditions or factors that are present, showing the variation of the dependent variable or outcome of interest (Peters, 2013; Toshkov, Dimiter, 2016).

Analysis of the Levels of Collective Rights in the Region

This section shows the results and analysis per each type of collective rights, strong, moderate, and weak, including the factors or conditions that are more important for achieving the outcome.

When All Conditions Meet: Strong Collective Rights

According to the truth table (table 3.4), the conditions that are sufficient for achieving strong collective rights (InCR) is the presence of coalitions between indigenous peoples (CA), coalitions with non-indigenous allies (CB), a weak party system (PS), and the presence of constitutional replacement (CC), as figure 3.1 shows. The formula is as follows:

$$CA + CB + PS(0) + CC = InCR$$

The conditions present in the formula for strong collective rights are necessary conditions, which means that in every case that the outcome is present, strong collective rights, the conditions are always present with the same combination of conditions (Schneider & Wageman, 2012). This is the case for Bolivia 3, Colombia 2, Ecuador 2 and 3, and Peru 2. This means indigenous peoples are entitled to have their organizational system without the opinion or intervention of the state and national governments in these countries. The government decreases its power in favor of indigenous peoples establishing spaces of self-determination, indigenous customary law, even recognizing them as a nation, forming a plurinational state.

The figure shows four rectangles, each representing one condition: short dashes for coalitions between indigenous peoples, long dashes and dots for the presence of coalitions with other non-indigenous allies, continuous line for the weak party system, and long dashes for constitutional replacement. I used a dichotomous party system condition for doing the figure: weak party system value 1, otherwise 0. Moreover, for strong collective rights, the value is 1, otherwise 0. The rest of the variables use the original value of the truth table. All the cases that present strong collective rights are inside the square where all conditions are present. In all these cases, the analysis of the necessary conditions presents a value of consistency[1] of 1 and a value of coverage of 0.4,[2] including the 16 cases. This means the combination of the conditions is in line with the statement of necessity, and it is relevant to achieve the outcome.[3]

The Diverse Path for Moderate Collective Rights

According to the truth table (table 3.4), there are four paths to achieve a moderate indigenous collective rights level. Figure 3.3 shows the different cases

Table 3.4   Truth Table with the Four Conditions under Analysis, Outcomes, and Cases

Row	Conditions				Outcomes	Cases[a]
	CA[b]	CB[c]	PS[d]	CC[e]	CR[f]	
1	1	1	0	1	2	Bolivia 3; Colombia 2; Ecuador 3; Peru 2; Ecuador 2
2	1	1	1 (2*)	0	1	Bolivia 1; Mexico 2[g]
3	1	0	1	1	1	Bolivia 2; Guatemala 2
4	1	0	1	0	1	Guatemala 1
5	1	0	0	0	1	Colombia 1
6	0	0	1 (2*)	0	0	Ecuador 1; Chile 1; Chile 2[g]
7	0	0	0	0	0	Peru 1
8	1	1	1	0	0	Mexico 1

Source: own elaboration.
[a] Cases: number 1 means before ILO's 169 Convention; number 2 means after ILO's 169 Convention; number 3 means the declaration of plutinational state. For more information see table 3.2.
[b] CA: Coalitions between Indigenous peoples. Presence 1; Absent 0.
[c] CB: Coalitions with other non-indigenous allies. Presence 1; Absent 0.
[d] PS: Party System. Weak 0; Mid-institutionalization 1; Institutionalization 2.
[e] CC: Constitutional Replacement. No replacement 0; Replacement 1.
[f] CR: Collective Rights. Weak 0; Moderate 1; Strong 2.
[g] In the case of Mexico 2 and Chile 2, the level of party system is institutionalized. Coded as 2.

in a Venn diagram. It shows the diversity of the combination of conditions that make collective rights a reality.

For doing figure 3.2, I use a dichotomous party system condition: weak party system value of 1, otherwise 0. For moderate collective rights, the value is 1, otherwise 0. The rest of the variables use the original value of the truth table. For the graphical representation, I use the same lines that are shown in figure 3.1: short dashes for coalitions between indigenous peoples, long dashes and dots for the presence of coalitions with other non-indigenous allies, continuous line for the weak party system, and long dashes for constitutional replacement.

For Bolivia 2 and Guatemala 2, the path for recognizing indigenous peoples includes one coalition and one institutional condition. These cases present national indigenous organizations, mid-levels of party system institutionalization, and constitutional replacement with a lack of coalitions between indigenous peoples and non-indigenous allies. Therefore, they are represented in the figure at the short dashes and long dashes rectange intersection. Colombia 1 also presents one condition of each set but with a different combination. This country presents the national organization of indigenous peoples, a weak party system, constitutional stability, and a lack of coalitions with non-indigenous peoples. This combination of conditions shows Colombia 1 in the intersection of the continuous line and short dashes rectangle.

Bolivia 1 and Mexico 2 demonstrate the presence of coalitions between indigenous peoples, a coalition with other non-indigenous allies, a lack of a

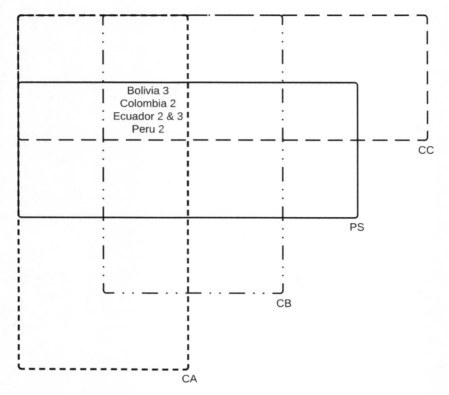

Figure 3.1   Venn Diagram with the Four Conditions and Cases for Strong Collective Rights. *Source*: Katherine Becerra Valdivia.

weak party system, and the absence of constitutional replacement. The graphical representation shows these two countries inside the intersection between the short dashes and long dashes and dots rectangles. Guatemala 1 follows the path of coalitions between indigenous peoples and a mid-level of party system institutionalization for achieving moderate collective rights, and with a lack of coalitions with other allies and no constitutional replacement, graphically represented in the continuous line square with no other intersection.

It is possible to analyze with these diverse paths two main issues: the theory presented in chapter 2, which states that one coalition condition and one institutional coalition create moderate collective rights, and the role of mid-level institutionalization of the party system. Regarding the theory, Bolivia 2, Guatemala 2, and Colombia 1 are the only cases that follow the theory stated in chapter 2, presenting one condition for coalitions and one condition for institutions, as shown in the following formula:

$$(CA \vee CB) + (PS(0) \vee CC)$$

Bolivia 2 and Guatemala 2 present indigenous national organizations and a new constitution. Colombia 1 also presents indigenous national coalitions, but the condition from the institutional variables is a weak party system.

It is essential to point out the role of party system institutionalization, all the analysis in this section was made considering three levels in measuring party system organization. This analysis shows that excluding Colombia 1 and Mexico 2, the other cases present a mid-level of party institutionalization. This means that Bolivia 1 and 2 and Guatemala 1 and 2 do not have a weak party system, but they are neither fully institutionalized. In these cases, this factor is critical to understand that there is an opening for indigenous national organizations to dialogue with the state's authorities who are more willing to introduce changes in the political and juridical system.

Applying logical minimization in the case of moderate collective rights, the role of coalitions between indigenous peoples is central. In all these cases, Bolivia 1 and 2, Mexico 2, Guatemala 1 and 2, and Colombia 1 have indigenous national organizations that create spaces to recognize indigenous collective rights. Thus, formula 3 shows the sufficient condition as:

$$CA = MoCR$$

One Condition or None of Them: Weak Collective Rights

According to the truth table (table 3.4), there are three combinations to have weak collective rights. Figure 3.3 shows the conditions and cases in a Venn diagram. For doing figure 3.3 a dichotomous party system condition is used: weak party system value of 1, otherwise 0. For weak collective rights, the value is 1, otherwise 0. The rest of the variables use the original value of the truth table. As in the other two previous figures, I use the same lines: short dashes for coalitions between indigenous peoples, long dashes and dots for the presence of coalitions with other non-indigenous allies, continuous line for the weak party system, and long dashes for constitutional replacement.

In the case of Chile 1 and 2, and Ecuador 1, the conditions that are sufficient for achieving weak collective rights (BaCR) is the lack of coalitions between indigenous peoples (CA) and with other non-indigenous allies (CB), the lack of a weak party system (PS(0)) and the absence of constitutional replacement (CC). Therefore, they are graphically represented outside the intersections of the four rectangles. Below, Formula 4 shows these conditions as follows:

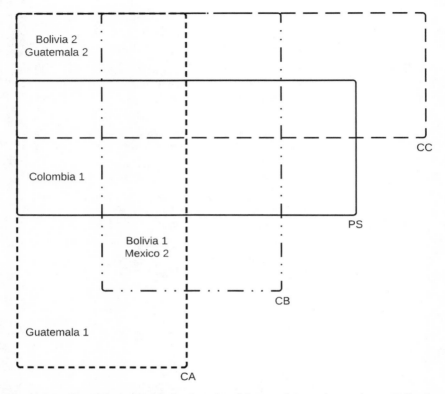

Figure 3.2   Venn Diagram with the Four Conditions and Cases for Moderate Collective Rights. *Source*: Katherine Becerra Valdivia.

$$\sim CA \sim CB \sim PS(0) \sim CC = BaCR$$

These cases present a lack of indigenous national organizations and constitutional replacement, the absence of coalitions with other non-indigenous allies, producing weak collective rights. In fact, in the case of Chile, its constitution is one of the most stable in the region. The difference between these three cases is the level of party system institutionalization. Ecuador 1 presents a mid-level of institutionalization, the highest in its history. It is essential to point out that Chile, in both cases, presents a fully institutionalized party system. It is the unique country where all its cases present a high level of institutional stability.

The lack of conditions produces a scenario that is adverse to the recognition of indigenous collective rights. Indigenous peoples are not seen as political actors because they do not have cohesion between them to represent their demands in a unitary form. Consequently, they cannot create coalitions with other non-indigenous groups, like minorities or left parties, unable to gain support to create any change. Having stability in the constitution and party system produces fewer chances to recognize collective rights. In these cases, the institutional structure is close to any change that contests the liberal paradigm. Nation-state authorities only recognize a few rights that allow a low level of differentiation, making the homogenization of the state a priority. Thus, indigenous peoples have fewer opportunities to obtain more rights.

The conditions present in the formula for weak collective rights can be understood as necessary, which means that the combination of conditions must be present to have weak collective rights (Schneider & Wageman, 2012). The level of necessary consistency is 1, and the coverage for necessity is 0.5.

There is a second path to get weak collective rights. Peru 1 shows a lack of coalitions between indigenous peoples and non-indigenous allies and a lack of constitutional replacement in that time frame, but with a weak party system. This solution is graphically shown in figure 3.3 in the only green square without any intersection with the rest of the rectangles. Mexico 1 also has a different solution. It presents the two coalitions with the lack of a weak party system and no constitutional replacement. This combination of conditions enhances the idea of the absence of institutional conditions as an essential set of factors. Nevertheless, the presence of indigenous national organizations and coalitions with peasant unions makes a difference, but they cannot increase the level of protection of indigenous collective rights. This solution is graphically represented in figure 3.3, showing Mexico 1 in the square where the short dashes and long dashes and dots intersect. Peru 1 and Mexico 1 are deviant case coverage for weak collective rights.

The role of constitutional replacement is central by applying logical minimization in the case for weak collective rights, due to Mexico 1, as formula 5 shows:

$$\sim CC = BaCR$$

The absence of constitutional replacement is sufficient to have weak collective rights. This means that the constitutions in these cases do not allow the increase of recognition for indigenous peoples. With the lack of recognition of collective rights at the constitutional level, the rest of the legal instruments cannot implement these rights or enshrine laws that recognize the indigenous way of life. These cases do not show an inclusive paradigm.

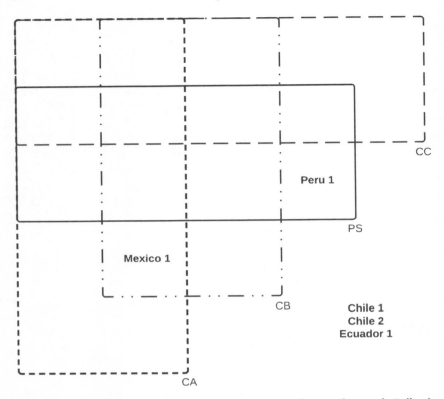

Figure 3.3　Venn Diagram with the Four Conditions and Cases for Weak Collective Rights. *Source*: Katherine Becerra Valdivia.

SUMMARY OF THE QCA ANALYSIS

In general, several cases follow the theory stated in chapter 2. Table 3.5 shows the cases and theory.

All the cases with a level of strong collective rights, Bolivia 3, Colombia 2, Ecuador 2 and 3, and Peru 2, present coalitions between indigenous peoples, coalitions with non-indigenous allies, constitutional replacement, and a weak party system. Formula (1) shows this case. That is the current situation for all cases. The cases with moderate collective rights, Bolivia 2, Guatemala 2, and Colombia 1, present one institutional factor and one coalition condition. In the case of weak collective rights, Chile 1 and 2 and Ecuador 1 show the lack of all the conditions. As a result, in the case of moderate and weak collective rights, logical minimization shows that the sufficient condition for moderate collective rights is coalitions between indigenous peoples and the lack of constitutional replacement for weak collective rights. Formulas (3) and (5) show these conditions.

There are five deviant cases: Bolivia 1, Mexico 1 and 2, Guatemala 1, and Peru 1. The first three show only the organizational conditions: both types of coalitions. The difference is the level of outcome and the level of the party system. Bolivia 1 and Mexico 2 have a moderate level of collective rights with a mid-level party system and institutionalized party system. Mexico 1 shows a weak level of collective rights with a mid-level party system. In the case of Guatemala 1, it only shows a coalition between indigenous peoples and lack of all the other conditions, with a moderate level of collective rights. Peru 1 only shows one condition, a weak party system, and the absence of the other three.

COUNTRIES AND THEIR TRAJECTORIES: MOVING FORWARD AND STAGNATION

It is interesting to review the trajectories of the diverse countries in this study and the presence of the conditions. The different levels of indigenous collective rights in diverse periods help us to recognize each country's uneven trajectories. This information makes it possible to infer the level of respect, protection, and promotion of these rights from a Latin American comparative perspective. Countries are moving forward in these endeavors, while others present stagnation in their trajectories. It is essential to point out that none of the countries under study present a regression in their processes. This is excellent news and agrees with the consolidation and progress of rights in a democratic society.

Regarding the countries that move forward in the inclusion of these rights, there are three trajectories: countries from moderate to strong level not having weak level of indigenous collective rights; countries with weak indigenous collective rights that move forward to strong collective rights, with no moderate state; and countries with weak collective rights to moderate levels.

In the first case, Bolivia and Colombia move from moderate to strong collective rights. At the beginning of the 1990s, both countries moved from a moderate level of indigenous collective rights, meaning some level of autonomy and differentiation for indigenous peoples. In these cases, the coalitions between indigenous peoples and a weak party system produce the recognition of these levels of rights. In both countries, the new constitutions, in 1990 for Colombia and 2008 and 2009 for Bolivia, and the creation of coalitions with non-indigenous peoples made the difference to recognize more inclusive indigenous rights allowing them to have the right to self-determination and the right to use their customary indigenous law, with a high level of autonomy

Table 3.5   Presence/Absence of the Conditions to Obtain Collective Rights with Cases

	Collective Rights		
Conditions	Strong	Moderate	Weak
Coalitions: between Indigenous peoples and with others.	Both	Only One	Neither
Institutions: weak party system and constitutional instability	Both	Only One	Neither
Cases[a]	Bolivia 3	Bolivia 2	Chile 1
	Colombia 2	Guatemala 2	Chile 2
	Ecuador 2	Colombia 1	Ecuador 1
	Ecuador 3		
	Peru 2		

Source: own elaboration.
[a] Cases: number 1 means before ILO's 169 Convention; number 2 means after ILO's 169 Convention; number 3 means the declaration of plutinational state. For more information see table 3.2.

and differentiation from the hegemonic group in the society. This successful transition from moderate to strong collective rights reveals a significant impact of the indigenous coalitions powered by the institutions, such as a new constitution and the party system that allows more radical decisions. The trajectory of Colombia will be described in detail in the next chapter.

It is possible to find Ecuador and Peru moving from weak to strong indigenous collective rights. The coalition between indigenous peoples and other non-indigenous allies significantly increased collective rights in these cases. Additionally, the 1993 Constitution in Peru and the 1998 Constitution in Ecuador were transcendental to make the change. Peru is one of the case studies, and it is presented in chapter 5, emphasizing this transition.

Finally, Mexico is the only country that started with weak collective rights that move forward to moderate collective rights. In Mexico, the indigenous organizations are constantly present. The significant difference is the level of party institutionalization, moving from a mid-level to an institutionalized one in this transition. The constitution of Mexico is the same as in 1917. It only has several amendments increasing the protection of indigenous peoples. For these conditions, precisely the last one, Mexico stays at a moderate level of collective rights.

Only two countries present the same level of indigenous collective rights in all the cases: Guatemala with a moderate level and Chile with a weak level. In Guatemala, the only conditions that changed in both cases were the party system's institutionalization. It started with a weak party system in 1988, changing by 1996 to a mid-level. The 1996 constitutional amendments did not make a profound difference in the level of collective rights. In this case, the national legislation is constant in time, showing an important level of inclusion of collective rights. Chile is the only case that presents a weak level of indigenous collective rights from 1988. The lack of indigenous coalitions, a highly institutionalized party system, and the same constitution since 1980 make invisible any recognition to indigenous rights. It is the only case presenting indigenous collective rights at this weak level. The individualistic structure of its legal instruments, as the constitutions and several acts, impedes the recognition of indigenous peoples as political actors. Furthermore, it is one of the few countries in South America that does not recognize indigenous peoples in its constitution, and there is no word about them in the Magna Carta. Chile is a paradigmatic case of weak collective right, but in chapter 6 I will demonstrate its complexities and future perspectives.

These trajectories show the importance of the conditions to achieve more indigenous collective rights. Without a doubt, when all of them are present, the country will show strong collective rights because all of them collaborated to push for more recognition: coalitions, a political system that accepts radical ideas and a new constitution. For those countries with a moderate level of collective rights, the coalitions between indigenous are central because they can negotiate with national authorities as equal political actors. Finally, when a country does not change its constitution is more likely to have weak collective rights.

NOTES

1. Consistency "indicates to what degree the empirical data are in line with a postulated subset relation" (Schneider & Wageman, 2012, p. 324). The consistency value is 1 if a condition is entirely consistent. The conventional value for assessing consistency is above 0.9.

2. Coverage "assesses the relation in size between the condition set and the outcome set [. . .] Coverage necessity is better understood in terms of relevance and trivialness of a necessary condition" (Schneider & Wageman, 2012, p. 325). The higher the value, the better.

3. It is not possible to achieve high values of consistency and coverage at the same time. There is a trade off between the two, which means having high value of consistency there will be less value of coverage and vice versa (Schneider & Wageman, 2012).

Chapter 4

Colombia

A Paradigmatic Case of More Indigenous Collective Rights

At present, Colombia is a typical case of strong collective rights. They were achieved with great efforts by indigenous national organizations with strong ties with other movements and left political parties, a weak party system, and a constitutional change. However, before 1991, the level of collective rights was moderate. The only conditions that existed were the indigenous organizations and the weak party system. In the following chapter, I will explain the level of collective rights in depth and how indigenous peoples could make coalitions with other non-indigenous allies and change their constitutions, thereby becoming a model for the rest of Latin America (Barié, 2003).

In the following sections, I will describe the Colombian context, explain each condition, its causal mechanism to create collective rights, the interaction between the conditions, and the transition to achieve from moderate collective rights to strong collective rights.

COLOMBIAN CONTEXT: POLITICAL CRISIS AND VIOLENCE

Colombia is the fourth largest country in South America (*BBC News*, 2018), with more than 50 million inhabitants. Like many countries in the region, their culture is a mixture of Spaniards, indigenous peoples, and Afro-descendants heritage. The society is highly stratified with an elite formed by descendants of wealthy Spanish families and a high number of the mixed-race working population in the other extreme of the social order (*BBC News*, 2018). The primary natural resource of the country is the oil reserves, and it is also a significant producer of gold, silver, emeralds, platinum, and coal

(*BBC News*, 2018). According to Dugas (2015), Colombia has been defined as a formal constitutional democracy with a history of civilian rule. However, even today, it fails to provide adequate protection to all its citizens, with several episodes of violent relationships between the political system and the guerillas.

About 1946 and the early 1960s, Colombia experienced a bloody episode of conflict between the two political parties: liberal and conservative (Dugas, 2015). This time is known as "La Violencia" (The Violence). It all started with the murder of Jorge Eliécer Gaitán, president of the liberal party. Consequently, there was an uprising in Bogota, a short alliance between liberals and conservatives, the election of an extreme conservative president, a coup, and a military government until 1957 (Dugas, 2015). This scenario was the key event for liberals and conservatives to sign a pact to make an opposition to the military government and to start to call it the National Front Regime, defined as a bipartisan civilian regime, in which the power was divided into equal parts between liberals and conservatives. Regarding guerillas, during the years 1964 and 1971, four paramilitary groups emerged, the Leftist National Liberation Army (ELN), the Maoist People's Liberation Army (EPL), the Revolutionary Armed Forces of Colombia (FARC), and M-19 (*BBC News*, 2018), but all of them were disarmed from 1988 to 2016.

In the late 1970s and early 1980s, Colombia experienced a political crisis due to several factors, such as the quasi-monopoly of the liberal and conservative parties in the political system, an increase in clientelism, abstentionism, and a general weakness of the institutions (Laurent, 2005). Before the 1990s, these political problems increased, adding a series of issues to the narco-terrorism uprising (Laurent, 2005). This term expresses a tight relationship between drug cartels and terrorism. The Medellín cartel was one of the most violent ones, assassinating several political figures at the time (Dugas, 2015). President Virgilio Barco (1986–1990) announced a "total war" against narco traffickers, so the level of conflict and violence escalated as never seen before. The narco traffickers responded with several deadly attacks across different cities in the region (Laurent, 2005), for example, the massacre of twelve judicial staffers in Santander; the murder of one leader from a social movement; the bomb attack on a newspaper, El Espectador; the fatality of 107 passengers from an Avianca airplane, among others (Cardona Alzate, 2011).

In August 1989, a very important event took place to originate a mobilization from the country's people: the murder of the liberal candidate for the presidency Luis Carlos Galán. This event created chaos and internal war; so the politicians, specifically President Barco and the new President Belisario Betancourt (1990–1994), started to believe that the peaceful solution would be achieved by an institutional change to create space for the opposition and a stronger ruling state (Laurent, 2005). The solution was to start a process of constitutional change and the National Constituent Assembly to generate a new constitution.

In spite of generating a new constitution, the levels of violence and social peace did not decrease. Peace negotiations started between the government and FARC in 1998–1999. However, in 2002, the violence and social disorder escalated with this group when the peace agreement was broken after FARC hijacked an airplane. The peace was only restored in 2016 with another peace agreement after fifty-two years of armed resistance from this group (*BBC News*, 2018).

It is in this context of profound violence that different conditions and causal mechanisms emerge to recognize the collective rights of indigenous peoples.

RECOGNIZING COLLECTIVE RIGHTS: THE ROLE OF WEAK PARTY SYSTEM AND PERSONALISTIC LEADERS

Before 1991, Colombia showed a weak party system and several coalitions between indigenous peoples. These conditions were necessary to achieve a level of moderate collective rights. In the case of a weak party system, the causal mechanism that allows this level of collective rights was the presence of personalistic leaders taking radical decisions.

It can be controversial to state that Colombia had a moderate level of collective rights before 1991, as I do in this chapter. The problem lies in Act No. 1889–1890, which –"determine how the savage must be governed to reduce them to a civilize life," this use of the discriminatory term "savages" influenced the national narrative against indigenous peoples. However, even that legislation established essential protection for them. It allowed them to have self-government through "cabildos"[1] and the possibility to claim respect for their territories (Semper, 2018). Before 1991, other collective rights were enshrined as ethnic education for indigenous peoples, definitions related to their territories, and preferences regarding mines on indigenous lands. All of these rights represented some level of autonomy for indigenous peoples. They all together did not represent full autonomy, but at least it was a starting point for indigenous peoples. As I will explain in further paragraphs, this level of collective rights is a consequence of two conditions: a party system crisis that impacts instability and the creation of several indigenous organizations that generate a new narrative regarding indigenous rights.

Concerning the party system, the literature states that "[u]ntil 1991, Colombia usually had one of the purest two-party systems in the world" (Albarracín et al., 2018, p. 228). Regarding the majoritarian political parties, liberal and conservative, the evidence shows a high level of clientelism and "caciquismo" (caciquism) (Alcántara Saez, 2013a; Laurent, 2005). This means that the political parties are led by one person who makes all the decisions and also creates the principles of the political parties from a more personalistic than ideological ones. These parties also present a lack of internal discipline, a weak organization and structure, and a high level of regionalism (Alcántara Saez, 2013a). This is coherent with the data provided by V-Dem 2019 related to party organization. Colombia presents a weak party organization.[2]

In this context of instability for the political parties and their leaders, some of them were more prone to make decisions regarding indigenous peoples, recognizing their cosmovision and culture, and two presidents were crucial for increasing the level of indigenous rights in Colombia: Alfonso López Michelsen (1974–1978) and Virgilio Barco (1986–1990). President Alfonso López Michelsen, from the liberal party and founder of Movimiento Revolucionario Liberal, was critical regarding the Washington consensus and liberal politics (Ardila Duarte, 2008). In 1977, he experienced one of the most intense protests in the country (Archila Neira, 2016), in which indigenous peoples and parts of the urban population, workers, and students came together. According to Ardila (2008), he tried to protect minority groups, and this goal allowed him to enshrine legal documents that start the protection of indigenous peoples. In the 1970s, he recognized, under his government, bilingual and bicultural education in decree No. 1142–1978. This was a radical decision at that period because it was one of the first times that a legal instrument recognized the difference between indigenous education and mainstream education.

President Virgilio Barco belonged to the liberal party, former executive director of the World Bank in DC and ambassador to the United States. Their opponents highly criticized him for following the Washington consensus (Treaster, 1989). However, two legal instruments on his own terms were signed to increase the level of indigenous rights: decree no. 2001–1988 concerning indigenous lands and the decree no. 2655–1988 which gives priority rights to indigenous peoples regarding mines. He has a particular sensitivity related to environmental issues (Von Hildebrand, 2017). In an intervention in the United Nations General Assembly on September 29, 1989, he was clear in declaring the role of industrialized countries in helping third-world countries to preserve their natural resources, especially the Amazon area. His government gives back the land to indigenous peoples (Barco, 1989). This occurred in applying the decree 2001–1988 regarding indigenous lands, and President Barco gave back to indigenous communities five million hectares in Amazon and Putumayo (M. T. Valenzuela, 2013). According to his collaborators, Barco made a tremendous difference in indigenous issues. He had a policy of giving back the lands, recognizing the indigenous peoples, indigenous knowledge, and their organizations (Von Hildebrand, 2017). This means he made decisions regarding indigenous peoples, thinking about protecting natural resources over extractive activities, presenting an alternative point of view amid his liberal policies.

The liberal party supported these two presidents; but, in both terms, the party was highly fragmented. López Michelsen faced several divisions and opposition from their liberal fellows (Redacción Política, 2017). The term "Barco" was a government without political parties (Bejarano, 1990). This means that each president and his team created a government plan without acknowledging the party, and consequently they did not respond to the party's ideology. This was an incentive to increase the protection of indigenous peoples in the case of López Michelsen and believe in the importance of indigenous rights to protect the environment, according to Barco (Von Hildebrand, 2017). In the 1990s, President Samper Ernesto Samper (1994–1998) followed the same pattern.

Thus, in the context of weak party systems, the role of personalistic leaders, mainly presidents, has been important for recognizing a moderate level of indigenous collective rights. Their decisions were considered radical in a framework of liberal decisions, challenging the status quo.

RECOGNIZING COLLECTIVE RIGHTS: THE ROLE OF NATIONAL ORGANIZATIONS OF INDIGENOUS PEOPLES AND THEIR INFLUENCE IN POLITICS

These leaders' decisions were highly influenced by indigenous organizations establishing their agenda. They influenced political power, mainly by protesting and implementing programs in their organizations to have some level of rights. This level of influence is the causal mechanism to achieve the level of moderate collective rights. Thus, indigenous organizations had a central role (G. A. Rodríguez, 2015). As stated in chapter 3, since 1971, the CRIC (Consejo Regional Indígena del Cauca) organized indigenous peoples in Colombia,[3] which was created in the region of Cauca, one of the most impoverished areas of Colombia with a high level of indigenous population and an even distribution of lands (Laurent, 2005). This organization states two postulates: "we are peasants" and "we are Indians." These two positions as peasants and indigenous helped them to develop strong ties among different groups in the region, such as unions, left political leaders, intellectuals, and administrative personnel (Duque Daza, 2008; Rappaport, 2003). In 1982, the ONIC was created with one specific goal: the self-determination as a central element of their revindications (Duque Daza, 2008; Laurent, 2005). This self-determination would allow them to take control of their collective lands, administrate their national resources, implement bilingual and bicultural education, participate in their political traditions, and, in general, implement programs to be representative of their culture (Laurent, 2005).

These organizations were made possible thanks to the notions of pan-Indianism and "indigenous fraternity." According to Laurent (2005), pan-Indianism creates organizations at the national level, including diverse types of associations to survive amid social conflicts. The glue that generates these associations is the belief that besides their internal differences based on ethnicity, language, and culture, all indigenous tribes decide to become political actors. Thanks to the coordination of ONIC, several organizations were starting to develop[4] in the country. By 1990, ONIC included thirty-eight regional and local organizations, representing 90% of organized indigenous peoples (Laurent, 2005; Van Cott, 2007).

At the same time, in the Cauca region between 1974 and 1977 other organizations emerge to defend indigenous peoples: the Movimiento Armado Quintin Lame (MAQL) and Autoridades Indígenas de Colombia. The MAQL was created in 1974–1975. They stated that they did not want to achieve political power but to protect indigenous peoples from landowners and other arm movements or "guerillas," such as FARC or EPL (Laurent, 2005). This was a social movement defending indigenous rights in a time of violence (Peñaranda, 2010). With the passing of time, and after achieving several goals, the existence of MAQL was contrary to the agreements signed by the CRIC. Therefore, in 1990, this group was successfully demilitarized after a peace agreement that was signed with the president of Colombia Cesar Gaviria (1990–1994) (Gobierno Nacional de Colombia & Quintin Lame, 1991). The agreement included one position for a representative of MAQL in the National Constituent Assembly in 1991 and the recognition of the movement as a legal organization (Duque Daza, 2008; Laurent, 2005).

In 1977, Autoridades Indígenas del Suroccidente de Colombia (AISO) also started to defend the rights of indigenous peoples in Colombia (Van Cott, 2007). It was formed by groups from the south occident of the country, with the unification of the Guambianos peoples and Pastos peoples in the department of Cauca and Nariño. The members were highly critical regarding the decisions and approach of CRIC (Laurent, 2010). The base principle for their organization was the respect of traditional authorities (Laurent, 2010; Van Cott, 2007). This organization played an essential role in the National Constituent Assembly, and in the 1990s, they became a political party named Movimiento de Autoridades Indígenas de Colombia (AICO) (Van Cott, 2007).

The central idea of coalitions among indigenous peoples was to influence the political system to recognize indigenous culture. The goal was not easy to accomplish due to multiple internal conflicts, difficulties between organizations, and problems with guerilla groups (Laurent, 2005, 2010). However, they started to have their first successes with the recognition of education that embraces their culture. In some cases, these coalitions-controlled education and in others the religious groups were in charge (Romero Loaiza, 2002). The CRIC established this accomplishment as the model for its relationship with the government (Del Rosario Rodríguez, 2011; Guido Guevara & Bonilla García, 2013).

ONIC was also essential in pushing new legislation regarding territories. The decree 2001–1988 established a right to land, in which indigenous peoples can recover "los resguardos," a colonial term that is used for naming the territories owned by indigenous peoples. By the end of the 1980s, ONIC pushed for the recognition of 80% of the "resguardos" that Colombia still has to this day (Muñoz Onofre & Rodríguez, 2016). According to Semper (2006), the survival of this figure is due to the resistance of indigenous peoples against state power. All these rights can be considered moderate collective rights that allow indigenous peoples to exercise some levels of autonomy, protecting critical cultural topics.

In these cases, the indigenous organizations could influence the political field, pushing for collective rights. Actually, in both cases, they were part of the implementation of the indigenous educational plan and the increase of land for indigenous peoples. These indigenous organizations implemented their own goal and negotiated with the government to achieve these rights.

Briefly the political crisis and authorities that were critics of the liberal paradigm and the mobilization of several indigenous associations, with regional and national scope, created the conditions to develop a legislative and executive agenda that increased the recognition of indigenous collective rights, achieving a moderate level. These two conditions maintained great importance until the beginning of the 1990s and allowed them to establish coalitions with other groups and have a central role in a new constitution.

A MOMENT OF PROFOUND CHANGE: MORE COALITIONS AND A NEW CONSTITUTION

At the end of the 1980s, the political crisis in Colombia created the scenario for enshrining a new constitution and establishing coalitions between indigenous peoples and other groups at the National Constituent Assembly. Moreover, left parties, in particular, and political parties extended the influence of the indigenous movements. All these conditions were necessary for increasing the level of recognition of collective rights in Colombia, going from a moderate level of them to one of the strongest in the Latin American region. The causal mechanisms of these changes are two. In the case of constitutional instability, the constitution was a solution to the political and social crisis, thus it became a new agreement between several groups of society. The coalitions with non-indigenous peoples were part of building a united front calling for differentiation as a mechanism for more collective rights. Thus, agreements and united front of ideas are the causal mechanisms.

At the end of the 1980s, the violence that Colombia experienced and the solution for the political leaders, in particular Presidents Barco and Betancourt, a process of constitutional change started, I mean a National Constituent Assembly to create a new constitution. In this case, the internal conflict was an opportunity to resolve the crisis with new institutions, with a new constitution based on a new political agreement.

The option for a new constitution was won in the presidential elections of May 1990,[5] and the elections for the member of the National Constituent Assembly were held in December 1990. As legitimate candidates, the indigenous movements presented two representatives: Francisco Rojas Birry (ONIC) and Lorenzo Muelas (AISO). They were elected from seventy representatives who worked in the Assembly. This election was an act of repair for all the pain caused to indigenous peoples over five centuries (Redacción, 1990). In May 1991, another indigenous representative became part of the Assembly, Alfonso Peña. His incorporation was part of the peace agreement between the government and the Quintin Lame movement. He had the right to participate in debates, but he could not vote (Correa Henao, 2005).

The indigenous representatives quickly declared their goals in the Assembly: recognize Colombia as a multiethnic and pluricultural country (Laurent, 2005) and enshrine several collective rights for protecting their cosmovision. To accomplish this, they started to create alliances and coalitions with other groups in the constituent work, including environmentalist groups, the presence of women, and the association of Afro-descendants (ONIC, 1991). According to ONIC (1991), the indigenous movements needed to dialogue and create a relationship with sectors that worked toward constitutional change, to be united at the Assembly. Progressive representatives lead these first alliances (Santamaría Chavarro, 2013). The traditional politicians represented 45% of conservatives and liberals of the Assembly, and they were not willing to recognize the participation of indigenous peoples at the constitutional level (Santamaría Chavarro, 2013). Also, indigenous organizations were reluctant to participate with traditional parties because "they oppose their material interest" (Van Cott, 2007, p. 181).

At this time, the most critical coalition was the groups of Afro-descendants (ONIC, 1991). This coalition was notable for helping indigenous peoples to obtain more substantial political leverage at the Assembly, and it gave them more power and a broader base of representation. The

Afro-descendants groups could not incorporate their representatives into the Assembly, even if they had several candidates (Laurent, 2005). Therefore, they found indigenous associations and representatives, in particular Rojas Birry (Agudelo, 2001), to support and give voice to their demands. Indigenous representatives used this coalition to elevate the importance of their ethnic demands, making a point of the need for a multiethnic country, not only for indigenous peoples but for Afro-descendants as well (Agudelo, 2001; Durán Durán, 2016; ONIC, 1991).[6] According to ONIC (1991), during the period of Assembly in February 1991, they had meetings with Afro-descendants' communities to analyze the diverse proposals and create an integration with ONIC, forming a group to support the Assembly. These groups wanted to define cultural particularities in the new constitution (ONIC, 1991).

Regarding environmentalist groups and the presence of women, they did not participate with representatives in the Assembly (Correa Henao, 2005). There were women as representatives, but they were not part of any feminist groups. At the time, women were part of traditional political parties or movements. Thus, the lobby groups that tried to influence the representatives were part of these coalitions (Correa Henao, 2005). Also, it was important for the participation of these groups through the citizen participation agenda, which allows social movements to present proposals for the new legal document (Rojas Betancourt et al., 2019). For indigenous peoples, these relationships brought more support for the claims of different perspectives in the Assembly. The relationship between the environmentalist movements, feminist groups, and indigenous organizations produced the inclusion at the constitutional level of articles regarding the protection of land and natural resources, quotas for women and indigenous peoples in Congress, and indigenous rights (Correa Henao, 2005; Tobasura Acuña, 2003).

Certainly, the process of achieving a new constitution was not easy. There was tension in the Assembly. The actors in this process were three: the national government; the traditional political parties, liberal and conservatives; and the representatives of social movements participating for the first time in a political process (Correa Henao, 1990). The traditional forces resisted any radical change (Correa Henao, 1990), and of course each group used strategies to achieve the final goal. The narrative from the indigenous representatives was broader than the push for recognizing indigenous rights. The focus was on defending human rights in a broader context, in which the indigenous topics were articulated with the international law of human rights and constitutional law (Santamaría Chavarro, 2013). At the end of the Assembly, the tension in the process was tangible especially when indigenous representative named Muelas denounced that nearly all articles incorporated into the new constitution regarding the indigenous rights were deleted from the document (Santamaría Chavarro, 2013). However, after a few days of conflict between the government and the Assembly, the articles were restored.

As a consequence of this new constitution process, indigenous peoples developed relationships with political parties. They created their own parties to achieve a stronger position in the new institutional framework. In 1990s, the AISO became a political party, now AICO, and in 1991, ASI, Alianza Social Indígena[7] (Indigenous Social Alliance), developed the political representation of the CRIC (Laurent, 2005; Van Cott, 2007). Today, MAIS, Movimiento Alternativo Indígena y Social (Alternative Indigenous Social Movement), represents the ONIC (Van Cott, 2007). These two political parties gave the indigenous associations the platform to act in the political field, accessing positions of power in diverse institutions and fields: senators, representatives, governors, and local governments (Laurent, 2005). In these coalitions, indigenous peoples can participate in the political field, enhancing their differences translated into laws and public policies.

Consequently, the causal mechanism for recognizing strong indigenous collective rights is the agreement for a new political understanding between opposite groups in a new institutional agreement that influences the rest of the juridical system. The coalitions with non-indigenous allies also provide a causal mechanism to recognize more collective rights. The creation of a united front for differentiation establishes the conditions to add diverse paradigms to the individual liberal paradigm.

THE AFTERWARDS OF THE 1991 CONSTITUTION: MORE COLLECTIVE RIGHTS FOR INDIGENOUS PEOPLES

In 1991, the new constitution established a new period for developing more collective rights and deep institutional transformation for indigenous peoples. The Colombian Constitution of 1991 became the central body to protect indigenous peoples. It is still one of the strongest constitutions on this issue (Aguilar et al., 2010). This constitution recognizes and protects ethnic diversity and the Colombian culture in article 7 (Aguilar et al., 2010; Semper, 2006, 2018). This principle shows the importance of ethnicity in the country; it is the starting point for achieving autonomy for indigenous peoples (Semper, 2006, 2018) and has become embedded in the constitution and other legal instruments since 1991. The constitutional document enshrined a series of collective rights for indigenous peoples, such as

- intercultural education (article 10);
- official indigenous languages (Article 10);

- right to land as archeological territories (Article 72);
- the right to use customary indigenous law and special jurisdiction for indigenous peoples (Article 246); and
- rights of autonomy (Articles 286; 287; 309; among others).

According to Aguilar et al. (2010), "the indigenous territories constitute one of the territorial entities of the State and indigenous communities keep autonomy for the 'management of their interests,' including the right to govern through their authority and administration of resources" (p. 62). The constitutional change in Colombia was an inspiration for other movements in the region (Barié, 2003).

At the constitutional level, these rules allow other rights to develop across legal instruments, such as the decree 1088-1993 that enshrines rights for indigenous peoples to have their traditional authorities, the act regarding general education no. 115-1994, the decree 620-2000 which established an ethnic education, the decree 1320-1998, and decree 649-2001 that states prior consultation and political rights for indigenous peoples (Ayuda en Acción, 2018a; G. A. Rodríguez, 2007). Furthermore, in decree 1088-1993 regarding indigenous authorities, President Gaviria expressly stated the importance of new conditions for the organization of indigenous peoples based on the new order of the constitution.[8] In the case of decree 1320-1998, President Samper also stated the role of the constitution for regulating the right to prior consultation for indigenous peoples.[9]

Interestingly, most of these instruments are decrees and not acts that need to start as bills in the Congress. In these cases, the president is fundamental in supporting the recognition and implementation of collective rights. As an example, President Samper from the liberal party, also the leader of the movement "Poder Popular," took power with the support of the "Alliance for Colombia," formed by Christians, conservatives, ex-members of guerrillas, and indigenous peoples (Ortiz Nieves, 1994). During his term, Samper was accused of corruption and to have relationships with narcotraffickers. This scenario of political instability was present throughout his term.[10] This setting and relationship with indigenous peoples led him to support indigenous rights, even allocating 2% of the national budget toward a plan of national development for indigenous peoples, which after this term was deleted from the national budget (Macdonald & Edeli, 2005). Thus, the following support for indigenous collective rights is a combination of implementing the constitution and national leaders who decide to make more radical decisions.

Consequently, this recognition of indigenous peoples' rights changed all the characteristics of the state in Colombia; it creates more spaces of participation for indigenous peoples and their leaders. For example, the Congress now has special quotas for indigenous representatives and senators (Aguilar et al., 2010), protecting the participation of indigenous peoples with political rights. Also, the Constitutional Court of Colombia has become a prominent protector of indigenous peoples, working on interpreting the current constitution and making sure that the state fulfills its constitutional obligations. The constant work that the Constitutional Court has done and continues to carry out with the right of indigenous peoples to participate in the decision-making process, which is enshrined in the ILO's Convention No. 169 (Instituto Interamericano de Derechos Humanos, 2016), is remarkable. Thus, it is possible to state that there are more tools than ever for indigenous peoples to live out their cosmovision in Colombia peacefully. They are using these tools to create recognition for more rights and beneficial conditions for them and their families, but not without new challenges.

These different juridical tools enhanced the importance of a new agreement for institutional stability, the influence of indigenous associations, and their ties to build a united front for differentiation that impacts leaders who are more willing to support changes in the context of fragmentation of political parties. These causal mechanisms are the key points to have more collective rights in Colombia.

COLOMBIA IN CURRENT TIMES: NEW COALITIONS AND NEW CHALLENGES

Colombia is one of the strongest countries in the recognition of indigenous collective rights. It has become a model for the rest of Latin America to move toward recognizing indigenous rights. However, new challenges, and the conditions and causal mechanisms that create these rights, continue to play a role but differ. Currently, the coalitions cooperate to ensure the implementation of those collective rights. The political system since 2010 is considered a mid-level institution, and the constitution is a reliable instrument that will not change in the foreseeable future. However, it needs to be interpreted by the Constitutional Court, which has a significant role in protecting and recognizing indigenous collective rights.

Indigenous national and regional organizations are very active in promoting, protecting, and helping to implement indigenous collective rights. Specifically, ONIC is active in participating in international organizations such as the International Forum for indigenous issues, in which one of their members, Dario Mejias Montalvo, represents Latin America and the Caribbean (ONIC, 2020). This organization has been influential in the process of mobilization that occurred in Colombia at the end of 2019 and the beginning of 2020. The CRIC is also a relevant actor in Colombian society, working with the government to implement collective rights. To highlight one example is the meeting between CRIC and the National Agency of Lands to retrieve indigenous territories (CRIC, 2020), implementing this collective right. CRIC and ONIC are both highly active, and these organizations still influence the decision-making of the national leaders.

Regarding coalitions with other movements and left parties, the relationships between indigenous associations and political parties remain stable. Their representation in national and local positions is not now in high proportions, but it remains steady. For example, at the Congress of 2018–2022, there is the presence of MAIS and AICO in the Senate and MAIS in the House of Representatives.[11] This presence in formal institutions helps to shape national public policies including indigenous peoples. Also, there is an increase in coalitions between indigenous peoples and organizations that regard human rights. This can be visualized by the presentation of legal claims from these organizations in favor of the protection of indigenous rights. For example, several human rights organizations[12] presented a protection claim at the Superior Court of Bogota in favor of several leaders that work for peace in Colombia. These leaders, including indigenous leaders who promote the right to lands and territories, had been threatened by unknown people (Thomas, 2019). Hence, indigenous organizations and other movements still work together, creating this united front from a broader perspective to maintain and implement indigenous collective rights.

Another important condition for including collective rights has been the party system. From 1987 to 2009, the party organization index shows a weak level organization.[13] From 2010 to 2018, the index has increased to a mid-level institutionalization of the party system. According to Tanaka (2015), the 1991 constitution opened the space for the participation of several excluded groups; however, the adverse effects of this were the increase in political fragmentation and weak political parties. Congress passed from having five political parties to nearly forty. Furthermore, this fragmentation did not collapse the party system (Tanaka, 2015). In 2003, it implemented reforms to institutionalize the political parties, so the Congress passed from having forty-two political parties to ten in 2006 (Tanaka, 2015). This mid-level institutionalization period is correlated with fewer legal instruments of indigenous collective rights. Despite this correlation, the protection of indigenous peoples is not only from the president but also from the Colombian Constitutional Court, the institution that has been rigorously active in the interpretation of the constitution and its rights.

The Constitutional Court has expanded the collective rights of indigenous peoples. For example, the right to recognize and protect traditional medicinal practices.[14] It has also helped to make these rights more concrete and visible. Another example is the right to prior consultation, in which the court has "develop[ed] not only the elements of prior consultation but also establishes the general rules for its proper application" (Vallejo Trujillo, 2016, p. 143). In most of these cases, the petitioners are indigenous peoples or indigenous organizations. Thus, in this case, the causal mechanism has shifted to implement collective rights thanks to a collective court in a more stable political background. This is an outstanding and interesting theory to be developed in this research.

In conclusion, the trajectory from moderate collective rights to strong collective rights is marked by the presence of several conditions. At the end of the 1980s, the pressure and influence of indigenous organizations and the presence of a weak party system helped national authorities, particularly the figure of the president, to recognize several rights for indigenous peoples. The evidence of this case shows the importance of indigenous national and regional organizations to influence the political field with mobilizations, but mainly with programs from ONIC and CRIC to enhance the role of indigenous peoples in society. These programs mainly influenced education and territorial policies, implementing collective rights. The actions of President López Michelsen and Barco, without the support of a strong party system, gave them the liberty to make radical decisions regarding indigenous peoples, enshrining important legislation increasing the protection of collective rights regarding bilingual and bicultural education and indigenous land. The influences of indigenous organizations and the personalistic decisions of national authorities within a fragmented party system were the causal mechanisms to achieve a moderate level of collective rights.

As in 1991, the new Colombian Constitution was implemented and a new institutional agreement was created, alongside the coalitions that indigenous organizations created at the Assembly make altogether elements to implement a united front to get more recognition of indigenous rights. The 1991 Constitution was an institutional solution for the profound crisis that Colombia was experiencing. It was a mechanism for including all the ideological sectors of the country in one endeavor. This specific situation allowed indigenous peoples to participate in the process, forming coalitions with environmentalist groups, including women's participation and the association of Afro-descendants. According to the evidence, the latter was the most important because it allowed them to be positioned in discussion with a broader support base, pushing for more collective rights at the constitutional level, including self-determination and particular indigenous jurisdiction. Since 1991, these conditions and mechanisms allowed to increase the levels of collective rights, adding a new body of legislation regarding indigenous peoples, such as rights to have their traditional authorities, general education, ethnic education, and prior consultation and political rights for indigenous peoples. Currently, the conditions remain, shifting their role in a context of consolidation of indigenous collective rights. All these terms place Colombia as an innovator and leader in recognizing indigenous collective rights making it a protagonist to other countries in Latin America.

NOTES

1. Cabildo means "a town council or a town hall in a country formerly a Spanish colony." Source: Merriam-Webster online dictionary.

2. The average value between 1987 and 1990 is 0.7. The average for the seven countries in the QCA analysis is 1.17. Party Organization Variable, ordinal, converted to interval by the measurement model. Min: -.222 Max: 2.6. V-Dem (2018).

3. The tribes that are part of CRIC are Nasas, Guambianos y Coconucos (Laurent, 2005, p. 71).

4. For example, Organización Indigena Cuna de Antioquia (1982), Cabildo Caguán Dujos de los indígenas nasas y tamas de Huila, Organización regional Indígena del Casanare (1983), primera asamblea indígena del Cauca, Caquetá y Putumayo (1984), Organización Ingano del Sur Colombiano (1985), Musu-rucanuca, Organización de las comunidades ingas del valle del Sibunsoy (Putumayo) (1985), Consejo regional indígenas del Medio Amazonas (1985), Consejo Indígenas del Amazonas (1985), Consejo Regional Indígena del Vichada (1988), Consejo Regional Indígena del Guaviare (1989), Consejo Regional Indigena de Arauca (1989), Cabildo Mayor de Socorpa (1986), Movimiento Civico Wayuu, Waya Wayuu, Organización Zonal Indígena Wayuu del sur de la Guajira (all of them in 1986), Organización regional Indígena del Valle del Cauca (1989), Cabildo Mayor Esperara- Siapidara (1990), Organización Uitoto del Caquetá, Amazonas y Putumayo (1987), Organización Zonal Indígena del Putumayo (1987), Organización Zonal Indígena Marití Amazonas (1990), Organización Indígena binacional de los ríos Querari y Vaupés (1990), among others (Laurent, 2005).

5. The presidential election was added a "seventieth ballot" to make the consultation concerning a process of a new constitution. The Electoral Council did not validate this consultation. However, the Supreme Court decides that the popular will of the majority is wanting a new constitution, thus this will should prevail.

6. This coalition was more fruitful for afro-descendants groups because in the Assembly, thanks to Francisco Rojas Birry and Orlando Fals Borda, another representative, they incorporate in the constitution a transitory article (55). This article order to form a special commission to create a bill regarding territorial rights for Afro-descendants (Durán Durán, 2016).

7. According to the National Electoral Council of Colombia, currently, the ASI is called Alianza Social Independiente (Independent Social Alliance). Source: www .registraduria.gov.co.

8. See the "Considerando" part at the decree.

9. See the "Considerando" part at the decree.

10. According to V-Dem Data Set (2019), the average index of party organization in his term (1994–1998) was 0.364, considerate weak in this research.

11. For more information regarding the Congress of Colombia: *Organización Congreso Visible.*

12. Cumbre Agraria, Campesina, Étnica y Popular; la Coordinación Colombia-Europa-Estados Unidos; la Alianza de Organizaciones Sociales y Afines; la Plataforma Colombiana de Derechos Humanos, Democracia y Desarrollo; junto con la Asociación Nacional de Afrocolombianos (AFRODES), la Comisión Colombiana de Juristas y Dejusticia.

13. Each year the index was below 0.9 according to V-Dem Data Set (2021). The average for the seven countries in the QCA analysis is 1.17. Party Organization Variable, ordinal, converted to interval by the measurement model. Min: -.222 Max: 2.8.

14. Sentence No. C-377-1994 and T-214-1997 Constitutional Court of Colombia.

Chapter 5

Peru

Diverse Condition Roles to Achieve Strong Level of Indigenous Collective Rights

In the typology of a case study by Seawright and Gerring (2008), Peru would be classified as a diverse case; it means to show all the conditions for having strong collective rights, but the process of achieving them is quite different from Colombia. First, it is possible to notice a weak party system that recognized more collective rights due to personalistic leaders making radical decisions at that time. Second, in the 1990s, a new constitution became the institutional instrument to achieve political stability after a political crisis. It became a new agreement for the country to recognize more indigenous collective rights. Third, at the end of the 1990s, the indigenous organizations obtained influence in the government, mainly through meetings with national authorities. This was the mechanism to recognize and implement strong collective rights in the country. Finally, in the 2000s, these indigenous national organizations developed relationships with non-indigenous left parties, creating a united front to recognize the indigenous cosmovision, thereby achieving more collective rights for indigenous peoples.

In this chapter, Peru becomes a central subject of analysis because it represents a case of transition from weak to strong collective rights. Before 1994, the level of collective rights was weak, with no coalitions of any type and without any constitutional change since 1979. The only condition that was present was a weak party system. The next sections will address the context of Peru. Subsequently, it will unfold what kind of causal mechanisms were created to have more collective rights and how indigenous peoples were able to pass or transit from a weak level to a strong level of collective rights.

PERU: A CONTEXT OF POLITICAL INSTABILITY

Peru is a country located in the Andean region of South America. It has a tremendous and rich geography that includes physical properties of Earth's surface such as coasts, highlands, and rainforest. Currently, the population is 32 million inhabitants (source: Work Bank). The ethnic composition of the country is mixed, including indigenous peoples, mestizos, afro-descendants, and immigrants from Europe and Asia, mainly Chinese and Japanese peoples (Hudson, 1992).

The political history of Peru shows periods of democratic and authoritarian regimes but is distinguished by a background of violence. In the 1960s and 1970s, "Shining Path Movement" emerged. This movement was opposed to Lima-based, a centralized government, a city that usurped the resources from the rest of the country (Hudson, 1992). Their members came from universities and high schools, urban-lower class neighborhoods, schoolteachers, and peasants from Ayacucho, Huancavelica, and adjacent areas (Hudson, 1992). The methods of this movement to achieve their purposes were violent, developing a popular war against the representatives of the status quo and civilian population, with more intense actions since 1980 (Comisión de la Verdad y Reconciliación, 2003). Thus,

> [f]rom 1980 to 1990, an estimated 200,000 persons were driven from their homes, with about 18,000 murdered people mostly in the department of Ayacucho and neighboring areas. In five provinces in Ayacucho, the resident population dropped by two-thirds, and many villages were virtual ghost towns. (Hudson, 1992)

It is in this context that multiple governments led the conduction of the country. President Fernando Belaúnde took power by force from 1963 to 1968. In 1968, the government was overthrown by the armed forces led by Juan Velasco Alvarado. This "revolutionary government" was a "progressive and left-wing military regime, which attempted to implement a series of structural reforms, such as land and educational reforms; it maintained dictatorial powers, but it was only mildly repressive" (Hudson, 1992). After an intra-regime coup, the military government called a civilian Constitutional Assembly to work on a new constitution.

A new constitution was drafted and ratified, so, two democratic governments took place: Fernando Belaunde Terry (1980–1985) and Alan García (1985–1990). In 1990, political parties were in crisis, a low level of institutionalization, an excess of personalism, authoritarianism emerged (Alcántara Saez, 2013a), and finally President Alberto Fujimori (1990–2000) took power. Fujimori was a figure without any political experience, supported by political parties, and without a majority in Congress. He was leading a country sat in a severe crisis: hyperinflation, terrorism, and a collapse of the state (Tanaka, 2015; Tanaka & Vera Rojas, 2010). All these features could be the perfect recipe for failure. However, Fujimori led the country to keep power, stabilize it, and succeed in front of his adversaries (Tanaka, 2015). This includes controlling the level of violence from the Shining Path Movements.

Furthermore, Fujimori organized a self-coup to dissolve Congress, calling for new elections and a new constitution, reorganized the power of the governments, and built a stable competitive authoritarian government (Tanaka, 2015). The citizens supported these measures.[1] After a scandal in which the head of the intelligence service was bribing members of Congress (Heuser, 2018), in 2000, Fujimori resigned from the presidency on a visit to Japan. However, "Peru's Congress, in turn, refused to accept his resignation and instead ousted him, declaring him 'morally unfit' for office" (*The New York Times*, 2000). After this, Congress called for a new election. Fujimori was found guilty of committing several human rights violations during his term.

After this second authoritarian government, a series of democratic regimes took place: Alejandro Toledo (2001–2006), Alan García (2006–2011), Ollanta Humala (2011–2016), and a short presidential term of Pedro Pablo Kuczynski (2016–2018) who resigned from the position due to the accusation of impeachment on corruption, and Pedro Castillo[2] (2021 to current).[3] All of them had the destabilizing problem of the Fujimori term: pervasive corruption. Moreover, drug trafficking is entwined with the political system, creating a perception of insecurity (Heuser, 2018). The Odebrecht scandal in 2017 showed illegal party financing by a Brazilian construction company involving all the presidents after Fujimori (Heuser, 2018).

In this context of changing political regimes, a high level of violence and corruption from Peruvian elites, the conditions and causal mechanisms for more collective rights found their way to pass from weak to a strong level of rights. In the case of Peru, the two most important conditions were a weak party system and a new constitution which are institutional ones. The coalitions between indigenous peoples or indigenous associations and coalitions with non-indigenous allies were developed in the process, but sometime later, influencing changes of non-beneficial plans for indigenous communities and increasing collective rights.

WEAK PARTY SYSTEM: WEAK COLLECTIVE RIGHTS FOR INDIGENOUS "COMMUNITIES"

Peru presents as a first condition in the case of a weak party system that recognizes weak collective rights. For this presence, Peru is a deviant case of weak collective rights because, according to the theory, none of the conditions should be present to have that level. However, the weak party system incentivizes an ambivalent relationship with indigenous peoples, called peasant communities or native communities, decreasing their level of influence in the political field. The following passages will refer to the weak party system's characteristics, the weak level of collective rights, and the transition from indigenous peoples to peasant communities.

Peru has had ambivalent relationships with indigenous peoples since the beginning of its history. In the nineteenth century, they had the right to vote and participate in the political field, but they lost these rights in 1890 because most indigenous peoples could not fulfill the voting requirement of knowing how to read and write (Chuecas, 2008). One of the essential features of this complicated relationship is the denomination of "indigenous communities" or "native communities." Since colonial times, indigenous peoples became known as communities, not as peoples. The consequences of this mislabeling minimized their participation in the political field. Despite this fact, the 1920 Constitution recognized these communities as part of Peru's cultural and ethnic diversity (Chuecas, 2008). These characteristics show an uncertain dialogue with the communities embedded in a particular political system that reinforce the instability of a weak party system.

Throughout its history, Peru has had a weak party system (Aragón Trelles, 2016; Grompone, 2016; Levistsky, 2018; Mainwaring, 2018a; Meléndez, 2019; Sulmont, 2018), and is likely one with the most problems in Latin America (Levistsky, 2018; Mainwaring, 2018a). According to the data provided by the V-Dem data set, the party organization from 1987 to 1993 was present in less than half of the parties,[4] which means that party systems were unorganized and only present for election periods. Before this time frame, the party system was highly personalistic and based on movements more than political parties (Alcántara Saez, 2013a). The consequence of this is national leaders prioritizing their interests and not collective projects, taking undisciplined and erratic decisions (Fernando Tuesta Soldevilla et al., 2019). Therefore, it is not easy to understand their motives. However, this mechanism of a personalistic approach is the one that will allow more collective rights in the country.

The political parties have tried to become institutionalized and modernized since 1956. However, they became technocratic groups (Alcántara Saez, 2013a), with a high level of technical experts only in time of elections. During the 1980s election, a redefinition of the party system took place, keeping some of the previous characteristics but increasing the visibility of three ideological tendencies: a conservative approach with the Acción Popular and the Partido Popular Cristiano; a center-left with the Partido Aprista Peruano; and the nonviolent Marxism approach with the Izquierda Unida (Alcántara Saez, 2013). According to Levistsky (2018), "[t]he Peruvian party system collapsed in the late 1980s and early 1990s in a context of deep socio-economic crisis and a mounting Shining Path insurgency" (Levistsky, 2018, p. 327). This collapse showed a system with a high degree of fragmentation and problems of political articulation between parties (Fernando Tuesta Soldevilla et al., 2019) that impacted the level of collective rights.

One of the consequences of this instability of the party system is that Peru has politicians but no political parties, and the alliances they can form are through independent coalitions with other politicians (Aragón Trelles, 2016). These coalitions are highly unstable, with politicians who can decide with a high level of discretion without any opposition (Grompone, 2016). Thus, the level of personalism in politicians changes the type of decisions they will implement and the party alliances they are going to build (Meléndez, 2019). These two elements become essential for policies that these politicians are willing to support.

It was possible to recognize necessary collective rights for indigenous peoples, within this context of instability, such as using indigenous land for the communities (not "property") and some type of autonomy for them. These rights are hallmark of strong collective rights. However, indigenous peoples did not have other rights because they were not recognized as political actors. The subject of these rights is the communities, not the peoples themselves. The imposition of the term "peasant," labeled indigenous peoples, eliminated them as political actors. Therefore, their conditions were different compared to other indigenous peoples in Latin America, putting them at a weak level of collective rights.

In 1974, the revolutionary government of the army, led by General Juan Velasco Alvarado (1968–1975), enshrined the decree-law 20653, in which indigenous communities obtained the right to their collective lands (Chuecas, 2008), in the context of agrarian reform. This legal document defines who are the native communities, recognizing the Amazon tribes, and enshrines that the lands are imprescriptible, inalienable, and unattachable (Chuecas, 2008; Millones, 2016). In 1978, this decree-law was modified, including a significant limitation of the lands, specifically for forest lands. They could use the land but could not obtain ownership of the property (Chuecas, 2008). This changed the legal entitlement considerably for the communities.

The military government then recognized Quechua and Spanish as the official language in 1975, in the decree-law 21156. According to Cuadros Sánchez (2018), this measure was revolutionary for the time because it enabled the improved living conditions of Quechua speakers and "peasants." The same was true for the right to land: the same decree-law, 20653.[5] This bill was presented by President Alan García (1984–1990), who espoused an anti-imperialist stance during his term (A. García, 1986, 1987), making economic decisions against the Washington consensus. These decisions were helpful for peasant and indigenous communities because their land and the use of those lands for agriculture were seen as an anti-imperialism measure[6] (A. García, 1986). However, the relationship with García was not as peaceful as it could have been because his second term increased the distance between indigenous communities and the government, which I will develop in other sections. Thus, it is possible to see that the categories of indigenous and peasants are the same in Peru.

The action of Velasco Alvarado, and to some extent García, is based on highly conflicting narratives. They were able to change the status quo because they did not need to explain their decisions to fellow political party members or even to the opposition in the case of Velasco. This process is the same pattern followed by Presidents Toledo and Humala. In any case, Velasco and García were highly ambivalent with indigenous peoples, increasing the level of protection with one action but decreasing their role in society substantially with another action.

THE STATUS QUO PERSISTS: NEW CONSTITUTION AND MAINTAINING THE WEAK COLLECTIVE RIGHTS

After Velasco, in the process of a new constitution, indigenous and peasant communities maintained the status quo with some collective rights, but it lacked the denomination of indigenous peoples. This situation produced a low level of indigenous participation and recognition of indigenous peoples and political subjects.

General elections for a Constituent Assembly occurred after the military government of Velasco, looking for a democratic exit. The political parties were once again legalized to compete. In June of 1978, after several tensions the elections took place. In July 1978, the same year, the president of the Constituent Assembly Haya de la Torre established in his speech the idea of addressing an article to recognize Peru as an indigenous-American country (Haya de la Torre, 1978). Within this context, the 1979 Constitution followed the rights of previous legal instruments, implementing the autonomy for peasants and native communities. This autonomy is regarding their organizations, local work, land use, economic role, and administrative measures (Chuecas, 2008). This constitution and the Civil Code (1984) repeated the characteristics of the lands of previous legal instruments: imprescriptible, inalienable, and unattached. However, the land could be sold with two-thirds of the community votes, and it can be expropriated for the public domain (Chuecas, 2008). All of these represent rights for the peasants and native communities. However, their representation as indigenous peoples did not exist in this first period.

In the process of a new constitution from 1978 to 1979, indigenous communities did not participate. According to Millones (1999), when the World Bank wanted to provide funds to indigenous peoples in Latin America and wanted to speak with leaders of indigenous organizations, it was not able because of the lack of indigenous organizations in Peru. One of the possibilities for this lack of indigenous organizations is the mix between indigenous peoples and peasants. Other explanations are the migration from rural areas to the capital and the process of "mestizaje" (Salazar-Soler, 2014). García and Lucero (2004) propose another possibility. In Peru, the indigenous associations were local, not national, like other countries in Latin America. What is certain is that indigenous organizations appeared in the late 1990s and the beginning of the 2000s (M. E. García & Lucero, 2004; Van Cott, 2008).

POLITICAL INSTABILITY AND A NEW CONSTITUTION: THE INSTITUTIONAL CONDITIONS

At the end of 1980, the party system was still weak, but it began a process to modify the existing constitution. This weak party system brought to power a personalistic leader who made decisions that indirectly helped recognize some indigenous rights but removed the recognition of others. Also, to contain a political crisis, a new constitution worked as a new institutional agreement in which indigenous collective rights became a part. Thus, the causal mechanisms with the institutional conditions are personalistic leaders who change the status quo and a new institution that creates a new constitutional pact to resolve a crisis.

In 1990, Alberto Fujimori took office, with an electoral campaign focused on his figure as an outsider of the party system and speeches against the political establishment (Alcántara Saez, 2013a). At this time, the traditional political forces disappeared from the political arena. This change of forces increased with the succession of elections: general elections in 1995, local elections in 1995 and 1998, and national elections in 2000.

In May 1992 after the self-coup, Fujimori called for a Democratic Constituent Congress (hereafter, Congress) to enforce a new constitution. The elections for the members of the Congress were held on November 22, 1992 (Toshiyama Tanaka, 1992). The process finished in December of 1993[7] with a new constitution.

During this time, Congress did not have any indigenous representatives as members of any political movement, like in the Colombian case. However, there is evidence of representatives who acted as allies for indigenous issues. Tuesday, July 6th, 1993, in the Congress session marriage was discussed. The representatives Luis Enrique Tord Romero and Lourdes Flores Nano explained the importance of allowing any form of marriage in the constitution, supporting the norms of native communities regarding marriage and its relationship to the customary law of indigenous peoples (Congreso Constituyente Democrático, 1998). In the session on Tuesday, July 13th, 1993, in a discussion regarding the state and nation, the representative Tord Romero praised the inclusion of several official languages in article 42 (actual 49) as recognition of Peruvian culture. This article was conflictive, and several conservative representatives pushed it back because of the lack of resources to translate all the official actions to Quechua, Aymara, and other newly officialized languages (Congreso Constituyente Democrático, 1998). However, the pushback was not enough, and the article was eventually enshrined in the constitution.

Additionally, there is evidence of how the different commissions of Congress developed indigenous rights, holding meetings with some groups that represented peasant and human rights organizations. For example, the Commission of Human Rights and Peace held meetings with several groups defending human rights, and it supported the actions of peasants and farmers in Lima (Congreso Constituyente Democrático, n.d.).

Thus, it is in this context of political instability and a Congress that has non-indigenous allies and no indigenous representatives, the 1993 Constitution contained several collective rights such as the right to self-determination and autonomy (Article 89); the right to cultural identity (Articles 2 and 89); right to participation (Articles 2, 31, 191, and 197); right to a special jurisdiction (Articles 149 and 139.8); right to land and territories (Articles 88 and 89); and right to natural resources (Article 89) with a high level of control by the government (Merino, 2018). For the first time, the government recognized peasant and native communities as an ethnic and cultural plurality; however, this recognition was not the consequence of a political agreement with indigenous communities (Gálvez Revollar, 2001), and it deleted several protections for them that were part of the juridical system since 1974 (Merino, 2018). Here, it is possible to observe the ambivalent relationship with indigenous communities.

Therefore, some indigenous groups and anthropologists were against several of these changes. Mainly, they fought against eliminating indigenous land attributes (imprescriptible, inalienable, and unattachable), but they were unable to achieve this goal (Merino, 2018; Van Cott, 2007). For Van Cott (2007) and Merino (2018), the constitution of 1993 and the government of Fujimori were disastrous for indigenous communities due to the neoliberal policies that the government imposed, such as the liberalization of the trading system, privatization of state industries, ending subsidies. All of these harmed the well-being of indigenous communities and their economy.

Thus, the first two conditions and causal mechanisms that are present in the Peruvian case is a weak party system that allows a personalistic leader with no political party support to take power, who makes decisions against the status quo, and calls for a new Congress to create a constitution that improves rights for indigenous communities. However, indigenous communities suffered a regression in land rights at the same time. This new constitution produced this ambivalent result by becoming a legal instrument to improve the political crisis. In this case, indigenous communities lost necessary rights from previous constitutions, such as the right to land. Nevertheless, they were able to recognize other collective rights due to institutional decisions, not indigenous social movements or organizations. Indigenous organizations have a diverse role in this puzzle.

ORGANIZATIONS AND SOME LEVEL OF COALITIONS FOR INDIGENOUS PEOPLES FOR RECOGNIZING INDIGENOUS COLLECTIVE RIGHTS

The Peruvian case includes the other two conditions that improve the level of indigenous collective rights in the process but later, at the end of the 1990s, indigenous national organizations and coalitions with non-indigenous allies appeared. The causal mechanisms are the same as in the Colombian case. Indigenous national organizations influence the political field to make decisions that improve collective rights. Moreover, these organizations make coalitions with non-indigenous peoples, becoming a united front to increase the level of differentiation. This front is the causal mechanism necessary to achieve more collective rights. In this case, it is not only about the recognition of indigenous communities but also the implementation of previous standards.

Since 1947 Peru has had several organizations related to indigenous communities with the CCP (Confederación Campesina del Perú) and in 1974 with the CNA (Confederación Nacional Agraria) (Karp-Toledo, 2014). However, these organizations were more centered on peasants than indigenous peoples. According to García and Lucero (2004), these organizations avoided indigenous issues. Thus, in 1999, the CONACAMI started to assume the agenda of the CCP and CNA, positioning itself as an organization with ethnic roots, using the indigenous identity as the center of their demands (Karp-Toledo, 2014). There were also organizations in the Amazon area, such as AIDESEP (Asociación interétnica de Desarrollo de la Selva Peruana), formally operative since 1985, and the CONAP (Confederación de Nacionalidades Amazónicas del Perú) since 1987.

A national organization that represented indigenous communities was founded in 1998, the COPPIP[8] (*Confederación Permanente de los Pueblos*

Indígenas del Perú. Later known as *Coordinadora Permanente de los Pueblos Indígenas del Perú).* According to García and Lucero (2004), "COPPIP represents a truly unprecedented space for the articulation of an indigenous political project and subject and a potentially crucial counterweight to the co-optive power of the state" (p. 180). According to Madrid (2012), the organization split in 2002; however, there is evidence of organizational actions further in time.

This organization was famous for pushing an indigenous policy that fitted the indigenous cosmovision. In 1998, they tried to influence an act regarding indigenous rights at the Peruvian Congress. In 2000, they held a meeting to organize a five-year plan with specific objectives. In 2003, they were able to postpone a congressional vote regarding a constitutional amendment to have indigenous consultation. They presented those results to Congress without success (Van Cott, 2007). In 2003–2004, the organization pushed back against CONAPA, Comisión Nacional de Pueblos Andinos, Amazonicos y Afroperuanos, an indigenous organization created by President Toledo and chaired by his Belgian Quechua-speaking wife, Eliane Karp-Toledo (S. Greene, 2005; Van Cott, 2007). The goal of this organization was to lead a process of developmental change in which it respects the value of indigenous culture and does not discriminate against indigenous peoples in any national institution (Alza Barco & Zambrano Chávez, 2014). This organization was a first step and an effort from the government to institutionalize indigenous communities. In these cases, indigenous organizations were crucial for increasing the protection of indigenous collective rights through a process of influence in the political system.

In this scenario, the organization of indigenous communities is highly fragmented. This characteristic does not mean they were nonexistent, as other studies claim (Van Cott, 2007; Yashar, 2005), but it shows the difficulties of articulating central answers to government actions. This also impacts coalitions with other non-indigenous allies. With indigenous coalitions highly fragmented, having strong ties with others is difficult. Therefore, Peru only shows one coalition with a left political party.

In the government of President Toledo, peasants' organizations (which include indigenous peoples) formed a coalition with the political party, Perú Posible, the party supporting the president. This coalition incorporated one peasant/indigenous leader at the Congress, Paulina Arpasi Velásquez, secretary of CCP (Cedillo Delgado, 2018), an important action for that time. The coalition aimed to embrace the differentiation and role of indigenous communities while emphasizing the indigenous identity of the president. Pending the term of President Toledo, several laws developed and enacted the collective rights of indigenous peoples: Act no. 27908-2003, regarding jurisdiction for peasant communities; act no. 28106-2003, concerning indigenous languages;

act no. 27818-2002, for bilingual education for indigenous peoples; act no. 27811-2002 regarding collective knowledge; lastly, the Supreme Decree 028-2003-AG-2003 concerning the land's territorial, economic, and ecological integrity for voluntarily isolated ethnic groups. According to the information gathered, this is the period with the most significant number of laws and regulations regarding the collective rights of indigenous communities in Peru.

Furthermore, regarding jurisdiction for peasant communities and the right to speak indigenous languages, there is also evidence that these legal documents passed because a large majority of Congress were members of Perú Posible. In all the voting processes (one for the jurisdiction of peasant communities and two for the right to speak indigenous languages), the party was the one that voted more in favor to pass the laws. In the case of jurisdiction for peasant communities, it had thirty-two votes in favor out of eighty.[9] For the right to speak indigenous languages, twenty-eight votes out of fifty-six for the first vote[10] and twenty-four votes out of seventy-one for the second vote.[11] Thus, the coalition successfully recognized more collective rights of indigenous peoples throughout the term of President Toledo.

During this time, any other type of coalitions with non-indigenous allies, including ethnic political parties, has been impossible. According to Van Cott (2007), this is due to a lack of maturity of indigenous organizations. Madrid (2012) agreed with Van Cott regarding the lack of power and fragmentation of the organization of native communities. However, Madrid is more optimistic, stating that there has been an increase in local ethnic political parties in the past decade. This modest achievement is not replicated nationally (Madrid, 2012). Coalitions with non-indigenous peoples become a challenge. Thus, coalitions will not improve if indigenous communities' national or regional associations are fragmented. Thus, if coalitions between indigenous peoples do not improve, it will be impossible to collaborate with other institutions.

The relations between indigenous organizations and national authorities have been conflictive with more recent governments. In the second term of Alan García (2006–2011), his several editorial opinions (from 2007 to 2008) in the prestigious newspaper *El Comercio* started a debate related to the use of natural resources in Peru. He argued that Peru has several natural resources that are not being used for bureaucratic and ideological reasons, thereby not contributing to the national economy. He used the proverbial term "a dog in the manger" to explain his point:

> There are many resources that are left unused, that don't receive investment and don't generate employment. All of that is due to ideology, idleness, laziness or the law of the perro del hortelano "dog in the manger": "If I don't do it, no one should do it" (si no lo hago yo, que no lo haga nadie). The first such resource is the Amazon." (A. García, 2007).[12]

This term is used when a person selfishly keeps something that he or she does not really need or want so that others may not use or enjoy it. President García stated that those suffering from that syndrome are patrimonialists against the modern economy.

In his second editorial opinion called "Recipe for terminating the dog in the manger," he was more explicit in exposing his neoliberal beliefs: "It emphasized the need to 'change the attitude to investments,' replacing 'exaggerated criteria' with the 'market and private competition fixing the conditions.' [. . .] Depleted forestlands were not being put to productive use due to inadequate property rights" (Larsen, 2018). The declarations were problematic because most natural resources and lands that are not utilized by the state are in the hands of peasants and native communities. These ideas soon become massive new bills.

Historically, indigenous peoples protect land and resources from indiscriminate private use and governmental abuse. The narrative of President García was seen as racist, in which indigenous peoples are considered dangerous, subject to manipulation, and passive subjects while expressing they live at the margin of modernity (Karp-Toledo, 2014). Thus, this declaration is an affront to those communities.

In June 2009 occurred the "Baguazo," a blooded confrontation between native communities, mainly the Awajún peoples, and the central government in Bagua, "with thousands of Amazonian and mestizo protestors blocking a stretch of highway, with police and military forces sent in to reopen it" (Larsen, 2018). According to official information, there were 33 fatalities, including 23 police officers, 5 indigenous civilians, 5 non-indigenous civilians, 200 wounded, and 1 missing person (Cavero, 2011). This confrontation occurred due to the enforcement of decree-law 1090, known as the forest law, and decree-law 1064, which stripped the land of native communities for national interest, giving it to private sectors for exploitation. This regulation had significant opposition from native communities, particularly from the AIDESEP, mainly because it was unconstitutional and the government did not open a process for consultation with indigenous peoples, as it was mandated to do according to Convention No. 169 (Che Piú, 2009). The confrontation lasted five days. In this process, CONACAMI supported AIDESEP (Salazar-Soler, 2014). In this context, CONACAMI and AIDESEP decided to sign a "National Agreement of Andean, Amazon, and Costal Organizations" to collaborate in future endeavors (Salazar-Soler, 2014). The confrontation results were the suspension and the revocation of the decree-laws (Cavero, 2011; Che Piú, 2009) and a high degree of distrust between the parties. These organizations now tied together and backing a unified front became central in influencing the government in revoking the unconstitutional decrees.

During Ollanta Humala government (2011–2016), and after a period of reflection regarding the Bagua conflict, it was time to regulate the process for prior consultation of communities. Several indigenous organizations, such as AIDESEP, CONACAMI, and CONAP, supported the bill's legislative process (AIDESEP et al., 2011). In 2011, act no. 29785 was enforced, and the rights to prior consultation became law. However, there were voices from the indigenous communities regarding how the government regulated it. According to Urteaga-Crovetto (2018), "[i]ndigenous organizations contend that through regulations the core substance of the right to consultation had been downgraded" (p. 17). There are significant differences between Convention No. 169, the law, and the regulations made in 2012 (AIDESEP et al., 2011). For the communities, the government became known for being full of contradictions. In the government of García, the lands were conceded to extractive companies, and President Humala followed that tendency throughout his term (AIDESEP et al., 2012). By June 2012, 25.3% of the national territory had mining concessions (AIDESEP et al., 2012) without considering the indigenous communities' opinion or approval.

Peruvian conditions stated in this research are necessary enough to create more collective rights; however, if we compare the case of Colombia the Peruvian process was totally different. The role of the presidents in an unstable system and the decision to have a new constitution in 1993 enabled more collective rights for indigenous peoples. The national authorities supported recognizing indigenous rights (Remy, 2014), but not in all cases. In this process, the role of organizations and coalitions is secondary, focusing more on contesting the amendments and regulations that the government implemented. The causal mechanisms in all the conditions are similar to the Colombian case. Therefore, Peru is a diverse case in the analysis.

PERU IN CURRENT TIMES: CHALLENGES FOR "INDIGENOUS PEOPLES"

There are two critical challenges that indigenous peoples must address in Peru. One is the use of the term "indigenous peoples," which peasant and native communities need to adopt because they are nations and not just "communities" (AIDESEP et al., 2012; Chuecas, 2008; Salazar-Soler, 2014), and the other is building strong associations and coalitions with non-indigenous peoples.

Regarding the first challenge, the lack of respect and rights that acknowledge indigenous, native, and peasant "communities" as their own nation has created obstacles to the full implementation of this level of strong collective rights: President Humala stated that the only indigenous peoples that are the object of prior consultation are isolated communities because in the "sierra" there are no native communities, only peasant communities (Remy, 2013). This statement created adverse conditions in the exercising of indigenous rights.

The following acts define indigenous peoples in the country: act no. 28736-2006 about isolated indigenous groups and first contact, act no. 29785-2011 regarding prior consultation, and act no. 27811-2002 concerning collective knowledge. All of them define indigenous peoples as those who recognize themselves as such, who have their own cultures and lands, and form a part of the Peruvian state.[13] The prior consultation act requires that one must have direct descendants from native populations to be considered indigenous. According to indigenous organizations, there are two problems with these definitions: the first one is related to the requirement of being a direct descendant from indigenous peoples, which does not recognize the contribution and identification of indigenous peoples from indirect descendants; the second problem is concerning the application of these definitions to the specific rights the acts enshrine. For the rest of the collective rights, indigenous peoples are still communities (AIDESEP et al., 2011). So, they are not general definitions for all the legal instruments in Peru.

The peasant communities like the ones organized by CONACAMI understand they need to use an ethnic denomination (indigenous peoples) to access a series of rights from the international human rights law (Salazar-Soler, 2014). This understanding is instrumental because it is related to the participation of communities in society (Salazar-Soler, 2014), and it is legitimized because peasant communities are indigenous peoples.

The government has also made efforts to use "indigenous peoples" instead of using the terms peasant and native communities. In a series of educational materials and documents issued to the public by the Ministry of Culture, they use the term "indigenous peoples" to explain several collective rights. These documents are a step forward in re-representing indigenous "communities" as indigenous peoples. However, there is evidence that in implementing the right to prior consultation, there are still public-private collaborations that continue to confuse the terms of communities and peoples. Thus, indigenous peoples cannot exercise their rights (Guevara-Gil & Verona-Badajoz, 2018). There is a slow transition from peasant and native communities to use the term indigenous peoples, supported by the indigenous associations and, to some extent, the government. Hopefully, this transition will allow the recognition of indigenous peoples as valued actors in Peruvian politics and society.

The impact of not using the term indigenous peoples affects the level of fragmentation of the diverse associations related to indigenous activities or territories. Stronger associations and more coalitions with non-indigenous allies will evolve into more representation of indigenous peoples in national politics. So far, the most important association is AIDESEP, which is very active in defending indigenous peoples' rights. They mainly operate in the Amazon region; however, they are becoming a reference for indigenous topics. Currently, they are implementing several projects with different institutions to increase the level of indigenous protections. Most recently, they signed an agreement with Equitable Origin ONG to have digital access to information related to the prior consultation process in other countries (AIDESEP, 2020). These alliances are the first step to create more stable relationships.

In sum, Peru is a compelling case because, after 1993, it presents all the necessary conditions to achieve strong collective rights. In the QCA analysis, Peru displays a higher level of indigenous rights than other countries in the region. However, how the conditions relate to each other is entirely different from the Colombian case. Perú passed from having weak to strong collective rights, and the most important conditions were institutional. The weak party system elevated personalistic leaders interested in recognizing some level of indigenous rights, such as General Velasco and President Toledo. In both cases, the presidents made radical decisions about political instability to increase the level of rights. Velasco was an important actor in including Quechua as an official language and the collective rights of peasant communities, including indigenous peoples. In the term of Toledo, it is possible to find the majority of indigenous legislation: jurisdiction for peasant communities, indigenous languages, bilingual education, collective knowledge, and the territorial, economic, and ecological integrity of the land for voluntarily isolated ethnic groups. They supported and approved these rights in the context of political instability.

The Congress and its new constitution were the causal mechanisms that enshrined several collective rights in 1993. This constitution was an instrument to solve a crisis created by Fujimori's self-coup. The Congress that drafted and signed the 1993 Constitution did not have any indigenous representation, only non-indigenous allies that helped to recognize several collective rights. The associations and coalitions with non-indigenous allies were developed later in the process. The most important is the COPPIP because it influences policies that fit the indigenous cosmovision. The role of associations has been a tool for modifying the non-beneficial plan for indigenous communities, set in place by personalistic leaders. For example, COPPIP pushed back against CONAPA. The coalitions with non-indigenous allies have been influential with President Toledo to spread the constitutional protection of indigenous peoples by laws. Thanks to this coalition, the body of legislation regarding collective rights was easier to approve in Congress regarding the evidence gathered from official reports. The process of recognizing peasant and native communities as indigenous peoples is ongoing and necessary to achieve the full implementation of strong collective rights.

NOTES

1. POP Survey, 73% of the interviewee agreed with the self-coup (*Anexo 1. Cronología 1978-2000*, s. f.).

2. Castillo was elected with high support of indigenous peoples and rural areas of Peru. Therefore, Keiko Fujimori, also a candidate for the election, claims for voter tampering, focusing on ballots coming from rurals regions of the Andean highlands and Amazon rainforest, ignoring Lima and other big cities.

3. From 2018 to 2021, there were several presidents due to the resignation of Kuczynski: Martin Vizcarra (2018–2020), vice president of Kuczynski who was declared with a permanent moral incapacity by the Congress for a corruption case in 2020. Manuel Merino (2020) was in power only for five days; he resigned after several protests against him. Francisco Sagasti (2020–2021) was president of the Congress when he had to take office.

4. The average index for this time is 0.8. The average for the seven countries in the QCA analysis is 1.17. Party Organization Variable, ordinal, converted to interval by the measurement model. Min: -.222 Max: 2.8. V-Dem Data Set 11v.1.

5. Others explain that the term "peasant community" is for the tribes of the sierra, and native communities for the Amazon tribes (Laats, 2000). According to Merino (2018), the act regarding the agrarian reform started using the term "peasant communities," and the act no. 20653 created the native communities in the Amazon.

6. In 1986, President García has several meetings with leaders from the peasant communities called "Rimanacuyó." These assemblies took place in Pira, Huancayo, and Cusco. The principal claim of these leaders was the legal recognition of the peasant communities.

7. The Democratic Constituent Congress keep their endeavors as a Legislative Congress until July 1995.

8. Fifteen organizations: Asociación de Defensa y Desarrollo de las Comunidades Andinas del Perú (ADECAP); Comisión de Emergencia Asháninka (CEA) ñ Comunidad Indígena Asháninka Marankiari Bajo (CIAMB); Confederación Campesina del Perú (CCP); Confederación de Nacionalidades Amazónicas del Perú (CONAP); Confederación Nacional Agraria (CNA); Consejo Aguaruna Huambisa (CAH)ñ Coordinadora Nacional de Comunidades afectadas por la minería (CONA-CAMI); Coordinadora Nacional de Comunidades Campesinas e Indígenas del Perú (CONACCIP); Federación Departamental de Comunidades Campesinas de Pasco; Federación Provincial de Comunidades Campesinas de Huaral; Federación Puquinañ Organización de Comunidades Aymara, Amazonenses y Quechuas (OBAAQ), Taller Permanente de Mujeres Indígenas Andinas y Amazónicas - Chirapaq; and, Unión Nacional de Comunidades Aymara (UNCA) (Source: www.gloobal.net).

9. Voting process on 12/12/2002. There were ninety-eight congresspersons present. Eighty votes for the approval of the bill. Thirty-three from Peru Possible (PP); twenty from Partido Aprista Peruano (PAP); eight from Union Parlamentaria Descentralista (UPD); eight from Frente Independiente Moralizador (FIM); five from Unidad Popular (UP); five from Democratico Independiente (GPDI); and two from

representatives without political parties (NA). There were six votes against the bill and seven abstentions (Congreso de la República del Perú, 2002).

10. Voting process on 10/23/2003. There were ninety-five congresspersons present. Fifty-six votes for the approval of the bill. Twenty-eight from PP; nine from PAP; five from GPDI; five from Peru Ahora (PA); four from FIM; three from SP-AP-VPP (SAU); and one from UN. There were fourteen votes against the bill and twenty-two abstentions (Congreso de la República del Perú, 2003a).

11. Voting process on 10/30/2003. There were seventy-one congresspersons present. Fifty-six votes for the approval of the bill. Twenty-four from PP; fifteen from PAP; five from GPDI; one from PA; four from FIM; four from SAU; and four from UN. There were four votes against the bill and seven abstentions (Congreso de la República del Perú, 2003b).

12. Translated in Larsen (2018).

13. Act no. 28736-2006 article 2, a; act no. 29785-2011 article 7; act no. 27811-2002 article 2, a.

Chapter 6

Chile

The Consequences of Stability: A Case of Weak Collective Rights

Chile is a typical case of weak collective rights before and after the ratification of the ILO's Convention No. 169. However, the level of collective rights improved after the ratification. This improvement was only related to recognize one type of political participation for indigenous peoples: the right to prior consultation. In this case, the party system is institutionalized and shows constitutional stability, showing lack of coalitions between indigenous peoples and other non-indigenous allies. Therefore, the causal mechanisms are different from those in other cases.

Chile has become one of the most stable political systems in Latin America (Mainwaring, 2018a); previously and after the dictatorship of Pinochet (1973–1990), left and right political parties are predictable. Thus, political parties align the decisions of national authorities, maintaining the status quo and a weak level of indigenous collective rights. The constitution has remained the same since 1980, without recognition of any collective rights due to a robust liberal paradigm. In terms of coalitions, the fragmentation of indigenous peoples is high, so they are unable to have national or regional organizations that can negotiate with the government to recognize more collective rights. Furthermore, indigenous peoples are not able to form coalitions with non-indigenous allies because they do not have national organizations that influence national authorities to promote significant changes. Due to these causal mechanisms, Chile has a weak level of collective rights.

CONTEXT OF CHILE: A STABLE COUNTRY

Chile is located in the western seaboard of South America with 17 million inhabitants who mainly live in urban areas (Silva, 2015). Chile has been one of the countries in Latin America with the fastest-growing economy in recent decades. The Chilean economy is based in the extractive industry. Chile is the main exporter and producer of copper in the world followed by Peru and China. The country's heritage is primarily Spanish culture including some appreciation of the indigenous cosmovision.

In the political history of the country, there were two military dictatorships. In 1927, General Carlos Ibañez del Campo took power, and in 1973, the chief of staff General Augusto Pinochet Ugarte started a period of authoritarianism until 1989 (BBC Mundo, 2017). Besides these standalone events, Chile has one of the most stable political systems in Latin America, along with Mexico and Uruguay (Mainwaring, 2018b).

The second period of military dictatorship has been one of the most important historical events in the current political field. The military meeting led by Pinochet took power on September 11, 1973, after a coup in opposition to the socialist president Salvador Allende (1970–1973). The military meeting decided to close the National Congress, they prohibited political parties, and the press became heavily censored (Government of Chile, 2014). This dictatorship was one of the bloodiest in modern Chilean history. According to official sources, "[o]ver 3,000 people were executed or made to disappear, thousands of people had to go into exile, universities and work centers were intervened or put under surveillance" (Government of Chile, 2014).

Turning into the economy, the dictatorship decided to implement the free-market model of Milton Friedman, professor at the University of Chicago (Government of Chile, 2014). Several members of the Chilean elite attended the university as graduate students to learn the model and apply it in Chile (they were known as "Chicago boys") (Silva, 2015). From 1975 to 1979, they implemented an orthodox program to stabilize the country, including a reduction in social spending, the privatization of companies, promoting exporting goods, and implementing a market system (Government of Chile, 2014; Silva, 2015). The constitution of 1980 cemented these ideas into national policy. This introduction was the beginning of a liberal paradigm adhered to by the following democratic presidents.

Following the economic crisis in 1982, left-social movements led by the Christian Democratic Party and the Communist Party emerged. After a failed assassination attempt on General Pinochet, the democratic transition followed an institutional structure (Silva, 2015). In 1988, following the provisions of the 1980 Constitution,[1] a plebiscite decided between maintaining the authoritarian regime for eight more years or calling for a new democratic government—the majority vote to end the authoritarian regime. Accepting failure, Pinochet called for elections that began a new democratic time. Patricio Aylwin Azocar (1990–1994) was the first transition president, after him, followed by three left party presidents: Eduardo Frei Ruiz-Tagle

(1994–2000), Ricardo Lagos Escobar (2000–2006), and Michelle Bachelet Jeria (2006–2010). The first right-wing president Sebastián Piñera Echenique was elected in 2011. Then the presidency returned to the left coalition with the second term of Michelle Bachelet (2014–2018). Sebastián Piñera returned to the office until 2022. In this period of dictatorship and post-dictatorship rule, with liberal policies from the left and right and a highly concentrated and organized system, the conditions and the causal mechanisms worked together to maintain a weak level of collective rights for indigenous peoples.

AN INSTITUTIONALIZED PARTY SYSTEM: THE ROLE OF A HIGH LEVEL OF PARTY ORGANIZATION FOR WEAK INDIGENOUS COLLECTIVE RIGHTS

The two institutional conditions, the party system and the constitution, remain constant in Chile. The party system is highly institutionalized, creating stable electoral game conditions and producing certain political conditions. A stable left and right wings, and the alignment of a liberal paradigm with the current constitution, create weak collective rights at the national level.

Regarding the institutionalized party system, acquiring stability means having a high level of professionalized politicians, with less space for inexperienced new candidates (Buquet, 2015). There are clear rules for obtaining power to elected positions, a complex organization for the public sector (Buquet, 2015) and a long-standing tradition of alignment between parties, different religions, and social classes (S. J. Valenzuela & Somma, 2018). Some authors state that "Chile constitutes a textbook case" (S. J. Valenzuela & Somma, 2018, p. 135) of stability. Chile has a multi-party system, "Chile's party system has been largely structured since the return of competitive politics around the two coalitions that were formed to support or oppose Pinochet's bid to continue rule" (Valenzuela & Somma, 2018, p. 136). For example, the radical and the communist party, which has a long political tradition from the end of the 1800s to the beginning of the 1900s, and other more recent right parties such as Union Democrata Independiente (UDI) and Renovación Nacional (RN), and left party Partido por la Democracia (PPD) (Buquet, 2015). Over time, this continuity of political parties produces low volatility, offering the same ideas in every election (Alcántara Saez, 2013a), not being a surprise to the electorate.

Since 1989, according to the V-Dem data set, the index of party organization has gone from 2.0 and upwards, showing a high level of institutionalization. Buquet (2015) explains that when this type of stability exists in the party system, political change will be incremental and predictable in a context of low confrontation.

Making decisions against the status quo are complex; thus, any collective rights become complex to be recognized because the change must be substantial and considerable to change the Chilean Constitution's liberal-individual perspective. There is no evidence of personalistic governments as in the cases of Colombia and Peru because the Chilean politicians follow the rules of their political parties. The only government that did not use the support of political parties was Pinochet, and he was against granting any rights to indigenous peoples. Furthermore, some evidence shows that the proposals are unsuccessful every time a bill and possible constitutional amendment recognizes indigenous collective rights in Chilean democracy.

PINOCHET AND INDIGENOUS PEOPLES: JURIDICAL ETHNOCIDE AND 1980 CONSTITUTION

During the dictatorship of Augusto Pinochet, the dialogue between the government and indigenous peoples was nonexistent. Pinochet enacted decree-law no. 2.568-1979, which decreased the number of lands and territories of indigenous peoples. According to several authors, this instrument showed indigenous peoples that the government wants to reduce their political influence (Bengoa, 2000; Figueroa Huencho, 2014; Navarrete Jara, 2019). This situation was called a juridical ethnocide (Guerrero Guerrero, 2016). The 1980 Constitution, prepared by Pinochet and his allies, followed the same pattern.

In 1977 after four years of dictatorship, Pinochet announced the reestablishment of civilian rule, with a new constitution enacted in 1980[2] (Heiss & Navia, 2007). The institution in charge of drafting this new constitution was the "Comisión de Estudios para una Nueva Constitución," which followed the instructions of Pinochet regarding the content, increasing executive powers (Directorate of Intelligence, 1988; Ensalaco, 1994). One of the most well-known members of this committee was Jaime Guzman, who was known for being an active proponent against democracy (Couso, 2006). In 1978, they finished the first draft. The "Council of the state" received the draft for comments. The second draft decreased the power of the president, and so, it was entirely ignored by the authoritarian regime (Directorate of Intelligence, 1988). Then, Pinochet assembled a small commission of lawyers (Couso, 2012) to enforce a draft more closely to the desire of the commission . The enforcement of the new constitution happened after a plebiscite (Directorate of Intelligence, 1988) in 1981.[3]

The original constitution entailed a "protected democracy" (Couso, 2012; Heiss & Navia, 2007) which shields the constitution against citizens, based on a teleological program and traditional values that are endangered by military forces (Heiss & Navia, 2007). For the citizens, this constitution represented restrictions in human rights, a weak separation of powers, a high degree of military control over democracy, and barriers to amendments (Ensalaco, 1994). This constitution has two essential characteristics regarding the topic of this research. First, it shows a liberal regime not only in politics but firmly in economics. Second, it does not recognize any indigenous peoples or their rights.

Regarding the liberal regime, the constitution only recognizes individual rights, and the state's participation in social activities is the exception. This paradigm is more robust in the economic sector than in others, in which the principle of subsidiarity is the general rule while extending its importance to several economic rights (Couso, 2012).[4] Thus, individual autonomy is a value of the highest importance in the Chilean Constitution, embedded in social, political, and juridical systems. In this context of the liberal-individual paradigm, the indigenous cosmovision is hard to recognize. The 1980 Constitution is a legal document with several constitutional amendments, which are central to affirm the liberal paradigm in Chile. Now, this paradigm keeps collective rights at a weak level.

Regarding the second characteristic, this constitution is silent regarding the recognition and the collective rights of indigenous peoples (Fuentes et al., 2017). All the potential constitutional amendments in that regard have failed. Until December 2019, the 1980 Constitution has had forty-two amendments (Biblioteca del Congreso Nacional de Chile, 2019), and none of them are related to indigenous rights. The only other countries in Latin America with this lack of recognition are Uruguay, Belize, French Guyana, and Suriname (Aguilar et al., 2010; Barié, 2003). The remaining laws have rights with a superficial level of differentiation and no autonomy, such as language and cultural diversity.

In the words of an indigenous scholar, the constitution is "ethnocentric," meaning that it represents only the majority of mestizos called Chileans as the only recognized ethnicity (Marimán, 2015). According to Aguilar et al. (2010), "During the 19th and 20th centuries, Chile promoted the notion of 'chilenidad,' a conception that refused to acknowledge the existence of indigenous peoples and marginalized certain ethnic groups" (p. 57). This idea does not mean that there are no legal standards that prescribe the indigenous topic; it means that the legal system has "failed to provide a role for indigenous group as a positive entity in the national society" (Worthen, 1998, p. 238). This lack of positive entity creates understanding problems: public policies are based on individual equality (Worthen, 1998). After several conversations between national authorities and indigenous communities, it has been impossible to include the notion of well-being and collective rights in the constitution since 1981.

THE NEW AGREEMENTS AND THE 1993
INDIGENOUS ACT: A GREAT EFFORT
WITHOUT SUBSTANTIAL CONSEQUENCES

In 1989, the democratization process opened the window for better relationships between the democratic government and indigenous peoples. Although this newfound relationship did not translate into constitutional provisions, it created the opportunity to enforce other legal documents. The first milestone in this relationship was the "Nueva Imperial Agreements," a document signed in 1989 by the candidate Patricio Aylwin and representatives of the Mapuches, Huilliches, Aymaras y Rapa Nui peoples (Aguilar et al., 2011). In this document, Aylwin recognized indigenous peoples and their right to be a part of the constitution. The expectation of indigenous peoples after this agreement was immense. Furthermore, due to the influence of his son, José Aylwin, who was the director of indigenous issues for the Chilean Commission of Human Rights, indigenous peoples saw a unique sensibility within the candidate, someone who would voice their concerns (Figueroa Huencho, 2014). This agreement was the first step toward enshrining Indigenous Act No. 19,253 of 1993 (henceforth, the Indigenous Act).

The Indigenous Act was the first step to fulfill the "Nueva Imperial Agreement" in recognizing indigenous peoples. The same indigenous peoples who signed the agreement worked with CEPI (Comisión Especial de los Pueblos Indígenas), a government institution created to manage indigenous issues (Figueroa Huencho, 2014). According to the presidential message added to the bill, 100,000 indigenous people contributed to working on the draft (Aylwin Azocar, 1991). The bill's first draft proposed a series of collective rights for indigenous peoples, such as rights to their language, education, traditional medicine, indigenous justice, and to unattached indigenous lands and territories (Figueroa Huencho, 2014).

Once the bill was submitted, the House of Representatives quickly modified the bill (Aylwin et al., 2013; Comisión Especial Pueblos Indígenas, 1992). One of the essential modifications was the erasure of the term "indigenous peoples." According to official documents, the right parties were part of the opposition and principal opponents to its use, based on the fear of giving sovereignty to indigenous peoples (Cámara de Diputados, 1993). According to the opposition, Chile is only one nation (Comisión Especial Pueblos Indígenas, 1992). The act was enacted in October 1993. The approach of Congress brings several problems for indigenous collective rights. The first one is that indigenous peoples are considered an ethnic group in the country (Figueroa Huencho, 2014), diminishing their participation as political actors (Sanhueza et al., 2013). Also, their political participation in the new indigenous institution, CONADI, is less than the bill's first draft. Some of the rights that were enshrined in the act are the recognition of culture and ethnic education, with fewer resources than expected, and limited land protection based on individual rights of an indigenous person or communities, but not to indigenous peoples (Aylwin et al., 2013; Figueroa Huencho, 2014). The Indigenous Act that brought so much hope for indigenous peoples was a solid first step, but not with a level of recognition that the indigenous peoples were expecting.

THE NEVER-ENDING STORY: THE FAILED PROCESS OF CONSTITUTIONAL AMENDMENTS

The history shows several commissions making recommendations regarding constitutional replacement or amendment (P. Rodríguez & Carruthers, 2008; Tomaselli, 2014). For example, in 2003, the report of the commission regarding Historical Truth and a New Deal for Indigenous Peoples[5] recommended the recognition of indigenous peoples and their political, territorial, and cultural collective rights (Comisión Verdad Histórica y Nuevo Trato, 2008). After several executive unsuccessful proposals of constitutional amendments, the fearfulness of authorities, particularly the legislative branch, is to establish a right to self-determination, implicitly if indigenous peoples have constitutional recognition (Román, 2014). Furthermore, in 1989 two significant constitutional amendments occurred, which decreased the role of Pinochet's "protected democracy" (Heiss & Navia, 2007), and in 2005, with the consolidation of civilian power over military power eliminating the remaining authoritarian enclaves. Both of these constitutional amendments did not include any provision regarding indigenous peoples, and other constitutional amendments failed in the process of consultation with indigenous in 2009,[6] 2011,[7] and in-between 2014 and 2015[8] (Ministerio de Desarrollo Social, 2015; Tomaselli, 2014). Thus, the Congress did not discuss these proposals.

In 2016 one of the last chances for altering this exclusion took place with the indigenous constitution-making process for participation and, in 2017, with the "Indigenous Constitutional Assembly Process." The objective was to have proposals and observations from indigenous peoples for a potential constitutional replacement in the former. In June 2017, the "Indigenous Constitutional Assembly Process" (Proceso de Consulta Constituyente Indígena) began with mixed results.

In this "Indigenous Constitutional Assembly Process," the indigenous peoples and the government of Michelle Bachelet agreed on five proposals: first, the recognition of indigenous peoples; second, the state must preserve, strengthen, and develop their history, identity, culture, languages, institutions, traditions, and ruling authorities; third, the obligation of the state to recognize the cultural diversity in the country; fourth, the recognition and protection of cultural and linguistic rights, and their material and immaterial cultural patrimony; and finally, the principle of equality and non-discrimination. There was partial agreement about other proposals: interpretation of the new constitution, the percentage of indigenous representation and political participation, and the right to health, consultation, and self-determination. This partial agreement meant a consensus about the topic, but it did not regard how to redact the articles. Moreover, it was not possible to achieve an agreement considering the concept of indigenous land (Ministerio de Desarrollo Social, 2017). The submission of the proposal for a new constitution to Congress happened the day before the end of the presidency of President Bachelet, on March 10, 2018. President Sebastián Piñera took office the day after, and he announced his government did not want to continue with the process for a new constitution that Bachelet started. Consequently, the liberal paradigm remains present in the Chilean Constitution, and there has been no formal change regarding this topic.

A NEW HOPE: ILO'S CONVENTION NO. 169 AND THE RIGHT TO PRIOR CONSULTATION

Although the "Nueva Imperial Agreement" included the ratification of ILO's convention No.169 as one of the commitments of President Aylwin, it was only ratified in 2008 and became active law in September 2009. Keeping in mind that the International Labor Organization issued the instrument in 1989, Chile became the last country in the region to ratify the treaty. The consequences of this late ratification were problems of interpretation, mainly in the level of compliance with international standards, with faltering jurisprudence (Román, 2014), and an executive power that was more silent than active in the process. The only right that has had any legal development in the country after the convention is the right to prior consultation for indigenous peoples.

During the first term of Michelle Bachelet (2006–2010), after the promulgation of the Convention in 2009, the government issued Supreme Decree No. 124, Ministry of Planning, to establish the process of consultation for indigenous peoples. This instrument recognized the process following confusing and frail rules regarding the consultation enshrined in article 34 of the Indigenous Act, not the rules of the convention (Tomaselli, 2014). Furthermore, the problem with this instrument was that indigenous peoples were not involved in elaborating this decree. The situation was a direct violation of the convention that prescribes consultation of indigenous peoples in their issues. The indigenous peoples were consulted on the legal standard to solve this problem. The outcome was Supreme Decree No. 66-2013, Ministry of

Social Development, for general consultation, and Supreme Decree No. 40-2012, Ministry of Environment, for issues related to the natural environment (Blanco, 2016; Contesse, 2012; ILO, 2016). Prior consultation became a reality for indigenous peoples having both instruments enacted.

THE ORGANIZATION CONDITION: HIGH LEVEL OF INDIGENOUS SOCIAL MOVEMENTS BUT LACK OF INDIGENOUS ORGANIZATIONS AND COALITIONS

The conditions that are absent in the Chilean context are the coalitions. There is a lack of coalitions between indigenous peoples, forming national organizations, and a lack of coalitions with other non-indigenous allies. This situation is due to several factors that I will explain in the following paragraphs, decreasing the political participation of indigenous peoples.

Chile has a high level of indigenous mobilization.[9] The level of the indigenous population is less than other countries in the Andean region. Nevertheless, indigenous mobilizations have been on the rise in recent years. Funk (2012) states,

> [t]hat Chilean political institutions have evinced greater stability than those of its northern neighbors is doubtless, as is the country's overall higher level of social and economic welfare. Nevertheless, given the widespread disenchantment in Chile with the country's political and economic systems—and such frequent eruptions of mass mobilizations by different social sectors in the country [. . .]—the differences between Chile and the other Andean states appear to be less of kind than degree. (p. 130)

This statement shows that despite the stability of the political systems, there are mobilizations and social movements, showing an ethnic perspective. This is the Chilean case.

The role of coalitions is scarce in the country. The lack of indigenous coalitions between indigenous peoples is due to two critical factors: the fragmentation of indigenous associations in the "Indigenous Act" and the elite narrative that indigenous peoples, notably the Mapuche, are "terrorists." The lack of coalitions with non-indigenous allies is a consequence of this fragmentation and narrative, having only specific purposes.

The Problem of Fragmentation and Indigenous National Coalitions

According to historical research, the coalitions between indigenous peoples were necessary to defend a territory during the colonial period, building a united front with peoples from the coast, plains, and pre-mountain and mountain ranges (Goicovich Videla, 2004). However, this reality does not exist anymore. Even if it is possible to find indigenous organizations beginning in 1990, there is no clear evidence of their participation as political actors. For example, according to Figueroa Huencho (2014), the indigenous representatives that signed the "Nueva Imperial Agreement" were part of the Consejo Nacional de Pueblos Indígenas. However, the signatures are representatives of diverse indigenous peoples in the document. A plausible explanation for this is the spontaneous creation of this organization in a time of erasure of indigenous peoples.

During this time, several organizations were established in the South and North of the country. In the South, "Consejo de Todas las Tierras" (Figueroa Huencho, 2014) or "Aukiñ Wallmapu Ngulam," a Mapuche organization that defends their peoples using the traditions and knowledge of Mapuche culture, and who demand an utterly separate government that is removed from any western institution or ruling Chilean authority (Marimán, 1995). This organization is still present in Chile. However, they only represent one indigenous people in the country, and its position as an anti-systemic movement makes participation in formal instances problematic. In 1987, in the North of the country, "the Coordinadora de Organizaciones Aymara" was created; it lasted for only three years due to several tensions between the leaders (Gundermann & Vergara, 2009). In 1988, they started to create the organization "Federación Andina Ayni," which disbanded in 1990 because their leaders became part of the new government, passing from the social to the political field (Gundermann & Vergara, 2009).

Several sectorial or specific indigenous organizations are created following the provisions of the Indigenous Act. According to this law, the indigenous associations need to have a specific interest and common objective[10] that must be related to education and culture, and ongoing professional activities of their members, or economic activities in the area of agriculture, livestock, handicrafts, and fishery.[11] However, there is an explicit prohibition for these organizations in that they cannot represent indigenous communities. Thus, these associations do not intend to be social movements; they are mainly for commercial purposes. Indigenous peoples often form these associations, which go against their traditions (Gundermann & Vergara, 2009), for monetary support from the government. According to official information, by 2015, there were 1,843 indigenous associations in Chile (CONADI, n.d.).

Specific recent events show the absence of political representation, in which indigenous social movements and indigenous people work alone, they are fragmented and dispersed within the political field. For example, the indigenous constitution-making process of 2017 came into tension between the indigenous peoples and the national authorities. Only 26% of the participants signed the final document, which would have established the points agreed upon by the indigenous peoples and that of the government. The participation was limited to official representatives from Chile's legally recognized indigenous peoples. Only 38 representatives out of 145 signed the document between indigenous peoples and the government (Plataforma Política Mapuche, 2017). The Yagan, Kaweskar, and Quechua peoples' representatives did not sign it, and they released the Statement of Withdrawal of the Conversations Between the Indigenous Nations and the Government. There were also public statements from the Council of Atacameño Peoples, the Mapuche peoples, and the Aymara Peoples from the Arica and Parinacota region. This incident shows a lack of unity and cohesion of indigenous peoples as one political actor.

The Worrisome Vision of Elites: The Narrative of Indigenous Peoples as Terrorist

The elite narrative regarding indigenous peoples is the action of labeling them as terrorists, a concept with a negative connotation toward indigenous differentiation. An assertion that they are traitors to western culture by not fulfilling western assimilation standards. The purpose of the term terrorism is a representation (Spivak, 1988), a portrait of indigenous peoples, an embodiment of their differences based on the fact that historically Mapuche peoples have been a nation that fights back against colonization, including from the Incas, Spanish, and Chileans, resisting "domination for hundreds of years" (Postero et al., 2018). Today, there are still a series of protests and mobilizations with a high level of criminalization of the indigenous social movements from these particular people (Figueroa Huencho, 2014; Postero et al., 2018). If Mapuche peoples act violently, organizations are less willing to work with them as a coalition. According to a survey applied by the National Institute of Human Rights in 2017, with 2047 surveyed, 81% stated that they believe indigenous peoples are violent (Instituto Nacional de Derechos Humanos Chile, 2017).

Thanks to fragmentation and the lack of national organizations that form coalitions with non-indigenous allies, the indigenous peoples in Chile have a weak level of collective rights. These are the causal mechanisms that do not allow higher levels of indigenous collective rights in Chile.

Some Organization: Specific Coalitions with Non-Indigenous Allies

Regarding the coalitions with non-indigenous allies, indigenous peoples only create them for anti-extractive purposes. Mapuche peoples have worked with environmentalists' social movements in the South of Chile against a hydro-electric project in the Ralco lake.[12] In that case, they worked with the organization named "Grupo de Acción por el BioBio," activating protests in the region (Gastaka Urruela, 2017). Another example is Pascua Lama, a gold mine project that a private company sought to build in Diaguita land in the north-central area of Chile. Indigenous peoples have formed alliances with Canadian networks, such as Mining Watch Canada and CorpWatch, which have been helpful in lobbying and creating mobilization for the project (Cuadra Montoya, 2014). There were other alliances between indigenous associations and unions. According to the ILO, some union associations maintain dynamic relationships with indigenous peoples, such as CUT, Central Unitaria de Trabajadores, with one secretary for peasants and indigenous peoples. This union organization has supported indigenous demands (OIT, 2015). These alliances, anti-extractive organizations, and union associations are not stable and permanent; there is not sufficient information to give an affirmative answer regarding the creation of coalitions.

The evidence regarding coalitions with left parties is not clear. Marimán (1995) states that in 1989 Mapuche people and other indigenous peoples signed a commitment letter with the left coalition to support the presidential candidate Patricio Aylwin. So far, Mapuche peoples are the only indigenous people who have attempted to become a political party, with the Wallmapuwen party in 2016 (Gutierrez Chong & Gálvez González, 2017). However, the ties of these alliances and their combined power are not enough to obtain more recognition for indigenous peoples.

CHILE IN CURRENTS TIME: A NEW CONSTITUTION AND THE ROLE OF INDIGENOUS PEOPLES

In October 2019, a social uprising changed the political scenario in Chile. The major protest started by high school students against the increase of the cost of public transportation initiated a snowball of mobilizations for more social justice. These events occurred in a violent atmosphere from the protesters and the police and military forces. There were several human rights violations of hundreds of citizens during this time.[13] The two most essential characteristics of this current uprising are the use of indigenous peoples' symbols, which help to spread awareness for the rights of indigenous peoples, and the strong demand for a new constitution. The use of Mapuche people's flag in the protest, the Wenufoye,[14] (Campos Muñoz & De la Maza, 2019; Caniuqueo Huircapan, 2019) helped to further the awareness of indigenous causes. Its use has become a symbol of the inequality and violence that Mapuche and Chilean people experience daily (Caniuqueo Huircapan, 2019a), also as a symbol of resistance and the change of the liberal paradigm.

Regarding constitutional change, one of the demands for more social justice is to change the constitution. The new constitution process began in Chile with a constitutional amendment approved on December 24, 2019. The first step was a plebiscite, on October 25, 2020, regarding the option to have a new constitution and the mechanism to carry out it: constitutional convention with all elected representatives or a mixed constitutional convention with members of Congress and members elected by the citizens.[15] The results of this plebiscite gave the new constitution support of 78.27% of the votes.[16] The chosen mechanism was a constitutional convention with 78.99% of the votes.[17]

One central part of the participation in this process is indigenous quotas. The inclusion of this topic was problematic for the constitutional amendment of December 2019 that allowed the plebiscite. Thus, the representatives presented a separate amendment with the topic. After a lengthy discussion at the Congress, the indigenous peoples achieved seventeen reserved seats and a different vote procedure for the indigenous peoples. These seats were distributed in proportion to the ten indigenous peoples recognized by law: seven to Mapuche, two to Aimara, and one for the rest of the indigenous peoples.[18]

On May 15 and 16, 2021, the 155 delegates to the constitutional convention, including the indigenous delegates, were elected in a special two-day election. Their work started on July 4, 2021. The delegates need to elect a president and a vice president on that day. In a complex process, the first president elected of the convention was Elisa Loncón Antileo, a Mapuche activist and scholar. She states as winning speech:

> I salute the people of Chile from the north to Patagonia, from the sea to the mountains, to the islands, all those who are watching us today [. . .] I'm grateful for the support of the different coalitions that placed their trust and their dreams in the hands of the Mapuche nation, who voted for a Mapuche person, a woman, to change the history of this country.[19]

It is in her words to feel faith and hope for significant changes for indigenous peoples.

The possibility of having a new constitution is a chance for indigenous peoples to participate in the process and change the liberal paradigm. It is the perfect opportunity for indigenous peoples to present their demands in a democratic context (Caniuqueo Huircapan, 2019b). So far, the demands are related to recognize indigenous peoples as a nation, implementing the concept of self-determination, and establishing a plurinational state with several collective rights (Albert, 2019; Caniuqueo Huircapan, 2019b, 2019a; Pairican, 2020).

It is possible to find the concepts of plurinational, interculturalism, and legal pluralism in the draft of the new constitutions. Also, the proposal recognizes collective rights as enforceable by indigenous peoples, including the right to prior consultation, self-determination and territorial autonomy, linguistic rights, the right to obtain the repatriation of cultural objects and human remains, the right to cultural identities, right to their own cosmovision, way of life and their own institutions. It also enshrined the right to ancestral knowledge and access to intercultural justice. The draft also prohibits the forced assimilation of indigenous peoples. In general, the Chilean transition is taking a direction from having weak to strong collective rights in a context of constitutional changes and party system instability.[20]

These potential changes are promising regarding the recognition of indigenous peoples in Chile. A constitutional change will force more collective rights for indigenous peoples in other types of legal documents. The current events in the country are pushing for a new level of social justice. It is in this context that indigenous peoples have the space to be recognized as an important social actor, with their own cosmovision in legal instruments. Hopefully, the changes will be implemented this time, moving away from previous promises that go unfulfilled.

In conclusion, Chile is a typical case of weak collective rights. This situation is due to an institutionalized party system that is strong in electing authorities following party ideologies, showing an absence of personalistic leaders. This makes decisions that tend to follow the status quo, influenced by the liberal paradigm present in the constitution. In the past, there were several attempts to recognize indigenous peoples' rights, and all of them failed. The evidence shows that indigenous organizations are highly fragmented because the system does not allow indigenous organizations to represent the communities and stops the formation of national organizations, keeping the groups as small economic and commercial groups. This lack of national organizations fails to help to create coalitions with non-indigenous allies. The evidence shows short-time alliances with some private institutions, but they vanished after a couple of actions together. These conditions and mechanisms create the perfect scenario conducive to the weak level of indigenous collective rights. The new changes in Chile's political and social fields were brought on by the recent social uprising and process for a new constitution. It will hopefully bring more recognition, position, historical, and social value to indigenous collective rights.

NOTES

1. Transitory articles 27 to 29.
2. The regime abolished the previous constitution in 1973.
3. Some of the characteristics of this plebiscite were: (1) Pinochet convoked the plebiscite with thirty days' notice, under an emergency state, with no room for

information. (2) The government spent a high number of resources in campaigning for this new constitution. The opposition did not have any resources. (3) Blank ballots would be counted toward "yes." (4) Absence of electoral registry, among others. Therefore, this plebiscite is considerate manipulated.

4. "This notion entails the idea that the state cannot intervene in the economy unless the private sector is unable to fulfill an economic function. Thus, the general rule is free markets, and state intervention is only the exception. In this approach, the state provides only the background to the real engine of economic activity, the market. The principle of subsidiarity is the foundation of specific economic precepts of the constitution. Among this specific set of norms can be mentioned: article 19 number 21, which guarantees the right to private entrepreneurial freedom (while requiring a super-majority legislative approval for the creation of state-owned companies); article 19, number 24, which fortifies the protection of existing private property rights, requiring that the state give up-front cash to any individual being expropriated; and article 19 number which for the first time in Chile's history guarantees the right to acquire private property of all classes of goods, subject to some exceptions" (Couso, 2012, p. 412).

5. This commission was created in January 2001 by the president of that time, Ricardo Lagos Escobar (2000–2006). They finished the report in October 2003. The government of Michelle Bachelet Jeria published the report in 2008.

6. Indigenous participation in Congress and creation of the Council of Indigenous Peoples; constitutional recognition of indigenous peoples (Tomaselli, 2014).

7. The Great Consultation (Tomaselli, 2014).

8. Creation of the Council of Indigenous Peoples (Ministerio de Desarrollo Social, 2015).

9. According to V-Dem Data Set (2021), the index of ethnic antisystem mobilizations has been increasing since 1998. The max value in Chile was 0.44. in 2017. The value of this ordinal variable goes from 0 to 1. For the seven countries under study, the minimum is 0; the maximum is 0.8.

10. Article 36 Indigenous Act.

11. Article 37 Indigenous Act.

12. This project wanted to build a dam of 3,500 hectares in a Mapuche-huilliche zone. Finally, in 2004 the dam was finished after several years of negotiations and compensations between the private companies and indigenous peoples (Cuadra Montoya, 2014).

13. From October 17 to November 30, 2019, The National Institute of Human Rights informed 11.180 injured people in Chile. 317 of them have eye trauma, eyeball burst, and loss of vision for eye trauma (Instituto Nacional de los Derechos Humanos, 2019).

14. El Consejo de Todas las Tierras established this flag in 1991.

15. Article 130, 1980 Constitution.

16. Official information provided by servel.cl.

17. Official information provided by servel.cl.

18. Transitory article 43, 1980 Constitution.

19. Translation by *BBC News* https://www.bbc.com/news/world-latin-america-57733539.

20. After the social uprising and the process for a new constitution the party system had experienced fragmentation of the political forces. This fragmentation was shown in the election to the National Congress in 2021. The Senate has an even distribution of left and right. However, the Chamber of Representatives shows a higher level of fragmentation and polarization. The right, including RN, UDI, and Evopoli, lead the Chamber with fifty-three members. Following the Socialist Party with thirteen members, Communist Party with twelve, and Republican party (far right) with fourteen. The rest of the chamber includes Christian Democratic Party (center left) with seven members, Partido de la Gente (center right) with six, Democratic Revolution (left) with seven, Communes (left) with three, Social Convergence (left) with eight, Partido por la Democracia (lef) with nine, Liberal Party (left) with four, Radical Party (left) with four, Humanist Action (left) with two, Humanist Party (left) with three, Ecologist Party (left) with two and, Green Social Regionalist Federation (left) with two, Unir Movement (left) with two, Commun Force (Left) with one and two independents.

Conclusion

STRONG COALITIONS AND UNSTABLE INSTITUTIONS FOR INCREASING THE LEVEL OF PROTECTION OF INDIGENOUS COLLECTIVE RIGHTS

The conventional wisdom is to attribute the increased level of collective rights to indigenous social movements; the current literature mainly focuses on recognizing collective rights at the constitutional level (Aguilar et al., 2010; Barié, 2003; Van Cott, 2004). However, there are many other factors that contribute to increasing collective rights and other legal instruments. This is the aim of the study of the current publication.

This research intends to clear up and give arguments that go beyond other more critical conditions than indigenous social movements in the way to get collective rights as recognized ones, which means to increase the level of autonomy and differentiation for indigenous peoples. Specifically, indigenous social movements are more likely to achieve collective rights if they create coalitions between the different indigenous peoples and other non-indigenous people. Furthermore, greater recognition of collective rights for indigenous peoples occurs when there is a weak party system and constitutional instability. The analysis is centered not only on the constitution but also on several legal instruments that enshrine diverse collective rights, organizing the cases in levels that allow more in-depth analysis and also looking for their recognition.

In the following sections, I will review the role of indigenous social movements and the evidence related to what conditions and causal mechanisms are necessary elements to increase collective rights in Latin America. This analysis includes the QCA, and the cases mentioned before. Finally, I will broadly reflect on future research regarding the collective rights of indigenous peoples in Latin America.

INDIGENOUS SOCIAL MOVEMENTS NEED COALITIONS TO BE SUCCESSFUL

This research contested and analyzed based on evidence the role of the indigenous social movement to increase the level of collective rights. The conventional wisdom explains that indigenous peoples look for the recognition of their cultural identities using various mobilization tools. This recognition is translated into collective rights. However, the role of indigenous social movements occurs in a context in which organization and institutional conditions play an essential role in the results obtained.

Therefore, it is more proper to state that this research entails an alternative explanation in which these new conditions are entwined with indigenous social movements to extend and refine the current theory. For example, in the case of organizations, the indigenous social movements become more powerful when they form coalitions between indigenous peoples or with other non-indigenous allies. The cases of Colombia, Ecuador, and Bolivia are the kind of organizations that result from these coalitions which are essential for conducting an official voice for the whole movement, using several tools as a mobilization method and becoming a stronger actor in the political field. Therefore, it is possible to recognize how indigenous social movements and organizations are two very closely related subjects to discuss.

In the case of institutional conditions, indigenous social movements are a tool for increasing significant changes if the personalistic leader is willing to recognize more collective rights in a weak party system context. This happened in Colombia, Ecuador, Peru, and Bolivia. These movements also help to accelerate constitutional replacement for increasing the level of protection of collective rights. Thus, the institutional conditions explain the context in which indigenous social movements are operating and predict specific results.

The organizations and coalitions of indigenous social movements provide a robust tool for influencing the political field. This theory stresses that it is not only about mobilizations, but it is also about having a strong structure of planning and analysis of the movement and its possibilities to be carried out. This is possible to identify in the CONAIE in Ecuador and ONIC in Colombia. The institutional conditions provide the context in which those organizations operate, creating positive or negative feedback for them. Therefore, this research expands conventional wisdom, using specific conditions that play an essential role in increasing the collective rights of indigenous peoples. This alternative explanation will be developed and explained in the next section.

SUMMARY AND FINDINGS

Due to the ongoing excluded role of indigenous peoples and the process of achieving collective rights in Latin America, it has become the greatest challenge to increase them, and a slow change toward recognizing the role and importance of indigenous peoples can be shown. Therefore, analyzing the necessary conditions to achieve these rights for indigenous peoples will provide answers for the process of recognition.

This research contributes to make a clear distinction between individual and collective rights for indigenous peoples, stressing the latter's importance in developing sensitive indigenous policies. The most important contribution of this research is shifting the analysis, expanding from social movements to other conditions, and causal mechanisms that generate collective rights in Latin America. The further sections will present the summary and findings out of each set of conditions and a complete analysis using the case studies to provide examples in more depth. The following section will present alternative explanations in the cases of Colombia, Peru, and Chile.

Separate Set of Conditions: Organizations and Institutions

The analysis recognizes the importance of two conditions, organizations and institutions. In complex relationships, it is vital to analyze the role of each of these conditions to have more accurate knowledge of the cases. There are a couple of elements to consider for the analysis, if we compare the results with the theory.

Concerning the organizational conditions, it is possible to confirm the role of these coalitions in increasing collective rights, as it was stated in hypothesis 1. This hypothesis indicates that strong collective rights are associated with the development of coalitions between indigenous peoples when there are coalitions with non-indigenous allies. Indigenous peoples are more successful in increasing their level of autonomy and obtaining recognition for necessary collective rights such as self-determination and some levels of indigenous jurisdiction when both types of coalitions are present, such as in the cases of Bolivia 3, Colombia 2, Ecuador 2 and 3, and Peru 2. The level of collective rights also increases in cases where there exist coalitions between indigenous peoples like Bolivia 2, Guatemala 1 and 2, and Colombia 1. Weak indigenous collective rights are more common when their coalitions are absent. The cases of Chile 1 and 2, Ecuador 1, and Peru 1 confirm this part of the theory.

There are no cases that show the presence of coalitions with non-indigenous peoples and the lack of coalitions between indigenous peoples. This result shows that the most crucial coalition of indigenous peoples is the one that they can make by and among themselves. This presence creates a strong political actor who can intervene in the process of making national decisions, such as CONAIE in Ecuador and ONIC in Colombia. After a national indigenous organization is created and becomes stable in time, there are higher possibilities of having coalitions with non-indigenous allies.

Turning into institutional conditions, the analysis confirms hypothesis 2: the presence of strong collective rights is associated with a weak party system when there is a high level of constitutional instability. These are the cases of Bolivia 3, Colombia 2, Ecuador 2 and 3, and Peru 2. Moderate collective rights are present when there is a non-institutionalized party system and the absence of constitutional replacement, such as in Bolivia 1, Mexico 2, Guatemala 1, and Colombia 1. Finally, the status quo prevails in an institutionalized political system without any constitutional replacement, like in Chile 1 and 2, Ecuador 1, and Mexico 2.

One interesting element to highlight is the absence of cases with moderate collective rights that have an institutionalized party system and the presence of a constitutional replacement—showing that if a country has political stability, a constitutional replacement is not likely to occur. Generally, a new constitution is an instrument to solve a political crisis, like in Peru with the 1993 constitutional replacement, Colombia in 1991, and potentially the case of Chile and its new constitution.

All the Conditions: Reviewing the Theory and the Causal Mechanisms for Strong Collective Rights

In terms of QCA, this research shows one path or conjunction to increase the collective rights of indigenous peoples in Latin America, so it can be a general view to other countries. There is a higher probability of having strong collective rights in the country, when all the conditions are present, the ones between indigenous peoples, coalitions with non-indigenous allies, weak party systems, and constitutional instability, The cases of Bolivia 3, Colombia 2, Ecuador 2 and 3, and Peru 2 confirm hypothesis 3. This is the most solid result regarding the theory.

The in-depth cases of Colombia and Peru point out the causal mechanism explaining why and how these levels increase. As established in theory, these cases show causal mechanisms depending on each condition. This increase in collective rights occurs because organizations and institutions open a possibility to include rights that allow indigenous peoples to develop a higher level of self-determination. A coalition between indigenous peoples or a national organization shows a coherent and strong political actor. These organizations influence the political field through protest and educational programs on collective rights (Colombian case) and meetings and mobilizations to resist prejudicial modifications (Peruvian case).

Furthermore, it is easier to find non-indigenous allies to present a more comprehensive proposal to national authorities when these national organizations, or coalitions between indigenous nationalities, are present. According to the cases of Colombia and Peru, these coalitions became a united front that pushed for more collective rights. Sometimes, the coalitions used a narrative that human rights apply to all minorities, like in the case of Colombia with the Afro-descendants and other minority groups. This also occurs with political parties that successfully achieved power, like in the case of Peru with President Toledo and the Perú Posible political party.

According to the theory, coalitions also push for a constitutional replacement, looking for the opportunity to make changes in the national constitution. In the discussion process, in Constituent Assemblies, these coalitions influence agreements among diverse actors to include the indigenous collective rights in the new constitution. However, this is partially supported by the evidence shown about Colombia and Peru. In the case of Colombia, national organizations were notable for including two representatives in the Assembly, and the coalitions with non-indigenous peoples allowed them to discuss indigenous recognition and more collective rights. However, Peruvian organizations and coalitions with non-indigenous allies were nonexistent in the process of the new constitution in 1993. Their role was more centered on stopping the implementation of legal standards that were not beneficial for indigenous peoples after the constitution was implemented.

The theory states that a weak party system enables indigenous coalitions to demand more collective rights from national leaders willing to make radical decisions to change aspects of the liberal paradigm, thereby recognizing indigenous collective rights. This change can be in the form of a new constitution and other legal instruments. The empirical results of the case study support this affirmation. However, these cases add two specifications: The president of each country is the one making radical decisions, and the regime has personalistic characteristics. This authority often makes decisions with no opposition and sometimes does not consult the political party. In the Colombian case, these leaders were Lopez Michelsen, Barco, and Samper, all of them having some level of counter-hegemonic narrative and a history of leading small groups inside their political parties. In the Peruvian Case, those leaders were Velasco Alvarado and Toledo. In both cases, they made decisions to improve the conditions of indigenous peoples, recognizing more rights for them.

According to the empirical analysis, the theory is confirmed: all conditions are necessary for achieving strong collective rights. This is the most reliable finding in the research. Also, the causal mechanisms for each condition are

supported by in-depth cases in Colombia and Peru. However, it is essential
to point out that the order of the conditions is different in these cases. I will
analyze this in a different section.

The Importance of Diverse Paths in Peru and Colombia

Colombia and Peru are two cases that have achieved strong collective rights.
The commonality between them is the presence of the same conditions and
causal mechanisms. The difference is the order of the conditions and causal
mechanisms. Colombia is a typical case, while Peru presents itself as a
diverse case (Seawright & Gerring, 2008).

Colombia passed from having a moderate level of collective rights to a
strong level of collective rights in 1991. The first two conditions that have
been present since 1970 are the coalition between indigenous peoples in
national organizations and a weak party system. The indigenous organizations influenced national leaders to make decisions regarding the level of
protection of indigenous peoples in an unstable context. The order of these
conditions and causal mechanisms are typical cases of moderate collective
rights. Moreover, the constitutional replacement in 1991 produced a new
national agreement to improve a national crisis, including diverse political
and social sectors. The National Assembly was the place for having indigenous representatives who could make coalitions with other minority groups
to create a united front. Later, with the new constitution enforced, indigenous
associations began to create relationships with indigenous political parties.
Colombia achieved strong collective rights that increased the number of
legal instruments, principally in the 1990s when these two new conditions
were added. This shows a sequential path for achieving collective rights, in
which all conditions have played an important role in the process. Coalitions
and institutional conditions worked toward increasing the protection of these
rights.

The case in Peru is different. Peru passed from having a weak level to a
strong level of collective rights in the past thirty years since 1990. However,
the most critical conditions and causal mechanisms that were institutional
dealt with a weak party system elevated personalistic leaders that had a particular interest in recognizing indigenous rights, such as Velasco and Toledo.
Furthermore, the constitutional replacement enshrined several new collective
rights at the end of 1993, but in the process, others were lost. Today, the
indigenous national associations and coalitions with non-indigenous allies
were and still are weak and fragmented in the country. The role of indigenous associations and coalitions has been a tool for modifying and influencing against non-beneficial plans from personalistic leaders. The coalitions
between indigenous peoples and non-indigenous allies were successful

during the entire term of President Toledo. This coalition spreads the constitutional protection of indigenous peoples through different laws, working with the indigenous identity of the president to create a united front. Some latter conditions were added in the late 1990s and at the beginning of 2000 when the level of protection for collective rights increased. The process for Peru has been slower with a central accent related to institutional conditions.

The trajectory of Colombia is closer to the cases of Ecuador and Bolivia, also for countries having strong collective rights. The role of coalitions between indigenous peoples in national organizations, such as CONAIE in Ecuador and CSUTCB and CIDOB in Bolivia, used their combined skills to influence the political context. There are coalitions between indigenous peoples and non-indigenous allies in all these countries. In the case of Ecuador, the coalitions are formed by diverse actors like the agrarian movements and human rights organizations which have helped to shape their united front. The same happened with Bolivia and several coalitions composed by other minorities and left parties.

Ecuador and Bolivia also follow the path of Colombia in having a weak party system with personalistic presidential leaders, such as Evo Morales in Bolivia and Rafael Correa in Ecuador. They both use narratives against the liberal paradigm and change the status quo. These countries also had several constitutional replacements: four in Bolivia beginning in 1995 and two in Ecuador since 1998. These constitutions were highly influential in having more indigenous collective rights. The case of Peru has a different order of conditions and causal mechanisms, showing that the path can be different, but the results will be more important when all the elements are present. This can be a lesson for countries with moderate levels of weak collective rights.

Alternative Explanations for Colombia and Peru

Colombia can be considered an overachiever in collective rights. It presents a low level of indigenous populations and indigenous social mobilizations; strong collective rights came by the result and influence of Convention No. 169, which gave new rights to indigenous peoples. However, this explanation does not account for the role of indigenous national organizations that are strong as political actors, influencing the result when getting more rights. This alternative does not consider the critical role of national authorities in making radical decisions for improving the level of recognition of indigenous peoples in significant historical moments in the Colombian political life.

In the case of Peru, its strong level of collective rights can be the result of historical patterns. Since 1920, the Peruvian constitutions have recognized indigenous rights. The 1993 Constitution maintained their current rights, while new rights were enshrined. In this case, the historical factor can be more important than the conditions. However, this explanation does not account for a phenomenon that has been multidimensional with different stages related to the role of the executive branch, and individual presidents are more willing to recognize indigenous rights and the incipient role of coalitions of indigenous peoples.

In both cases, the analysis of this research includes several conditions that together increase the level of collective indigenous rights. This phenomenon, like many others in social science, includes several variables. Each of the conditions plays a role in the outcome, giving more information regarding the state of the art of the collective rights of indigenous peoples in Latin America.

Diverse Paths for Achieving Moderate Collective Rights

According to the empirical evidence in achieving moderate collective rights, there are four different paths in the results of QCA. Two of these paths are based on the theory of this research: to achieve moderate collective rights, one type of coalition must be present, whether with indigenous peoples or non-indigenous allies, and one institutional condition, a weak party system, or constitutional instability. The cases of Bolivia 2, Guatemala 2, and Colombia 1 support this theory.

Two other paths are not based on the theory. Bolivia 1 and Mexico 2 only have the presence of the two coalitions. Guatemala 1 shows only a coalition between indigenous peoples. Thus, having a general view of the cases, the most critical factor for having moderate collective rights is the vital role of indigenous associations in influencing the national context. All the organizations, such as "Consejo Mexicano 500 años de Resistencia Indígena'" and EZLN in Mexico or COPMAGUA in Guatemala, became political actors with different levels of influence used to increase the protection of collective rights. These diverse paths for having moderate indigenous collective rights are part of the equifinality theory that this book wants to address.

Also, the role of the mid-institutionalized party system in achieving moderate collective rights is important. Bolivia 1 and 2 and Guatemala 1 and 2 present these party institutionalization levels. In these cases, the political system allows some flexibility to make radical decisions to include collective rights. This mid-level shows the capability of countries to get better levels of the party system that include collective rights, having national authorities that are willing to change some aspects of the liberal paradigm. It is also supported by the methodological decision to have three levels of the party organization index because it displays a difference in the case of moderate collective rights. A mid-level of party institutionalization can achieve moderate collective rights.

Weak Collective Rights and the Exception of the Chilean Case

It is more likely to have a weak level of collective rights in a country when there is a lack of organizations and institutional conditions. This is the case of Ecuador 1 and Chile 1 and 2. The expectation in these countries is that indigenous peoples are not political actors that can form coalitions between themselves or with other non-indigenous allies. In these countries, there can be high levels of indigenous social movements. However, fragmentation is too high to look for those connections that create a union among groups. In countries with weak collective rights, the stability of the institutions does not offer a possibility for modifying the status quo; the party system is highly institutionalized. Thus, the decisions made are moderate and follow the rules of capitalism in contraposition with indigenous cosmovision. The constitutional stability does not allow any opportunity for including collective rights, even if there are high levels of constitutional amendments. In the majority of the cases, the constitution does not allow any other cosmovision other than the liberal paradigm. According to the QCA analysis, the only current case of weak collective rights is in Chile, while Ecuador 1, Mexico 1, and Peru 1 passed this stage several years ago.

Chile is a typical case of weak collective rights. This situation is due to an institutionalized party system that is strong in electing authorities following party ideologies, with an absence of personalistic leaders. This makes decisions that tend to follow the status quo, influenced by the liberal paradigm presented in the constitution. In the past, there were several attempts to recognize indigenous peoples' rights, and all of them failed. The indigenous organizations are highly fragmented because the system does not allow indigenous organizations to represent the communities and peoples and aggressively stops the formation of national organizations. This lack of national organizations fails to create coalitions with non-indigenous allies. These conditions and mechanisms create the perfect scenario conducive to a weak level of indigenous collective rights. The alternative to increase collective rights in Chile would be to form coalitions between indigenous peoples. As the moderate collective rights analysis shows, to have indigenous national organizations is a sufficient condition.

There are two other paths for achieving weak collective rights: the lack of all conditions except a weak party system, as in Peru 1, and the presence of only two types of coalitions as in Mexico 1. Therefore, the sufficient condition to have weak indigenous collective rights is constitutional stability. The constitution is the most important legal document in a country. Their provisions help to organize all the rights to which citizens are entitled. If the constitution does not change, it keeps a paradigm that does not allow the flexibility to incorporate indigenous collective rights. This is particularly true in the case of Chile. The country's constitution entails a liberal paradigm that has been difficult to change even with several constitutional amendments. Thus, countries with constitutional stability tend to have weak collective rights.

Alternative Explanation for the Chilean Case

Multiple explanations can help to understand the presence of weak collective rights in Chile. For example, the role of indigenous associations asking to have their own internal governments may explain this underachievement. The influence of "El Consejo de Todas las Tierras" spreads the idea among some indigenous peoples to have a parallel and separate government with their rights. The indigenous social mobilizations are stronger because they are fighting to create a separate nation with no relationship to the national authorities. Thus, they are fighting for their own government, not to have more collective rights in a national paradigm. This explanation can be plausible.

However, the underlying assumption of this alternative explanation is the influence of Mapuche peoples on other indigenous peoples in the country. As I stated before, not all indigenous peoples agreed on the idea of a separated nation, and the level of fragmentation is high enough not to create this agreement. Also, the indigenous social movements in the country search for levels of autonomy and self-determination, but inside a context of juridical recognition and inclusion.

FUTURE RESEARCH AGENDA REGARDING COLLECTIVE RIGHTS

This research aimed to understand the conditions that explain why some countries recognize more collective rights and why others allow fewer. This research does not go into other aspects of the process, such as implementing or evaluating the role of collective rights and creating space to carry out other types of analysis. This research leaves space to reflect and think about several other indigenous collective rights topics.

First, to confirm the generalizability of this research, it would be essential to expand the study to other countries in Latin America, searching for the role of the same variable in countries like Costa Rica, Honduras, Paraguay, Nicaragua, Panama, and El Salvador. It is also possible to expand this research to other regions in the world.

Also, future research could explore the role of different conditions. Doing this research, it can be seen that the role of the federal system in some countries reveals the importance of having political decentralization for recognizing more collective rights of indigenous peoples. In countries with federal systems, there is a plurality of legal orders. Therefore, adding collective rights as self-determination or indigenous jurisdiction adds another layer to the complex state and federal relationships system. This is harder to achieve in systems with centralized legal orders, in which all the legal instruments respond to just one central paradigm. For this reason, Venezuela, Brazil, and Argentina, which were part of the first CQA analysis, were left aside to do a more in-depth study of their conditions, enhancing the role of the current federal system.

In terms of the implementation and evaluation of indigenous collective rights, future research should assess how important these rights are for improving the quality of life for indigenous peoples. It is essential to research empirically if having more rights for indigenous peoples means improving standards such as poverty, access to education, and cultural development. Furthermore, these collective rights are essential in influencing the western law system, for example, increasing the role of natural resources as a subject of law. Indigenous cosmovision is helping to decentralize the analysis, including mother nature and rivers as a subject of protection. This is the post-structuralist vision of law. Also, these analyses can be general, including all indigenous collective rights, as this book does, or researching some particular collective right, such as self-determination or indigenous justice, to enhance the role of the most essential collective rights for indigenous peoples.

In sum, this book has sought to explain the determinant of collective rights in Latin America, focusing on the first step of a long process: obtaining recognition. This research opens the door to explore other relevant questions, such as the implementation and evaluation of collective rights for indigenous peoples.

Appendix

Table A Indigenous Rules and Legislations, Explaining the Collective Rights and the Level of Indigenous Collective Rights

Case	Legal Instrument (Law, Decree, etc.)[1]	Collective Rights	Level of Indigenous Collective Rights	Source
Bolivia 1	Constitución de 1967	Indigenous justice, special protection to indigenous territories, autonomy (only these rights)	Moderate	Barié, 2003
Bolivia 2	Decreto Supremo 25.894de 2000	Indigenous language	Moderate	Barié, 2003
Bolivia 3	Constitucion de 2007	Collective rights, self-determination, consultation, indigenous as peoples, recognition of their political system, exploitation of their natural resources, indigenous language, multicultural and culturally plural nation	Strong	Fundación Tierra, n.d.; Aguilar et al, 2010
	Ley de educación	Intercultural, bilingual, productive and decolonize education		
	Ley 073	Indigenous jurisdiction		
	Ley 0727	Indigenous territories (collective)		
Chile 1	Ley 17.729 de 1972	Land (not collective)	Weak	Valenzuela & Oliva, 2017
	Ley 19.253 de 1993	Indigenous culture, land (individual and collective), indigenous language, intercultural and bilingual education		
Chile 2	Ley 20.500 de 2011	Participation (general not for indigenous peoples)	Weak	
	Decreto 66 de 2015 and decreto 40 de 2012	Previous consultation		
	Ley 89 de 1890	Self-government and territories		
Colombia 1	Decreto ley 88 de 1976 and 1142 de 1978	Bilingual and bicultural education; ethnic pluralism	Moderate	Rodriguez, 2007; Ayuda en Acción, 2018a
	Resolucion 3454 de 1984 del Min. de Educación Nacional	Program in ethnic development and ethnic education		
	Decreto 2001 de 1988	Land		
	Decreto 2655 de 1988	Priority rights of indigenous peoples regarding mines		

Colombia 2	Constitución 1991	Ethnic diversity, political participation, indigenous language, intercultural, bilingual education, indigenous as peoples, natural resources, collective land, includes self-determination and customary indigenous law	Strong	Aguilar et al, 2010; Rodriguez, 2007; Ayuda en Acción, 2018a
	Decreto 1088 de 1993 Ley 115 de 1994, Decreto 620 de 2000	Indigenous authorities Ethnic education		
	Decreto 1320 de 1998 Decreto 649 de 2001	Previous consultation Political rights		
Ecuador 1	Constitución de 1979 Ley 50 de 1994	Land (in all their forms) Indigenous traditions	Weak	Comisión Interamericana de Derechos Humanos, 1997 Diaz Garaycoa, 2002
Ecuador 2	Constitucion de 1998	Indigenous traditions, collective lands, natural resources, intercultural bilingual education, indigenous justice, autonomy in special territories, and participation in decisions related to natural resources	Strong	
Ecuador 3	Decreto 1642 Constitución de 2008	Indigenous health Indigenous language, cultural identities, culturally plural, traditional norms, indigenous as peoples, previous consultation, participatory rights, intercultural bilingual education, indigenous health, natural resources, collective land for indigenous peoples in voluntary isolation, self-determination, customary indigenous law	Strong	Barié, 2003 IWGIA, 2010; Aguilar et al, 2010

(continued)

Table A   **(Continued)**

Case	Legal Instrument (Law, Decree, etc.)¹	Collective Rights	Level of Indigenous Collective Rights	Source
Guatemala 1	Constitución de 1986	Language, bilingual education, special protection to territories, indigenous culture	Moderate	Barié, 2003
	Decreto 65 de 1990 Acuerdo Gubernativo No. 726-95	Mayan language Bilingual education		www.democraciamulti cultural.blogspot.com
	Decreto del Congreso 5-1995	Natural resources		
Guatemala 2	Constitución de 1998	Includes cultural diversity, land, and territories, indigenous language, bilingual education, consultation, and indigenous justice	Moderate	ACNUR (n.d.); Aguilar et al, 2010
	Acuerdo de la Corte Suprema de Justicia de 1998	Indigenous justice		ACNUR; Democraciam ulticultural.blogspot .com
	Decreto 24 de 1999 Decreto 42 de 2001	Respect for indigenous sacred land and collective lands Promote the social, economical, and cultural improvement of indigenous peoples		
	Acuerdo Ministerial 387-2001	Access to sacred land		
	Decreto 11 de 2002 Decreto 19-2003	Participation in public affairs National languages		
Mexico 1	Constitución de 1917	Collective land	Weak	López Bárcena, 2010
Mexico 2	Constitución de 1917, amendment 1992	Suppress collective land	Moderate	Aguilar et al 2010; López Barcena, 2010
	Constitución de 1917, amendment 2002	Includes self-determination under conditions, indigenous as peoples, own norms of social organization, indigenous justice, indigenous authorities, linguistic and cultural rights, protection to their lands (no collective), and priority for the use of natural resources, proportional representation at local level, federal legislation enshrine individual rights not collective		

	Legal instrument[1]	Content	Strength	Source
Peru 1	Decreto Ley 20653 de 1974, modified in 1978	Collective land, after the modification only use of their land (not property)	Weak	Chuecas, 2008; Merino, 2018
	Decreto Ley 21156 de 1975	Right to speak Quechua		Cuadros Sánchez, 2018
	Constitución 1979	Autonomy for peasants and native communities		Chuecas, 2008
	Ley 24656 de 1987	Property of collective land (Peasant)		Ministerio de Justicia y Derechos Humanos, 2013
	Código Civil, art. 126	Presumption of collective land		Ministerio de Justicia y Derechos Humanos, 2013
Peru 2	Constitution, 1993	Indigenous language, includes autonomy and self-government	Strong	Aguilar et al, 2010; Chuecas, 2008
	Código de los niños y adolescentes, 2000	Cultural identity in elementary education		Ministerio de Justicia, 2013
	Ley 29763 de 2011	Natural resources		
	Decreto Supremo 028-2003-AG, 2003	Territorial, economical, and ecologic integrity of land for ethnic groups that are voluntary isolated		
	Ley 28736 de 2006	Rights to isolated indigenous groups (definition of indigenous peoples)		
	Ley 29785 de 2011	Prior consultation		
	Ley 27908 de 2003	Jurisdiction for peasant communities		
	Resolución Adm 499-2012-P-PJ de 2012	Intercultural justice		
	Ley 26842 de 1997	Traditional health		
	Ley 28106 de 2003	Indigenous language		
	Ley 27811 de 2002	Collective knowledge		
	Ley 27818 de 2002; Ley 29735 de 2011	Bilingual intercultural education, cultural diversity, and bilingual collective rights		

[1]The name of the legal instruments are in Spanish.
Source: Katherine Becerra Valdivia.

Table B   Coalitions between Indigenous Peoples and Non-Indigenous Allies, with Their Sources

Case	Coalitions between Indigenous Peoples	Coalitions with Non-Indigenous Peoples	Source
Bolivia 1	CSUTCB Confederación Sindical Única de Trabajadores Campesinos de Bolivia; CIDOB Confederación de Indígenas del Oriente de Bolivia (since 1982)	Coalition between CIDOB and MNR Party	Postero, 2004; Van Cott, 2004, 2007; coica.org.ec
Bolivia 2	CSUTCB Confederación Sindical Única de Trabajadores Campesinos de Bolivia; CIDOB National Indigenous Federation (since 1982)	Coalitions felt apart. None.	Postero, 2004; Van Cott, 2004, 2007; coica.org.ec
Bolivia 3	CSUTCB Confederación Sindical Única de Trabajadores Campesinos de Bolivia; CIDOB National Indigenous Federation (since 1982)	From 2003 coalitions between indigenous and diverse groups. Important coalitions with MAS, Movimiento al Socialismo, Political Party	Madrid, 2012; Postero, 2004; Van Cott, 2004, 2007; coica.org.ec
Chile 1	None	None	
Chile 2	None	None	
Colombia 1	CRIC Consejo Regional Indígena del Cauca (since 1971); AICO Autoridades Indígenas de Colombia (since 1978); ONIC Organización Nacional Indígena de Colombia (since 1982)	None	Rathgeber, 2004; Laurent, 2005; Van Cott, 2004; ONIC, 1991
Colombia 2	CRIC; AICO; ONIC; OPIC Organización de los Pueblos Indígenas de la Amazonía Colombiana (Since 1995)	Coalitions with environmentalists, women and Afro-descendants, and left political parties. Mainly, ASI, Alianza Social Indígena (Independiente) and MIC, Movimiento Indígena de Colombia	Rathgeber, 2004; Van Cott, 2007; ONIC, 1991

Ecuador 1	CONAIE Confederación de Nacionalidades Indígenas (Since 1986)	CONAIE creates coordination with some sectors such as agrarian. And it was involved in the creation of Coordinadora de Movimientos Sociales, including union from the public sectors, neighbors association, human rights activities and development NGOs	Zamosc, 2004; Van Cott, 2004, 2007; conaie.org
Ecuador 2	CONAIE Confederación de Nacionalidades Indígenas (Since 1986)	CONAIE creates coalitions with trucker and small and medium entrepreneurs (1998–1999). Since 2002 there is a great relationship between CONAIE, Pachakutik Political Party, and Patriotic Society Party	Madrid, 2012; Zamosc, 2004; Van Cott, 2004, 2007; conaie.org
Ecuador 3	CONAIE Confederación de Nacionalidades Indígenas (Since 1986)	Since 2002 there is a great relationship between CONAIE, Pachakutik Political Party, and Patriotic Society Party	Zamosc, 2004; conaie.org
Guatemala 1	COMG Consejo de Organizaciones Mayas de Guatemala (90's); APM Asamblea del Pueblo Maya (1993); ASC Asamblea de la Sociedad Civil (1993)	None	Fischer, 2004; Rostica 2007
Guatemala 2	COPMAGUA Coordinadora de Organizaciones del Pueblo Maya de Guatemala (1996)	None	Fischer, 2004; Rostica 2007
Mexico 1	CNPA Coordinadora Nacional Plan de Ayala (since 1979)	CNPA forms coalition with the CIOAC Central independiente de Obreros Agrícolas y campesinos	Dietz, 2004; movimientocampe sinoplandeayalasigloxxl.org .mx

(continued)

Table B Continued

Case	Coalitions between Indigenous Peoples	Coalitions with Non-Indigenous Peoples	Source
Mexico 2	Consejo Mexicano 500 años de la Resistencia Indígena (Since 1992); EZLN Ejercito Zapatista de Liberación Nacional (Since 1994)	EZLN formed coalitions with other movements for the Democratic National Convention and the Transition Governor in Rebellion (mainly human rights organizations)	Dietz, 2004
Peru 1	None (a few with local representation)	None	Van Cott, 2007; Salazar-Soler, 2014; Coppedge et al (2021); Karp-Toledo, 2014
Peru 2	COPPIP Confederación (Coordinadora) Permanente de los Pueblos Indígenas del Perú (1997-1998); CONAMI Coordinadora Nacional de Comunidades Afectadas por la Minería (1999); COAI Coordinadora Andina de Organizaciones Indígenas (2006)	Coalitions of indigenous peoples with the political party "Perú Posible" (since the presidency of Toledo in 2001)	García & Lucero 2004; Van Cott, 2007, Salazar-Soler, 2014, Karp-Toledo,2014; Madrid, 2012

Source: Katherine Becerra Valdivia.

Table C   Presence of Coalitions for Each Case

Cases	Coalitions between Indigenous Peoples	Coalitions with Non-Indigenous Peoples
Bolivia 1	1	1
Bolivia 2	1	0
Bolivia 3	1	1
Chile 1	0	0
Chile 2	0	0
Colombia 1	1	0
Colombia 2	1	1
Ecuador 1	1	1
Ecuador 2	1	1
Ecuador 3	1	1
Guatemala 1	1	0
Guatemala 2	1	0
Mexico 1	1	1
Mexico 2	1	1
Peru 1	0	0
Peru 2	1	1

Source: Own elaboration. See table B for more details.
1: Presence; 0: Absent

Table D   Index of Party Organization

Cases	Index[a] (Average)	Level
Bolivia 1	1.6	1
Bolivia 2	1.2	1
Bolivia 3	0.8	0
Chile 1	1.8	1
Chile 2	2.5	2
Colombia 1	0.7	0
Colombia 2	0.8	0
Ecuador 1	1	1
Ecuador 2	0.8	0
Ecuador 3	0.7	0
Guatemala 1	1	1
Guatemala 2	1	1
Mexico 1	2.2	2
Mexico 2	2	1
Peru 1	0.8	0
Peru 2	0.05	0

[a] *Source*: Party Organization Variable, ordinal, converted to interval by the measurement model. Min: -.222 Max: 2.8. V-Dem Data Set v11.1 (Coppedge et al., 2021).

Table E   Standing Constitution, New Constitutions, and Constitutional Replacement

Case	Standing Constitution[a]	No. of New Constitution	Presence/Absent Constitutional Replacement[b]
Bolivia 1	Constitución de 1967	0	0
Bolivia 2	Constitución de 1967. Constitución Política del Estado de Bolivia del 6 de febrero de 1995. Constitución política del Estado del 2004 (Ley de 13 de abril de 2004)	2	1
Bolivia 3	Constitución política del Estado del 2004 (Ley de 13 de abril de 2004). Nueva Constitución Política del Estado, Congreso Nacional, octubre 2008. Constitución Política del Estado plurinacional de Bolivia, promulgada el 9 de febrero 2009	2	1
Chile 1	Constitución de 1980	0	0
Chile 2	Constitución de 1980	0	0
Colombia 1	Constitución de 1886	0	0
Colombia 2	Constitución Política de Colombia, 1991	1	1
Ecuador 1	Constitución de Ecuador de 1979	0	0
Ecuador 2	Constitución de Ecuador de 1979 Constitución de Ecuador de 1998	1	1
Ecuador 3	Constitución de Ecuador de 1998 Constitución de la República de Ecuador el 20 de octubre 2008	1	1
Guatemala 1	Constitución Política de la República de Guatemala de 1985	0	0
Guatemala 2	Constitución Política de la República de Guatemala de 1985. Proyecto de reforma constitucional del 16 de octubre de 1998	1	1
Mexico 1	Constitución Federal de 1917	0	0
Mexico 2	Constitución Federal de 1917	0	0
Peru 1	Constitución Política del Perú, 12 de julio 1979	0	0
Peru 2	Constitución Política del Perú, 1993	1	1

[a] *Source*: Biblioteca Virtual Miguel de Cervantes (www.cervantesvirtual.com); all the names are in Spanish.
[b] Present: 1 Absent: 0.

Table F   Formulas per Each Row of the Truth Table

Row	Formula[a]	Cases
1	$CA + CB + PS(0) + CC = InCR$	Bolivia 3; Colombia 2; Ecuador 3; Peru 2; Ecuador 2
2	$CA + CB + PS(1) \sim CC = MoCR$	Bolivia 1
2	$CA + CB + PS(2) \sim CC = MoCR$	Mexico 2
3	$CA \sim CB + PS(1) + CC = MoCR$	Bolivia 2; Guatemala 2
4	$CA \sim CB + PS(0) \sim CC = MoCR$	Guatemala 1
5	$CA \sim CB + PS(1) \sim CC = MoCR$	Colombia 1
6	$\sim CA \sim CB + PS(1) \sim CC = BaCR$	Ecuador 1; Chile 1
6	$\sim CA \sim CB + PS(2) \sim CC = BaCR$	Chile 2
7	$\sim CA \sim CB + PS(0) \sim CC = BaCR$	Peru 1
8	$CA + CB + PS(1) \sim CC = BaCR$	Mexico 1

Source: Own elaboration.
[a] Meaning:
CA: Coalitions between indigenous peoples. Presence 1; Absent 0.
CB: Coalitions with other non-indigenous allies. Presence 1; Absent 0.
PS: Party system. Weak 0; Mid-institutionalization 1; Institutionalization 2.
CC: Constitutional replacement. No replacement 0; Replacement 1.
InCR: Strong collective rights.
MoCR: Moderate collective rights.
BaCR: Weak collective rights.
+ Presence; ~ Absence.

References

Acevedo De la Harpe, C. (2021). Inclusión de derechos indígenas en Chile: Arquetipo constituyente desde América Latina. *Polis. Revista Latino.*

ACNUR. (n.d.). Guía para la aplicación judicial: Los Derechos de los Pueblos Indígenas en el Convenio 169 de la OIT (Organización Internacional del Trabajo). ACNUR.

Agudelo, C. (2001). Nuevos actores sociales y relegitimación del Estado. Estado y Construcción del Movimiento Social de Comunidades Negras en Colombia. *Análisis Político*, 43, 3–31.

Aguilar, G., LaFosse, S., Rojas, H., & Steward, R. (2010). South/North Exchange of 2009—The Constitutional Recognition of Indigenous Peoples in Latin America. Pace International Law Review Online Companion, 2010 [xiii]. https://heinonline.org/HOL/Page?handle=hein.journals/piliewco2010&id=347&div=&collection=

AIDESEP. (2020, December 2). Activarán herramienta digital sobre consulta previa para fortalecer derechos indígenas en Perú. http://www.aidesep.org.pe/noticias/activaran-herramienta-digital-sobre-consulta-previa-para-fortalecer-derechos-indigenas-en

AIDESEP, CONACAMI, CNA, Asociación Paz y Esperanza, APRODEH, CAAAP, CooperAcción, CNDH, Grupo de trabajos de los Pueblos Indígenas, DAR, FEDEPAZ, IDL, IBC, SERVINDI, ONAMIAP, Aprodeh, & Cedal. (2012). Perú: Informe Alternativo 2012. Sobre cumplimiento del Convenio 169 de la OIT. http://www.servindi.org/pdf/InformeAlternativo2012.pdf

AIDESEP, CONACAMI, CNA, CCP, CARE, Asociación Paz y Esperanza, APRODEH, CAAAP, CooperAcción, CNDH, Grupo de trabajos de los Pueblos Indígenas, DAR, FEDEPAZ, IDL, IBC, & SERVINDI. (2011). Perú: Informe Alternativo 2011. Sobre cumplimiento del Convenio 169 de la OIT. http://www.servindi.org/pdf/Informe_Alternativo_2011.pdf

Albarracín, J., Gamboa, L., & Mainwaring, S. (2018). Deinstitutionalization without Collapse: Colombia's Party System. In *Party System in Latin America. Institutionalization, Decay and Collapse*. Cambridge University Press.

Albert, C. (2019). Plurinacionalidad y reconocimiento de los pueblos: Las demandas indígenas para la nueva Constitución. CIPER/Académico.

Alcántara Sáez, M. (2013a). *Sistema Políticos de América Latina: Vol. Volumen I*. Tecnos.

Alcántara Sáez, M. (2013b). *Sistema Políticos de América Latina: Vol. Volumen II*. Tecnos.

Almeida, P., & Cordero Ulate, Allen. (2017). Movimientos Sociales en América Latina. In *Movimientos sociales en América Latina* (pp. 13–26). Clacso.

Altman, D., & Luna, J. P. (2015). ¿Partidos hidropónicos en un sistema de partidos muy institucionalizado? El caso de Chile. In *Sistema de Partidos en América Latina* (pp. 203–2019). Anthropos ediciones.

Altman, D., Luna, J. P., Piñeiro, R., & Toro, S. (2009). Partidos y sistemas de partidos en América Latina: Aproximaciones desde la encuesta a expertos 2009. *Revista de Ciencia Política*, 29(3), 775–798. https://scielo.conicyt.cl/scielo.php?script=sci _arttext&pid=S0718-090X2009000300005

Alza Barco, C., & Zambrano Chávez, G. (2014). Pueblos Indígenas y Establecimiento de Agenda: Cambios en la estructura institucional en el Estado Peruano (2000-2011). Clacso & PUCP.

Andrade, M. J. (2018). Pueblos indígenas y minorías nacionales: Similitudes y diferencias en la protección internacional de sus derechos. *Revista Campos En Ciencias Sociales*, 6(2), 13–48.

Andrés Santos, F. J., & Amezúa Amezúa, L. C. (2013). El multiculturalismo y los derechos colectivos en el primer constitucionalismo iberoamericano. *Revista de Derecho (Valparaíso)*, 41, 341–358. https://doi.org/10.4067/S0718-68512013000200010

Anexo 1. Cronología 1978-2000. (n.d.). http://www.cverdad.org.pe/ifinal/pdf/Tomo %20-%20ANEXOS/ANEXO%201Cronologia%201978-2000%20ultima%20revision.pdf

Aragón Trelles, J. (2016). Políticos en el Perú: Lo que ves es lo que hay. In *Participación, Competencia y Representación Política. Contribuciones para el Debate* (pp. 131–146). IEP Instituto de Estudios Peruanos.

Arce, M. (2010). Parties and Social Protest in Latin America's Neoliberal Era. *Party Politics*, 16(5), 669–686. https://doi.org/10.1177/1354068809346005

Archila Neira, M. (2016). El paro cívico nacional del 14 de septiembre de 1977. Un ejercicio de memoria colectiva. *Revista de Economia Institucional*, 18(25), 313–318.

Ardila Duarte, B. (2008). López Michelsen: Académico y demócrata. *Revista Temas Socio-Jurídicos*, 55, 69.

Aylwin Azocar, P. (1991). Mensaje de S.E. El Presidente la República. Fecha 15 de octubre, 1991. Cuenta en Sesión 08, Legislatura 323. Congreso Nacional. Historia de la Ley.

Aylwin, J. (2014). Los derechos de los pueblos indígenas en América Latina: Avances jurídicos y brechas de implementación. Derechos Humanos de Los Grupos Vulnerables, 275–300.

Aylwin, J., Meza-Lopehandía, M., & Yáñez, N. (2013). Los Pueblos Indígenas y el Derecho. Lom.

Ayuda en Acción. (2018a). Derechos de los pueblos indígenas. Derechos Humanos. https://ayudaenaccion.org/ong/blog/derechos-humanos/derechos-pueblos-indigenas/

Ayuda en Acción. (2018b, August 1). Las 102 comunidades indígenas en Colombia. Ayuda en Acción. https://ayudaenaccion.org/ong/blog/america-latina/comunidades-indigenas-colombia/

Badger, A. (2010). Collective v. Individual Human Rights in Membership Governance for Indigenous Peoples. *American University International Law Review*, 26, 485. https://heinonline.org/HOL/Page?handle=hein.journals/amuilr26&id=489&div=&collection=

Barad, K. (2007). *Meeting the Universe Halfway: Quantum Physics and the Entanglement of Matter and Meaning*. Duke University Press.

Barco, V. (1989). Intervención ante la Asamblea General de las Naciones Unidas. https://www.virgiliobarco.com/images/discursos/Intervencion-ante-la-Asamblea-General-de-las-Naciones-Unidas-Virgilio-Barco.pdf

Barelli, M. (2009). The Role of Soft Law in the International Legal System: The Case of the United Nations Declaration on the Rights of Indigenous Peoples. *The International and Comparative Law Quarterly*, 58(4), 957–983. JSTOR. https://www.jstor.org/stable/25622251

Barié, C. G. (2003). *Pueblos indígenas y derechos constitucionales en América Latina: Un panorama*. Editorial Abya Yala.

Barlow, M. (2001). BLUE GOLD the global water crisis and the commodification of the world's water supply A Special Report issued by the International Forum on Globalization (IFG). http://www.thirdworldtraveler.com/Water/Blue_Gold.html

Barvosa- Carter, E. (2001). Multiple Identity and Coalition Building: How Identity Differences within US Enable Radical Alliances among Us. In *Coalitions across Borders. Transnational Protest and the Neoliberal Order* (pp. 21–34). Rowman & Littlefield.

Barvosa-Carter, E. (1999). Multiple Identity and Coalition Building: How Identity Differences Within Us Enable Radical Alliances Among Us. *Contemporary Justice Review*, 2(2), 123–134.

BBCMundo. (2017, November 20). Chile Profile. *BBC News*. https://www.bbc.com/news/world-latin-america-19356356

BBCNews. (2018, August 8). Colombia Country Profile. *BBC News*. https://www.bbc.com/news/world-latin-america-19390026

Beamish, T., & Luebbers, A. (2009). Alliance Building across Social Movements: Bridging Difference in a Peace and Justice Coalition. *Social Problems*, 56(4), 647–676.

Becker, M. (2014). Correa, Indigenous Movements, and the Writing of a New Constitution. In *Rethinking Latin American Social Movements: Radical Action from Below* (pp. 267–283). Rowman & Littlefield.

Bejarano, A. M. (1990). La Paz en la Administración Barco: De la rehabilitación Social a la negociación política. *Análisis Político*, 9, 7–29.

Bellinger, P. T., & Arce, M. (2011). Protest and Democracy in Latin America's Market Era. *Political Research Quarterly*, 64(3), 688–704. https://doi.org/10.1177/1065912910373557

Benavides-Vanegas, F. S. (2009). Indigenous People's Mobilization and their Struggle for Rights in Colombia. *SSRN Electronic Journal*. https://doi.org/10.2139/ssrn.1884151

Bengoa, J. (2000). La Emergencia Indígena en América Latina (Third). Fondo de Cultura Economica.

Bennett, A. (2010). Process Tracing and Causal Inference. In *Rethinking Social Inquiry* (Second Edition, pp. 207–220). Rowman & Littlefield.

Biblioteca del Congreso Nacional de Chile. (2019). Reformas a la Constitución Política. Departamento Servicios Legislativos y Documentales. https://www.bcn.cl/obtienearchivo?id=repositorio/10221/28085/1/Constitucion_Reformas.pdf

Biddulph, S. (2015). *The Stability Imperative: Human Rights and Law in China*. UBC Press.

Blanco, C. (2016). Balance del Perú en el contexto regional: Una mirada comparativa del derecho a la consulta previa con relación a Colombia, Chile y Bolivia. In La Implementación del Derecho a Consulta Previa en el Perú. Aportes para el análisis y la garantía de los derechos colectivos de los pueblos indígenas.

Boulding, C., & Holzner, C. (2015). Vote and Inequality in Latin American Democracies. Paper presented at the 73rd Annual Conference of the Midwest Political Science Association, Chicago, IL, April 16–19.

Bowen, J. R. (2000). Should We Have a Universal Concept of "Indigenous Peoples" Rights'? Ethnicity and Essentialism in the Twenty-First Century. *Anthropology Today*, 16(4), 12–16. JSTOR. https://www.jstor.org/stable/2678305

Bresnahan, R. (2003). Introduction: Chile since 1990 the Contradictions of Neoliberal Democratization. *American Perspective*, 30(5), 3–15.

Buchanan, A. (1993). Role of Collective Rights in the Theory of Indigenous Peoples' Rights Symposium: Contemporary Perspectives on Self-Determination and Indigenous Peoples' rights. *Transnational Law & Contemporary Problems*, 1, 89–108. https://heinonline.org/HOL/LandingPage?handle=hein.journals/tlcp3&div=12&id=&page=

Buechler, S. M. (2013). New Social Movements and New Social Movement Theory. In *The Wiley-Blackwell Encyclopedia of Social and Political Movements*. Blackwell Publishing Ltd.

Bulmer-Thomas, V. (2017). *La historia económica de América Latina desde la Independencia*. Fondo de Cultura Economica.

Buquet, D. (2015). El cambio político en el Cono Sur: Institucionalización partidaria y alternancia en Argentina, Chile y Uruguay. In *Sistemas de Partidos en América Latina* (pp. 139–160). Anthropos ediciones.

Bystydzienski, J., & Schacht, S. (2001). Introduction. In *Forging Radical Alliances Cross Difference. Coalition Politics for the New Millenium* (pp. 1–17). Rowman & Littlefield.

Campos Muñoz, L., & De la Maza, F. (2019, December). Los pueblos indígenas y afrodescendientes frente a la nueva Constitución. *La Tercera*.

References 159

Campos Muñoz, L., & De la Maza, F. (2019, diciembre). Los pueblos indígenas y afrodescendientes frente a la nueva Constitución. *La Tercera.*

Caniuqueo Huircapan, S. (2019a, November). Pueblo Mapuche y Asamblea Constituyente: Una oportunidad para la convivencia. *The Clinic.* https://www.theclinic.cl/2019/11/18/pueblo-mapuche-y-asamblea-constituyente-una-oportunidad-para-la-convivencia/?fb_comment_id=3814955881863115_3816024988422871

Caniuqueo Huircapan, S. (2019b, November). Pueblo Mapuche y la inflexión histórica del 18/O. CIPER/Académico.

Cardona Alzate, J. (2011, July 3). El arduo camino de la Constituyente de 1991. *El Espectador.*

Carmona Caldera, C. (2013). Tomando los Derechos Colectivos en Serio: el derecho a consulta previa del convenio 169 de la OIT y las instituciones representativas de los pueblos indígenas. *Ius et Praxis,* 19(2), 301–334. https://doi.org/10.4067/S0718-00122013000200009

Carreras, M. (2012). Party Systems in Latin America after the Third Wave: A Critical Re-assessment. *Journal of Politics in Latin America,* 4(1), 135–153. https://journals.sub.uni-hamburg.de/giga/jpla/article/view/508

Cavero, O. (2011). Después del Baguazo: Informes, diálogo y debates. Departamento de Ciencias Sociales, Pontificia Universidad Católica del Perú. http://repositorio.pucp.edu.pe/index/bitstream/handle/123456789/52663/baguazo_cavero.pdf?sequence=1&isAllowed=y

Cedillo Delgado, R. (2018). Inclusión política indígena en el Perú del siglo xxi. *Apuntes Electorales,* XVII(59), 9–44.

CEPAL. (2014). Los pueblos Indígenas en América Latina. Avances en el decenio y retos pendientes para la garantía de sus derechos. Síntesis.

Che Piú, H. (2009). Conflicto entre Estado e indígenas por DL 1090 y 1064 nace en anteriores normas forestales. Inforegión.

Chuecas, A. (2008). El Derecho de los Pueblos Indígenas y comunidades en el contexto histórico del Perú. *Boletín de Estudios Amazónicos,* 4, 1–19.

Collier, D. (2011). Understanding Process Tracing. *PS: Political Science & Politics,* 44(4), 823–830.

Comisión de la Verdad y Reconciliación. (2003). Informe Final. CVR. http://cverdad.org.pe/ifinal/

Comisión Especial Pueblos Indígenas. (1992). Informe de la Comisión Especial para el Estudio de la Legislación referida a los pueblos indígenas, sobre el proyecto de ley relativo a la protección, fomento y desarrollo de los pueblos indígenas. Cámara de Diputados. Fecha 10 de noviembre, 1992. Cuenta en sesión 43, Legislatura 325. Cámara de Diputados. Historia de la Ley.

Comisión Interamericana de Derechos Humanos. (1997). Informe sobre la situaci'on de los Derechos Humanos en Ecuador. Capitulo IX. http://www.cidh.org/countryrep/Ecuador-sp/Capitulo%209.htm

Comisión Verdad Histórica y Nuevo Trato. (2008). Informe de la Comisión Verdad Histórica yHistórica y Nuevo Trato con los Pueblos Indígenas. Comisionado Presidencial para Asuntos Indigenas. Santiago.

CONADI. (n.d.). Registro de Comunidades y Asociaciones Indígenas. Retrieved February 24, 2020, from http://www.conadi.gob.cl/registro-de-comunidades-y -asociaciones-indigenas

Congreso Constituyente Democrático. (n.d.). Memoria 1993. http://www4.congreso .gob.pe/ccd/memorias/memo93.htm

Congreso Constituyente Democrático. (1998). Debate Constitucional. Pleno-1993. Tomo I. Congreso de la República. http://spij.minjus.gob.pe/Textos-PDF/Consti- tucion_1993/DebConst-Pleno93/DebConst-Pleno93TOMO1.pdf

Contesse, J. (2012). El derecho de consulta previa en el Convenio 169 de la OIT: Notas para su implementación en Chile. In El Convenio 169 de la OIT y el derecho chileno: Mecanismos y obstáculos para su implementación.

Coppedge, M., Gerring, J., Knutsen, C. H., Lindberg, S. I., Skaaning, S.-E., Teorell, J., Altman, D., Bernhard, M., Fish, M. S., Cornell, A., Dahlum, S., Gjerløw, H., Glynn, A., Hicken, A., Krusell, J., Lührmann, A., Marquardt, K. L., McMann, K., Mechkova, V., Olin, M., Paxton, P., Pemstein, D., Seim, B., Sigman, R., Staton, J., Sundtröm, A., Tzelgov, E., Uberti, L., Wang, Y., Wig, T., and Ziblatt, D. (2021). V-Dem Country-Year Dataset v11.1. Varieties of Democracy (V-Dem) Project.

Correa Henao, N. (1990). El proceso constituyente: El caso colombiano. *Revista Facultad de Derecho y Ciencias Políticas*, 91, 23–38.

Correa Henao, N. (2005). La Experiencia de Colombia (1991). In *Asamblea Consti- tuyente: Aprendiendo de otras experiencias. Colombia, Ecuador y Venezuela* (pp. 11–46). Friedrich Ebert Stiftung, Instituto Latinoamericano de Investigaciones Sociales (FES-ILDIS).

Couso, J. (2006). Trying Democracy in the Shadow of an Authoritarian Legality: Chile's Transition to Democracy and Pinochet's Constitution of 1980. *Wisconsin International Legal Journal*. 29(2), 393.

Cruz-Saco, M. A. (2018). Indigenous communities and social inclusion in Latin America. Prepared for the United Nations Expert Group Meeting on Families and Inclusive Societies New York Headquarters. United Nations.

Cuadra Montoya, X. (2014). Nuevas estrategias de los movimientos indígenas contra el extractivismo en Chile. *Revista CIDOB d'Afers Internacionals*, 105, 141–163.

Cuadros Sánchez, H. E. (2018). De Indio a Campesino: La Construcción de Cat- egorías Jurídicas en Contextos de Cambio Político e Ideológico en el Perú Repub- licano hasta el Último Militarismo. Forum Historiae Iuris.

Cullen, P. (2001). Coalitions Working for Social Justice: Transnational NGOs and International Governance. In *Coalitions across Borders. Transnational Protest and the Neoliberal Order* (pp. 249–263). Rowman & Littlefield.

Dawson, M. (1994). *Behind the Mule: Race and Class in African American Politics*. Princeton University Press.

De La Cadena, M. (2001). Reconstructing Race: Racism, Culture and Mestizaje in Latin America. *NACLA Report on the Americas*, 34(6), 16–23. https://doi.org/10 .1080/10714839.2001.11722585

De Meur, G., Rihoux, B., & Yamasaki, S. (2009). Addressing the Critiques of QCA. In *Configurational Comparative Methods. Qualitative Comparative Analysis (QCA) and Related Techniques*. Sage Publications.

De Varennes, F. (2012). Language, Rights and Opportunities: The Role of Language in the Inclusion and Exclusion of Indigenous Peoples. UN Expert Mechanism on the Rights of Indigenous Peoples.

Del Rosario Rodriguez, M. F. (2011). La supremacía constitucional: Naturaleza y alcances. *Díkaion: Revista de Actualidad Jurídica*, 20(1), 97–117.

Del Toro Huerta, M. I. (2008). Los aportes de la jurisprudencia de la Corte Interamericana de Derechos Humanos en la configuración del derecho de propiedad colectiva de los miembros de comunidades y pueblos indígenas. SELA (Seminario En Latinoamérica de Teoría Constitucional y Política), Paper 58. http://digitalcommons.law.yale.edu/yls_sela/58

Denzin, N. K., Lincoln, Y. S., & Smith, L. T. (2008). *Handbook of Critical and Indigenous Methodologies*. Sage.

Diario Financiero. (2019, July 30). Perú, Colombia y Chile liderarán crecimiento regional con expasión mayor a 3% en 2019 y 2020. https://www.df.cl/noticias/internacional/economia/peru-colombia-y-chile-lideraran-crecimiento-regional-con-expansion/2019-07-29/180134.html

Díaz Garaycoa, F. (2002). Indígenas: Convenios internacionales y legislación nacional. *Iuris Dictio*, 3(6), 33–40.

Dietz, G. (2004). From Indigenismo to Zapatismo: The Struggle for Multi-ethnic Mexican Society. In *The Struggle for Indigenous Rights in Latin America* (pp. 32–80). Sussex Academic Press.

Directorate of Intelligence. (1988). Chile: How Authoritarian is Pinochet's Constitution? CIA. https://www.cia.gov/library/readingroom/docs/DOC_0000451593.pdf

Disney, J. L., & Williams, V. S. (2014). Latin American Social Movements and a New Left Consensus: State and Civil Society Challenges to Neoliberal Globalization. *New Political Science*, 36(1), 1–31. https://doi.org/10.1080/07393148.2013.864897

Dugas, J. (2015). Colombia. In *Politics of Latin America* (Fifth edition, pp. 433–457). Oxford University Press.

Duque Daza, J. (2008). Las organizaciones políticas étnicas en Colombia. Los indígenas y las elecciones 1990-2006. *Iberoamericana*, 32(8), 7–30.

Durán Durán, A. (2016). Acciones colectivas configuradoras de lo étnico. EL Caso del Pacífico Sur Colombiano. *Revista Brasileira de Gestão e Desenvolvimento Regional*, 12(1), 3–32.

ECLAC. (2008). Indigenous People. Latin America and the Caribbean Demographic Observatory.

Ensalaco, M. (1994). In with the New, out with the Old? The Democratising Impact of Constitutional Reform in Chile. *Journal of Latin American Studies*, 26(2), 409–429. JSTOR. https://www.jstor.org/stable/157949

Estupiñan Silva, R., & Ibáñez Rivas, J. M. (2014). La jurisprudencia de la Corte Interamericana de Derechos Humanos en materia de pueblos indígenas y tribales. Derechos Humanos de Los Grupos Vulnerables, 301–336.

Figueroa Huencho, V. (2014). Formulación de políticas públicas indígenas en Chile: Evidencias de un fracaso sostenido. Editorial Universitaria.

Fischer, E. (2004). *Beyond Victimization: Maya Movements in Post-war Guatemala* (pp. 81–104). Sussex Academic Press.

Flores-Macias, G. A. (2012). *After Neoliberalism?: The Left and Economic Reforms in Latin America*. Oxford University Press.

Fuentes, C., & Cea, M. de (2017). Reconocimiento débil: Derechos de pueblos indígenas en Chile. *Perfiles Latinoamericanos*, 25(49), 55–75. https://doi.org/10.18504/pl2549-003-2017

Fundación Tierra. (n.d.). Los Pueblos Indígenas en la Normativa Nacional e Internacional. Módulo 2. Imprenta-Editorial "Tupac Katari."

Funk, K. (2012). "Today There Are No Indigenous People" in Chile?: Connecting the Mapuche Struggle to Anti-neoliberal Mobilizations in South America. *Journal of Politics in Latin America*, 4(2), 125–140.

Gagliardi, S. (2019). The Human Rights of Minority and Indigenous Women. In *International Human Rights of Women, International Human Rights* (pp. 1–20). Springer Science+Business Medi. https://www.researchgate.net/publication/334654347_The_Human_Rights_of_Minority_and_Indigenous_Women

Gálvez Revollar, C. (2001). El derecho consuetudinario indígena en la legislación indigenista republicana del Perú del siglo XX. *BIRA*, 28, 285–302. http://repositorio.pucp.edu.pe/index/bitstream/handle/123456789/113997/9900-Texto%20del%20art%C3%ADculo-39183-1-10-20140801.pdf?sequence=2

García, A. (1986). Mensaje del presidente constitucional del Perú, doctor Alán García Pérez, ante el Congreso Nacional, el 28 de Julio de 1986. http://www.congreso.gob.pe/participacion/museo/congreso/mensajes/mensaje-nacion-congreso-28-07-1986

García, A. (1987). Mensaje del presidente constitucional del Perú, doctor Alán García Pérez, ante el Congreso Nacional, el 28 de Julio de 1987. http://www.congreso.gob.pe/participacion/museo/congreso/mensajes/mensaje-nacion-congreso-28-07-1987

García, A. (2007). El síndrome del perro del hortelano. *El Comercio*. http://peruesmas.com/biblioteca-jorge/Alan-Garcia-Perez-y-el-perro-del-hortelano.pdf

García, M. E., & Lucero, J. A. (2004). Un país sin indigenas?: Re-thinking Indigenous Politics in Peru. In *The Struggle for Indigenous Rights in Latin America* (pp. 158–188). Sussex Academic Press.

Garcia-Huidobro, R. (2016). La narrativa como método desencadenante y producción teórica en la investigación cualitativa. Empiria. *Revista de metodología de ciencias sociales*, (34), 155–178. https://doi.org/10.5944/empiria.34.2016.16526

Gastaka Urruela, E. (2017). Movimiento Ecologistas y Mapuche en el Chile Postdictadura. Pueblos, Revista de Información y Debate.

Geddes, B. (1990). How the Cases you Choose Affect the Answers you Get: Selection Bias in Comparative Politics. *Political Analysis*, 2, 131–150.

George, A., & Bennett, A. (2005). *Case Studies and Theory Development in the Social Sciences*. MIT Press.

Gobierno Nacional de Colombia, & Quintín Lame. (1991). Acuerdo. https://peacemaker.un.org/sites/peacemaker.un.org/files/CO_910306_AcuerdoMAQLparaEstablecerCampamento.pdf

Goicovich Videla, F. (2004). José Bengoa: Historia de los antiguos mapuches del sur. Desde antes de la llegada de los españoles hasta las paces de Quilin. *Historia*, 37(1), 237–241.

Government of Chile. (2014, March 11). Military Regime. This Is Chile. https://www.thisischile.cl/history/institutional-breakdown/?lang=en

Goy, P. (2008). Introduction. In *Research in Social Movements, Conflicts and Change* (pp. ix–xv). Emerald Group.

Gramson, W. (1991). *The Strategy of Social Protest*. Wadsworth.

Green, L. (1991). Two Views of Collective Rights. *Canadian Journal of Law and Jurisprudence*, 4(2), 315–328.

Greene, K., & Sánchez - Talanquer, M. (2018). Authoritarian Legacies and Party System Stability in Mexico Party Systems in Latin America (p. 201). Kindle Edition. In *Party System in Latin America. Institutionalization, Decay and Collapse*. Cambridge University Press.

Greene, S. (2005). Incas, Indios and Indigenism in Peru. *NACLA Report on the Americas*, 38(4), 34–41.

Grompone, R. (2016). Lo que queda del día: Sobre partidos y sombras. In *Participación, Competencia y Representación Política. Contribuciones para el Debate* (pp. 113–129). IEP Instituto de Estudios Peruanos.

Grossman, Z. (2001). "Let's Not to create Evilness for This River": Interethnic Environmental Alliances of Native Americans and Rural Whites in Northen Wisconsin. In *Coalitions across Borders. Transnational Protest and the Neoliberal Order* (pp. 146–162). Rowman & Littlefield.

Grugel, J., & Riggirozzi, P. (n.d.). Post-neoliberalism in Latin America: Rebuilding and Reclaiming the State after Crisis. *Development and Change*, 43(1), 1–21. https://doi.org/10.1111/j.1467-7660.2011.01746.x

Guerrero, A. L. G. (2018). Reflexiones ético-políticas sobre los derechos colectivos de los pueblos indígenas. *Revista nuestrAmérica*, 6(11), 227–238. http://revista nuestramerica.cl/ojs/index.php/nuestramerica/article/view/129

Guerrero Guerrero, A. L. (2016). Demandas de derechos humanos de los mapuches en Chile y los discursos jurídicos. Latinoamérica. *Revista de Estudios Latinoamericanos*, 62, 103–134. https://www.redalyc.org/jatsRepo/640/64046034006/html/index.html

Guevara-Gil, A., & Verona-Badajoz, A. (2018). Si No Hay Sujeto, No Hay Derecho. *Forum Historie Iuris*. https://www.forhistiur.de

Guido Guevara, S., & Bonilla García, H. (2013). Pueblos indígenas y políticas educativas en Colombia: Encantos y desencantos. In *Experiencias de educación indígena en Colombia: Entre prácticas pedagógicas y políticas para la educación de grupos étnicos*. Universidad Pedagógica Nacional.

Gundermann, H., & Vergara, J. I. (2009). Comunidad, Organización y Complejidad Social Andina en el Norte de Chile. *Estudios Atacameños*, 38, 107–126. https://doi.org/10.4067/S0718-10432009000200008

Gutiérrez Chong, N., & Gálvez González, D. (2017). La cultura política en el pueblo mapuche: El caso Wallmapuwen. *Revista Mexicana de Ciencias Políticas y Sociales*, 62(231), 137–165. https://doi.org/10.1016/S0185-1918(17)30041-7

Gutiérrez Chong, N., Martínez Resémdiz, J., & Sará Espinosa, F. (2015). *Cultura política indígena Bolivia, Ecuador, Chile, México*. UNAM, Instituto de Investigaciones Sociales.

Haas Institute. (2016). *Inclusiveness Index. Measuring Inclusion and Marginality.* UC Berkeley. https://www.issuelab.org/resources/38259/38259.pdf

Hall, G. P., & Patrinos, H. A. (2004). *Indigenous Peoples, Poverty and Human Development in Latin America*. The World Bank. https://doi.org/10.1596/978-1 -4039-9938-2

Hall, T., & Fenelon, J. (2009). Indigenous Peoples: Global Perspective and Movements. In *Indigenous Peoples and Globalization: Resistance and Revitalization* (pp. 120–158). Routledge.

Hanna, P., Langdon, E. J., & Vanclay, F. (2016). Indigenous Rights, Performativity and Protest. *Land Use Policy*, 50, 490–506. https://doi.org/10.1016/j.landusepol .2015.06.034

Haya de la Torre, V. R. (1978). Discurso del Presidente de la Asamblea Constituyente, Victor Raúl Haya de la Torre, el 28 de julio de 1978. http://www.congreso .gob.pe/participacion/museo/congreso/mensajes/discurso_28_julio_1978.

Heiss, C., & Navia, P. (2007). You Win Some, You Lose Some: Constitutional Reforms in Chile's Transition to Democracy. *Latin American Politics & Society*, 49(3), 163–190.

Hernández Chavés, P. (2018). El sistema político peruano: Su principal nota característica y dos omitidas propuestas de reforma. *Vox Juris*, 35(1), 57–67.

Heuser, C. (2018). New President, Old Problems: Corruption and Organised Crime Keep Peru in Crisis. *GIGA Focus Lateinamerika*, 4, 1–14.

Hodgson, D. L. (2002). Introduction: Comparative Perspectives on the Indigenous Rights Movement in Africa and the Americas. *American Anthropologist*, 104(4), 1037–1049.

Hooker, J. (2005). Indigenous Inclusion/Black Exclusion: Race, Ethnicity and Multicultural Citizenship in Latin America. *Journal of Latin American Studies*, 37(2), 285–310. https://doi.org/10.1017/S0022216X05009016

Hsieh, J. (2006). *Collective Rights of Indigenous Peoples | Identity-based Movement of Plain Indigenous in Taiwan | Taylor & Francis Group*. Routledge.

Htun, M. (2016). *Inclusion without Representation in Latin America: Gender Quotas and Ethnic Reservations*. Cambridge University Press.

Hudson, R. A. (1992). *Peru: A Country Study*. GPO for the Library of Congress. http://countrystudies.us/peru/

Huntington, S. (1968). *Political Order in Changing Societies*. Yale University Press.

ILO. (2016). Reporte Regional Colombia Costa Rica Guatemala Chile Convenio núm. 169 de la OIT sobre Pueblos Indígenas y Tribales en Países Independientes y la consulta previa a los pueblos indígenas en proyectos de inversión.

Instituto Nacional de Derechos Humanos Chile. (2017). Informe de campo "Levantamiento de Encuesta sobre percepciones y manifestaciones del racismo en Chile." Instituto Nacional de Derechos Humanos. https://bibliotecadigital.indh.cl/bitstream /handle/123456789/1070/Informe%20de%20campo.pdf?sequence=3

Instituto Nacional de los Derechos Humanos. (2019). Informe Anual Situación de los Derechos Humanos en Chile 2019. Instituto Nacional de Derechos Humanos.

International Rights of Nature Tribunal. (2014). Indigenous Cosmovision and Tribunal Framework. Global Alliance for the Rights of Nature. https://therightsofnature.org/framework-for-tribunal/

IWGIA. (2010). Ecuador- Derechos colectivos de los pueblos y nacionalidades. Evolución de una décda 1998-2008.

Jovanović, M. A. (2005). Recognizing Minority Identities through Collective Rights. *Human Rights Quarterly*, 27, 625–651.

Jovanović, M. A. (2012). *Collective Rights: A Legal Theory*. Cambridge University Press.

Kane, J. (2002). "Democracy And Group Rights." In A. Carter and G. Stokes (eds). *Democratic Theory Today: Challenges for the 21st Century*, Oxford: Polity Press.

Karp-Toledo, E. (2014). *El Perú Invisible. En busca de los derechos indígenas en tiempos de democracia y globalización*. Planeta.

Kenrick, J., & Lewis, J. (2004). Indigenous Peoples' Rights and the Politics of the Term 'Indigenous.' *Anthropology Today*, 20(2), 4–9. https://doi.org/10.1111/j.0268-540X.2004.00256.x

Ketley, H. (2001). Exclusion by Definition: Access to International Tribunals for the Enforcement of the Collective Rights of Indigenous Peoples. *International Journal on Minority and Group Rights*, 8, 331. https://heinonline.org/HOL/Page?handle=hein.journals/ijmgr8&id=347&div=&collection=

Koop, G., & Tole, L. (2001). Deforestation, Distribution and Development. *Global Environmental Change*, 11(3), 193–202. https://doi.org/10.1016/S0959-3780(00)00057-1

Kovach, M. (2009). *Indigenous Methodologies: Characteristics, Conversations, and Contexts*. University of Toronto Press.

Kreimer, O. (2000). Collective Rights of Indigenous Peoples in the Inter-American Human Rights System, Organization of American States. *Proceedings of the ASIL Annual Meeting*, 94, 315–316. https://doi.org/10.1017/S0272503700056238

Krupa, C., & Nugent, D. (2015). Off-Centered States: Rethinking State Theory Through an Andean Lens. In *State Theory and Andean Politics. New Approaches to the Study of Rule*. University of Pennsylvania Press. http://www.upenn.edu/pennpress/book/15370.html

Kymlicka, W. (1995). *Multicultural Citizenship. A Liberal Theory of Minority Rights*. Claredon Press.

Larsen, P. (2018). "The Dog in the Manger": Neoliberal Slogans at War in the Peruvian Amazon. In *SlogansSubjection, Subversion, and the Politics of Neoliberalism*. Routledge.

Lauderdale, P. (2009). Collective Indigenous Rights and Global Social Movements in the Face of Global Development. From Resistance to Social Change. *Journal of Developing Societies*, 25(3), 371–391.

Laurent, V. (2005). *Comunidades Indígenas, espacios políticos y movilizaciones electoral en Colombia, 1990-1998. Motivaciones, campos de acción e impactos*. Instituto Colombiano de Antropologia e Historia e Instituto Francés de Estudios ANdinos.

Laurent, V. (2010). Con bastones de mando o en el tarjetón. *Colombia Internacional*, 71, 35–61. https://doi.org/10.7440/colombiaint71.2010.03

Levistsky, S. (2018). Peru: The Institutionalization of Politics without Parties. In *Party System in Latin America. Institutionalization, Decay and Collapse*. Cambridge University Press.

Liverman, D., & Vilas, S. (2006). Neoliberalism and the Environment in Latin America. *Annual Review of Environment and Resources*, 31, 327–363. https://doi.org/10.1146/annurev.energy.29.102403.140729

López Bárcenas, F. (2010). *Legislación y derechos indígenas en México* (Tercera Edición). CEDRSSA, H. Cámara de Diputados.

López Calera, N. (2003). The Concept of Collective Rights. *Rechtstheorie*, Issue 4, 351.

Lorente, R. (2010). An Analysis of Colombia's Democracy. E-international Relations Students. https://www.e-ir.info/2010/04/15/an-analysis-of-colombia's-democracy/

Lorenz, A. (2016). Explaining Constitutional Change: Comparing the Logic, Advantages and Shortcomings of Static and Dynamic Approaches. In *A New Constitutionalism in Latin America: Promises and Practices*. Routledge.

Macdonald, T., & Edeli, D. (2005). *Pueblos Indígenas y Plan Colombia*. Abya Yala.

Madrid, R. L. (2012). *The Rise of Ethnic Politics in Latin America*. Cambridge University Press.

Mainwaring, S. (1998). Party Systems in the Third Wave. *Journal of Democracy*, 9(3), 67–81. https://doi.org/10.1353/jod.1998.0049

Mainwaring, S. (2018a). Introduction. In *Party System in Latin America. Institutionalization, Decay and Collapse*. Cambridge University Press.

Mainwaring, S. (2018b). Party System Institutionalization in Contemporary Latin America. In *Party System in Latin America. Institutionalization, Decay and Collapse*. Cambridge University Press.

Mainwaring, S., & Scully, T. (1995). Party Systems in Latin America. In *Building Democratic Institutions: Party Systems in Latin America* (pp. 1–34). Standford University Press.

Mainwaring, S., & Torcal, M. (2006). Party System Institutionalization and Party System Theory After the Third Wave of Democratization. In *Handbook of Party Politics*. Sage Publications.

Marimán, J. (1995). Consejo de Todas Las Tierras (revised text). https://www.mapuche.info/mapuint/jmar2.htm

Marimán, J. (2015). Nueva constitución para Chile y Pueblos Indígenas. http://www.uchileindigena.cl/nueva-constitucion-para-chile-y-pueblos-indigenas/

McAdam, D. (1982). *Political Process and the Development of Black Insurgency*. University of Chicago Press.

Meléndez, C. (2019). *El Mal Menor. Vínculos Políticos en el Perú Posterior al Colapso del Sistema de Partidos*. IEP Instituto de Estudios Peruanos.

Merino, R. (2018). La Nación reimaginada: Autodeterminación Indígena y las olas del indigenismo legal en Perú. In Descolonizar el derecho. *Pueblos Indígenas derechos humanos y estado plurinacional* (pp. 97–129). IEP Instituto de Estudios Peruanos.

Meyer, D. (2005). Introduction. Social Movements and Public Policy: Eggs, Chicken, and Theory. In *Routing the Opposition: Social Movements, Public Policy, and Democracy* (pp. 1–26). University of Minnesota Press.

Millones, L. (1999). Hay un País sin Indígenas entre Ecuador y Bolivia. In *Hay un País sin Indígenas entre Ecuador y Bolivia*. GTZ.

Millones, L. (2016). Reflexiones sobre el Perú indígena y Afrodecendiente. In *El Perú en su Historia: Frácturas y Persistencias*. Éditions Le Manuscript.

Ministerio de Desarrollo Social. (2015). *Informe Final, Sistematización Proceso de Consulta Previa Indígena*. Ministerio de Desarrollo Social. http://www.min isteriodesarrollosocial.gob.cl/pdf/upload/Informe%20Nacional%20CONSULTA %20PREVIA%20INDIGENA.pdf

Ministerio de Desarrollo Social. (2017). *Informe Final. Sistematización Proceso de Consulta Constituyente Indígena*. Government of Chile (Gobierno de Chile).

Ministerio de Justicia y Derechos Humanos. (2013). Compendio Normativo y Jurisprudencial sobre los Derechos de los Pueblos Indígenas, Comunidades Campesinas y Nativas. Gobierno del Perú. https://www.minjus.gob.pe/wp-content /uploads/2014/09/DGDOJ-Compendio-Normativo-Derechos-de-los-Pueblos-Ind %C3%ADgenas.pdf

Moreno, J. L. (2013). Democracia, movimientos sociales y participación popular. Lógicas democráticas y lógicas de distinción en las asambleas del 15M. In *Movimientos sociales, participación y ciudadanía en Andalucía* (pp. 263–301). Aconcagua Libros.

Moseley, M. W. (2015). Contentious Engagement: Understanding Protest Participation in Latin American Democracies. *Journal of Politics in Latin America*, 7(3), 3–48. https://journals.sub.uni-hamburg.de/giga/jpla/article/view/899

Mosquera Caro, E. del R., & Hinestroza Cuesta, L. (2017). La acción de tutela: ¿Mecanismo transitorio o autónomo para la protección de derechos colectivos de los grupos étnicos en Colombia? / Tutela: Transient or autonomous mechanism for the protection of collective rights of ethnic groups in Colombia? *Justicia*, 31, 188. https://doi.org/10.17081/just.22.31.2606

Muñoz Onofre, J. P., & Rodríguez, G. A. (2016). Aproximación histórica al reconocimiento y configuración normativa del derecho al territorio de los pueblos indígenas. In *Retos del Constitucionalismo Pluralista* (pp. 273–338). Universidad del Rosario.

Murillo, M. V. (2001). *Labor Unions, Partisan Coalitions, and Market Reforms in Latin America*. Cambridge University Press.

Navarrete Jara, M. J. (2019). *Constitucionalización Indígena. Variaciones jurídicas y metajurídicas (Segunda Edición)*. Librotecnia.

Ndahinda, F. M. (2007). Victimization of African Indigenous Peoples: Appraisal of Violations of Collective Rights under Victimological and International Law Lenses. *International Journal on Minority and Group Rights*, 1, 1–24. https://hei-nonline.org/HOL/P?h=hein.journals/ijmgr14&i=5

Negretto, G. L. (2008). *The Durability of Constitutions in Changing Environment: Explaining Constitutional Replacements in Latin America*. Kellog Institute.

Negretto, G. L. (2016). Toward a Theory of Formal Constitutional Change: Mechanisms of Constitutionl Adaptation in Latin America. In *A New Constitutionalism in Latin America: Promises and Practices*. Routledge.

Nolte, D. & Schilling-Vacaflor, A. (2012). Introduction: The Times they are a Changin': Constitutional Transformations in Latin America since the 1990s, In Nolte & Schilling-Vacaflor, eds. *New Constitutionalism in Latin America: Promises and Practices*. Ashgate, 3–30.

North, D. (1990). *Institutions, Institutional Change and Economic Performance*. Cambridge University Press.

Obach, B. K. (2004). *Labor and the Environmental Movement. The Quest for Commond Ground*. Massachussetts Institute of Technology.

O'Faircheallaigh, C. (2012). International Recognition of Indigenous Rights, Indigenous Control of Development and Domestic Political Mobilisation. *Australian Journal of Political Science*, 47(4), 531–545. https://doi.org/10.1080/10361146.2012.731484

O'Faircheallaigh, C. (2013). Extractive Industries and Indigenous Peoples: A Changing Dynamic? *Journal of Rural Studies*, 30, 20–30. https://doi.org/10.1016/j.jrurstud.2012.11.003

OIT. (2015). *Alianzas entre sindicatos y pueblos indígenas: Experiencias en América Latina*. OIT.

ONIC. (1991). Constituyente Indígena 1. http://observatorioetnicocecoin.org.co/cecoin/files/Constituyente%20indigena%201.pdf

ONIC. (2020). Estos son los miembros del Foro Permanente para las cuestiones Indígenas 2020-2022. ONIC Noticias. https://www.onic.org.co/comunicados-internacionales/3552-estos-son-los-miembros-del-foro-permanente-para-las-cuestiones-indigenas-2020-2022

Ortiz Nieves, J. (1994, May 16). Ernesto Samper Lanza la Estrategia Final. *El Tiempo*. https://www.eltiempo.com/archivo/documento/MAM-128948

Pairican, F. (2020). Estado Plurinacional: La gran disyuntiva. *Le Monde Diplomatique*.

Peerenboom, R. (2005). Assessing Human Rights in China: Why the Double Standard. *Cornell International Law Journal*, 38(1), 72–172.

Peñaranda, R. (2010). *El movimiento armado Quintín Lame (MAQL): Una guerra dentro de otra guerra* (Primera edición). Agencia Sueca de Cooperación Internacional para el Desarrollo: Corporación Nuevo Arco Iris: Organización Internacional para las Migraciones.

Pepinsky, T. (2013). The Institutional Turn in Comparative Authoritarianism. *British Journal of Political Science*, 44(3), 631–653.

Pepinsky, T. (2019). The Return of the Single-Country Study. *Annual Review of Political Science*, 22, 187–203.

Peters, B. G. (2013). *Strategies for Comparative Research in Political Science*. Palgrave.

Plataforma Política Mapuche. (2017). Declaración Pública de la Plataforma Política Mapuche sobre el Proceso de consulta constituyente indígena que termina sin acuerdos consensuados con las naciones originarias. Plataforma Política Mapuche.

https://werkenrojo.cl/sobre-el-proceso-de-consulta-constituyente-indigena-que
-termina-sin-acuerdos-consensuados-con-las-naciones-originarias/

Postero, N. (2004). Articulation and Fragmentation. Indigenous Politics in Bolivia. In *The Struggles for Indigenous Rights in Latin America* (pp. 189–216). Sussex Academic Press.

Postero, N., Risør, H., & Montt, M. P. (2018). Introduction: The Politics of Identity in Neoliberal Chile. *Latin American and Caribbean Ethnic Studies*, 13(3), 203–213. https://doi.org/10.1080/17442222.2018.1513224

Postero, N., & Zamosc, L. (2006). *The Struggle for Indigenous Rights in Latin America*. Sussex Academic Press.

Potter, P. (2006). Selective Adaptation and Institutional Capacity: Perspectives on Human Rights in China. *International Journal: Cánada's Journal of Global Analysis*, 61(2), 389–407. https://doi.org/doi.org/10.1177/002070200606100210

Powell, G. B., & Whitten, G. D. (1993). A Cross-National Analysis of Economic Voting: Taking Account of the Political Context. *American Journal of Political Science*, 37(2), 391–414.

Quijano, A. (2004). El laberinto de América Latina: ¿Hay otras salidas? *Journal of Iberian and Latin American Research*, 10(2), 173–196. https://doi.org/10.1080/13260219.2004.10426802

Ragin, C. C. *What is Qualitative Comparative Analysis (QCA)?* 19. https://eprints.ncrm.ac.uk/id/eprint/250/1/What_is_QCA.pdf

Ragin, C. C. (1987). *The Comparative Method*. University of California Press.

Ragin, C. C., & Rihoux, B. (2009). *Configurational Comparative Methods. Qualitative Comparative Analysis (QCA) and Related Techniques*. Sage Publications.

Rappaport, J. (2003). El espacio del diálogo pluralista: Historia del Programa de Educación Bilingüe del Consejo Regional Indígena del Cauca. In *Políticas de identidades y diferencias sociales en tiempos de globalización* (pp. 257–281). FACES - UCV.

Rappaport, J. (2005). *Intercultural Utopias Public Intellectuals, Cultural Experimentation, and Ethnic Pluralism in Colombia*. Duke University Press.

Rathgeber, T. (2004). Indigenous Struggles in Colombia: Historical changes in perspectives. In *The Struggle for Indigenous Rights in Latin America* (pp. 105–130). Sussex Academic Press.

Raz, J. (1988). *The Morality of Freedom*. Clarendon Press.

Redacción. (1990, December 5). Indígenas en la Constituyente. *El Tiempo*. https://www.eltiempo.com/archivo/documento/MAM-37029

Redacción Política. (2017, November 17). El liberalismo y sus crisis históricas. *El Espectador*. https://www.elespectador.com/noticias/politica/el-liberalismo-y-sus-crisis-historicas-articulo-723660

Remy, M. I. (2013). *Historia de las comunidades indígenas y campesinas del Perú*. IEP Instituto de Estudios Peruanos.

Remy, M. I. (2014). Población Indígena y Construcción de la Democracia en el Perú. In *Etnicidades en Construcción. Identidad y acción social en contextos de desigualdad* (pp. 13–46). IEP Instituto de Estudios Peruanos.

Rivera, F. (2016). Liberalism in Latin America. In *The Stanford Encyclopedia of Philosophy* (Spring). Metaphysics Research Lab, Stanford University.

Robbins, P. (2012). *Political Ecology*. Wiley-Blackwell.

Roberts, K. M. (2013). Market Reform, Programmatic (De)alignment, and Party System Stability in Latin America. *Comparative Political Studies*, 46(11), 1422–1452. https://doi.org/10.1177/0010414012453449

Rodríguez, G. A. (2007). Breve reseña de los derechos y de la legislación sobre comunidades étnicas en Colombia. http://observatorioetnicocecoin.org.co/cecoin/files/Resena_Derechos_Legislacion_Comunidades_Etnicas(1).pdf.

Rodríguez, G. A. (2015). *Los Derechos de los Pueblos Indígenas de Colombia. Luchas, Contenido y Relaciones*. Editorial Universidad del Rosario.

Rodríguez, P., & Carruthers, D. (2008). Testing Democracy's Promise: Indigenous Mobilization and the Chilean State. *European Review of Latin American and Caribbean Studies*, 85, 3–21. https://doi.org/10.18352/erlacs.9616

Rojas Betancourt, M., Bocanument Arbeláez, M., Restrepo Yepes, O., & Molina, C. (2019). La participación ciudadana en el proceso constituyente de Colombia de 1991. El derecho a la Educación. *Historia Constitucional*, 20, 1043–1073.

Román, C. (2014). Reconocimiento constitucional de los pueblos originarios en Chile. *Revista de Derecho Público*, 137–147. https://doi.org/10.5354/rdpu.v0i0.31683

Romero Loaiza, F. (2002). La educacion indigena en Colombia: Referentes conceptuales y socio historicos. Congreso de Antropología. http://www.naya.org.ar/congreso2002/ponencias/fernando_romero_loaiza.htm

Rossi, F., & von Bulow, M. (2016). Introduction: Theory-Building Beyond Borders. In *Social Movements Dynamic. New Perspectives on Theory and Research from Latin America*. Routledge.

Rostica, J. C. (2007). Las organizaciones mayas de Guatemala y el diálogo intercultural. *Política y cultura*, (27), 75–97.

Rousseau, S. (2016). Indigenous Movement Politics in Bolivia. Forging New Citizens of a Plurinational and Decolonized State. In *Beyond Colonialism, Development and Globalization. Social Movements and Critical Perspective*. Zed Books.

Saito, N. T. (1996). Beyond Civil Rights: Considering "Third Generation" International Human Rights Law in the United States. *The University of Miami Inter-American Law Review*, 28(2), 387–412. http://www.jstor.org/stable/40176424

Salazar-Soler, C. (2014). ¿El Despertar Indio en el Perú Andino? In *De la Política indígena. Perú y Bolivia* (pp. 71–126). IEP Instituto de Estudios Peruanos.

Salinas de Dosch, A. L. (2012). Understanding Latin America indigenous movements: From marginalisation to selfdetermination and autonomy?. In 3rd International Seminar and Workshop on Latin American and Asian Studies (LASA III), Institute of Occidental Studies, Universiti Kebangsaan Malaysia (pp. 17–18).

Salmón, E. (2000). Kincentric Ecology: Indigenous Perceptions of the Human-Nature Relationship. *Ecological Applications*, 10(5), 1327–1332. JSTOR. https://doi.org/10.2307/2641288

Sanchez, O. (2008). Transformation and Decay: The De-Institutionalisation of Party Systems in South America. *Third World Quarterly*, 29(2), 315–337. JSTOR. https://www.jstor.org/stable/20455042

Sanhueza, C., Saver, D., Cavallaro, J., Contesse, J., & Rodriguez, C. (2013). *No nos toman en cuenta*. Ediciones Universidad Diego Portales.

Santamaría Chavarro, A. (2013). Lorenzo Muelas y el Constitucionalismo Indígena "Desde Abajo": Una Retrospectiva Crítica sobre el Proceso Constituyente de 1991. *Colombia Internacional*, 79, 77–120.

Sartori, G. (1976). *Parties and Party Systems. A Framework for Analysis* (Vol. 1). Cambridge University Press.

Sauca, M. J., & Wences, I. (2015). Derechos colectivos (en la doctrina de la Corte Interamericana de Derechos Humanos). Eunomía. *Revista En Cultura de La Legalidad*, 9, 195–204.

Schilling-Vacaflor, A., & Kuppe, R. (2012). Plurinational Constitutionalism: A New of Indigenous-state Relations? In *New Constitutionalism in Latin America. Promises and Practices*. Routledge. https://scholar.google.com/scholar?hl=en&as_sdt=0%2C26&q=schilling-+vacaflor+Kuppe+plurinational+constitutionalism&btnG=

Schneider, C. Q., & Wageman, C. (2012). *Set-Theoretic Methods for the Social Sciences. A Guide to Qualitative Comparative Analysis*. Cambridge University Press.

Seawright, J., & Gerring, J. (2008). Case Selection Techniques in Case Study Research: A Menu of Qualitative and Quantitative Options. *Political Research Quarterly*, 61(2), 294–308. https://doi.org/10.1177/1065912907313077

Segal, Z. (2010). Do Israeli Arabs Have Collective Rights. *Journal of Law in Society*, Issues 1 and 2, 94–115. https://heinonline.org/HOL/P?h=hein.journals/jls12&i=97

Semo, Ii. (2017, March 11). La Jornada: ¿Indígenas o pueblos originarios?: una reforma conceptual. https://www.jornada.com.mx/2017/03/11/opinion/015a1pol

Semper, F. (2006). Los derechos de los pueblos indígenas de Colombia en la jurisprudencia de la Corte Constitucional. *Anuario de Derecho Constitucional Latinoamericano*, 2, 761–778.

Semper, F. (2018). *Los Derechos de los Pueblos Indigenas en Colombia*. Editorial Temis.

Seymour, M. (2017). *A Liberal Theory of Collective Rights*. McGill-Queen's University Press.

SICETNO. (2013). *Sistema de Consulta de Organizaciones Indígenas y Conflictos Étnicos en las Américas*. Instituto de Investigaciones Sociales- Universidad Autónoma de México.

Sieder, R. (2012). The Challenge of Indigenous Legal Systems: Beyond Paradigms of Recognition. *Brown Journal of World Affairs*, 13(2), 103–114.

Silva, E. (2009). The Inconvenient Fact of Anti-neoliberal Mass Mobilization. https://doi.org/10.1017/CBO9780511803222.002

Silva, E. (2015). Chile. In *Politics of Latin America* (pp. 409–431). Oxford University Press.

Simien, E. M. (2005). Race, Gender, and Linked Fate. *Journal of Black Studies*, 35(5), 529–550. JSTOR. https://www.jstor.org/stable/40034336

Smith, J., & Bandy, J. (2005). Introduction: Cooperation and Conflict in Transnational Protest. In *Coalitions across Borders. Transnational Protest and the Neoliberal Order* (pp. 1–17). Rowman & Littlefield.

Sniderman, P., & Piazza, T. (2002). *Black Pride and Black Prejudice*. Princeton University Press.

Sonenshein, R. (2006). *Politics in Black and White: Race and Power in Los Angeles*. Princeton University Press.

Soriano González, M. L. (2019). *Los pueblos y comunidades indígenas de América Latina. Filosofía jurídico-política y derechos*. Dykinson, SL.

Spivak, G. C. (1988). Can the Subaltern Speak? Can the Subaltern Speak? Reflections on the History of an Idea. In Nelson & Grossberg (eds). *Marxism and the Interpretation of Culture*. Macmillan, 21–78.

Squella, A. (2000). *Introducción al Derecho*. Editorial Jurídica de Chile.

Stahler-Sholk, R., Vanden, H. E., & Becker, M. (2014). *Rethinking Latin American Social Movements: Radical Action from Below*. Rowman & Littlefield.

Stearns, L. B., & Almeida, P. (2004). The Formation of State Actor-social Movement Coalitions and Favorable Policy Outcomes. *Social Problems*, 51(4), 478–504.

Sulmont, D. (2018). ¿Existe el voto programático en elecciones con un sistema de partidos políticos débil? *Revista de Ciencias Políticas*, 38(3), 429–457.

Swanborn, P. (2010). *Case Study Research: What, Why and How?* Sage Publications.

Tanaka, M. (2015). Agencia y Estructura, y el Colapso de los Sistemas de Partidos en los Paises Andinos. In *Sistema de Partidos en América Latina* (pp. 161–182). Anthropos ediciones.

Tanaka, M., & Vera Rojas, S. (2010). La dinámica "neodualista" de una democracia sin sistema de partidos: La situación de la democracia en el Perú. *Revista de Ciencia Política*, 30(1), 87–114.

The New York Times. (2000, November 22). Peru After Fujimori. 26. https://www.nytimes.com/2000/11/22/opinion/peru-after-fujimori.html

Tobasura Acuña, I. (2003). El Movimiento Ambiental Colombiano, una aproximación a su historia reciente. *Ecología Política*, 26, 107–119.

Tomaselli, A. (2014). El derecho a la consulta de los pueblos indígenas en Chile: Avances y desafíos (2009-2012). *Iberoamericana – Nordic Journal of Latin American and Caribbean Studies*, 43(1–2), 113–142. https://doi.org/10.16993/ibero.25

Torres-Rivas, E. (2006). Guatemala: Desarrollo, democracia y los acuerdos de paz. *Revista Centroamericana de Ciencias Sociales (RCCS)*, 3(2), 11–48.

Toshiyama Tanaka, J. (1992). Discurso del Presidente del Congresso Constituyente Democrático del Perú, Ingeniero Jaime Yoshiyama Tanaka, el 30 de Diciembre de 1992. http://www.congreso.gob.pe/participacion/museo/congreso/mensajes/mensaje-ccd-30-12-1992

Toshkov, Dimiter. (2016). *Research Design in Political Science*. Palgrave.

Treaster, J. B. (1989, September 10). COLOMBIA'S VIRGILIO BARCO VARGAS; The President with the Biggest War on Drugs. *The New York Times*, 1. https://www.nytimes.com/1989/09/10/weekinreview/colombia-s-virgilio-barco-vargas-the-president-with-the-biggest-war-on-drugs.html

Ture, K., & Hamilton, C. (1992). *Black Power: The Politics of Liberation*. Vintage Books.

UN Environment. (2017). Indigenous People and Nature: A Tradition of Conservation. UN Environment. http://www.unenvironment.org/news-and-stories/story/indigenous-people-and-nature-tradition-conservation

Ungar, M. (2001). Lesbian, Gay, Bisexual, and Transgendedered International Alliances: The Perils of success. In *Coalitions across Borders. Transnational Protest and the Neoliberal Order* (pp. 235–249). Rowman & Littlefield.

Union Interparlamentaria. (2014). Más allá de los números: La participación parlamentaria de los pueblos indígenas. Informe sobre la encuesta. Oficina del Observador Permanente de la Unión Interparlamentaria ante las Naciones Unidas.

United Nation. (n.d.). Indigenous Peoples at the UN | United Nations for Indigenous Peoples. Retrieved August 8, 2019, from https://www.un.org/development/desa/indigenouspeoples/about-us.html

Urteaga-Crovetto, P. (2018). Implementation of the Right to Prior Consultation in the Andean Countries. A Comparative Perspective. *The Journal of Legal Pluralism and Unofficial Law*, 50(1), 7–30.

Valenzuela, J. S., Somma, N., & Scully, T. (2018). Resilience and Change: The Party System in Redemocratized Chile. In *Party System in Latin America. Institutionalization, Decay and Collapse*. Cambridge University Press.

Valenzuela, M. T. (2013, April 24). Entrega de tierra a indígenas del Amazonas. El colombiano. https://www.elcolombiano.com/blogs/casillerodeletras/indigenas-del-amazonas-con-resguardo-propio/11095

Valenzuela, M., & Oliva, S. (2017). *Recopilación de legislación indígena 1813-2017*. Tomo I y II. Librotecnia.

Valenzuela, S. J., & Somma, N. (2018). Resilience and Change: The Party System in Redemocratized Chile. In *Party System in Latin America. Institutionalization, Decay and Collapse*. Cambridge University Press.

Vallejo Trujillo, F. (2016). El proceso de Consulta Previa en los fallos de la Corte Constitucional Colombiana. *Estudios Constitucionales*, 14(2), 143–182.

Van Cott, D. L. (2000a). *The Friendly Liquidation of the Past: The Politics of Diversity in Latin America*. University of Pittsburgh Press.

Van Cott, D. L. (2000b). Party System Development and Indigenous Populations in Latin America: The Bolivian Case. *Party Politics*, 6(2), 155–174. https://doi.org/10.1177/1354068800006002002

Van Cott, D. L. (2003). From Exclusion to Inclusion: Bolivias 2002 Elections. *Journal of Latin American Studies*, 35(4), 751–775. https://doi.org/10.1017/S0022216X03006977

Van Cott, D. L. (2004). Los movimientos indígenas y sus logros: La representación y el reconocimiento jurídico en los Andes. *América Latina Hoy*, 36, 141–159. http://revistas.usal.es/index.php/1130-2887/article/view/7415

Van Cott, D. L. (2007). *From Movements to Parties in Latin America: The Evolution of Ethnic Politics* (1 Edition). Cambridge University Press.

Van Cott, D. L. (2008). *Radical Democracy in the Andes*. Cambridge: Cambridge University Press.

Van Cott, D. L. (2010). Indigenous Peoples' Politics in Latin America. *Annual Review of Political Science*, 13(1), 385–405. https://doi.org/10.1146/annurev.polisci.032708.133003

Van Dyke, N., & McCammon, H. (2010). Introduction: Social Movement Coalition Formation. In *Strategic Alliances: Coalition Building and Social Movements* (pp. xi–xxviii). University of Minnesota Press.

Vanden, H. E., & Prevost, G. (2015). Introduction. In *Politics of Latin America* (Fifth, pp. 1–17). Oxford University Press.

Vasquez, P. (2014). *Oil Sparks in the Amazon: Local Conflict, Indigenous Population, and Natural Resources*. The University of Georgia Press.

Von Hildebrand, M. (2017). Los Pueblos Indígenas y el Futuro de la Amazonía Colombiana. In *La presidencia de Virgilio Barco treinta años después* (p. 174). Ediciones Uniandes.

Wade, P. (2010). *Race and Ethnicity in Latin America*. Pluto Press. http://www.oapen.org/search?identifier=625258

Walsh, A., & Hemmens, C. (2008). *Law, Justice and Society. A Sociolegal Introduction*. Oxford University Press.

Warren, K. B., & Jackson, J. E. (2002). Introduction: Studying Indigenous Activism in Latin America. In *Indigenous Movements, Self-Representation, and the State in Latin America*. University of Texas Press; JSTOR. https://www.jstor.org/stable/10.7560/791381

Wheeler, D. (2001). Racing to the Bottom? Foreign Investment and Air Pollution in Developing Countries. *The Journal of Environment & Development*, 10(3), 225–245. https://doi.org/10.1177/10704965-0101003-02

Whitley, R. (1999). *Divergent Capitalism: The Social Structuring and Change of Business System*. Oxford University Press.

Williams, L. (2003). *The Constraint of Race: Legacies of White Skin Privilege in America*. Penn State University Press. http://www.psupress.org/books/titles/0-271-02253-1.html

Worthen, K. (1998). The Role of Indigenous Groups in Constitutional Democracies: A Lesson from Chile and the United States. In *The Human Rights of Indigenous Peoples*. Transnational Publisher.

Xanthaki, A. (2000). Collective Rights: The Case of Indigenous People. *Amicus Curiae*, 25, 7–11.

Yashar, D. J. (2005). *Contesting Citizenship in Latin America: The Rise of Indigenous Movements and the Postliberal Challenge*. Cambridge University Press.

Yrigoyen Fajardo, R. (2011). El horizonte del constitucionalismo pluralista: Del multiculturalismo a la descolonización. In *El derecho en América Latina: Un mapa para el pensamiento jurídico del siglo XXI* (pp. 139–159). Siglo XXI.

Zamosc, L. (2004). The Indian Movement in Ecuador: From Politics of Influence to Politics of Power. In *The Struggle for Indigenous Rights in Latin America* (pp. 131–157). Sussex Academic Press.

Index

Note: Page references for figures and tables are italicized

About the Author

Katherine Becerra Valdivia is assistant professor of law at Universidad Católica del Norte, Chile. She is an attorney (LL.B and LL.M) and PhD in political science (University of Missouri).